BUNYIPS and BIGFOOTS

In Search of Australia's Mystery Animals

Up-dated second edition

by

Malcolm Smith

Dedicated to

Paul Cropper and the late Bernard Heuvelmans

First published in 1996 by Millennium Books

Copyright © Malcolm Smith, 1996

Up-dated second edition independently published in 2021.

Copyright © Malcolm Smith, 2021

National Library of Australia
Cataloguing-in-Publication data
Smith, Malcolm, 1949 May 6 -
Bunyips and Bigfoots: in search of Australia's mystery animals.
Up-dated second edition.

ISBN: 9798703605486

1. Animals, folklore   2. Australia   3. Bunyips
4. Yowies   5. Sea Serpents 6. Mystery predators

CONTENTS

INTRODUCTION

I first began this work more than twenty years ago, while studying for my second zoology degree. Only in recent years did become obvious that pen would have to be put to paper. The evidence was being generated as fast as it could be collected. If I waited for a definitive solution to be found, most of these marvellous stories would be lost to posterity. Other individuals had actively attempted to solve individual aspects of the problem, and their evidence, for the most part, lies gathering dust in unpublished files.

The material in this book can be approached from two perspectives: folklore and cryptozoology. In the first category, it is surely significant that large numbers of people all over the continent are sincerely claiming to have seen animals which do not officially exist, and which, by all rights, should not exist. It is likely that the vast majority of the population - those who live in the capital cities - have no idea of the extent of the phenomenon. I certainly did not, until I started investigating. Generally, such stories are only recorded locally, and even the inhabitants of an area undergoing a "flap" of unknown animal sightings probably know little of events outside their own area.

Students of popular beliefs and crazes will also find much to interest them. They might like to consider, for example, how reports of bunyips cropped up every 20 years or so last century, and how, two thirds of the way into this century, the pages of a local newspaper ran hot with tales of bunyips, and was taken seriously, until after two weeks, they died in a peal of laughter without anyone disproving or investigating the original claims. It is also surely of significant sociological import that legends of hairy men were rife in southern New South Wales for more than 30 years last century. They then faded away, to return on a much larger scale 70 years later at the sole instigation of one man. And one phenomenon will be noted again and again: the vast majority of witnesses are too scared or embarrassed to come forth until some brave soul leads the way.

How one analyses this issue will depend on how much credence one places on the reports. This brings us to the second approach: cryptozoology, the study of animals known only from native tradition, eye-witness testimony, footprints, or other evidence not officially recognized by science. Few laymen, or even zoologists, are familiar with the scores of mystery animals, both large and small, which have be reported all over the world. Their horizon is limited to such high-profile wonders as the bigfoot and Loch Ness monster. Since these have entered the realm of popular mythology, and are often the subject of quite uncritical comment, the average zoologist will not touch them with a barge pole. The major problem facing cryptozoologists is still the perception that we are "monster hunters".

Fortunately, a group of zoologists have been prepared to put their reputations on the line to found the International Society of Cryptozoology, whose address is listed at the end of this book. At last the scientific community has a forum where the existence of such animals can be debated objectively. Were I to provide a list of the Board of Directors, nearly every vertebrate zoologist would recognize a major figure in his or her field.

So, on the assumption that what is true needs to be told, and what is not true is at least interesting, I set about to write a book which would be informative to both zoologists and non-zoologists. My aim has been to set forth the evidence for all unknown Australian animals in a systematic manner. So that readers can decide for themselves, and check the evidence for themselves, every item has been referenced. As far as possible, I have sought to cite original sources. Where secondary sources have had to be relied on, I have made that clear.

Where I have considered that a simple explanation is available, I have voiced my opinion. When I have felt that a certain story contains contradictions, or is otherwise unreliable, I have also said so. However, by and large, I have chosen to let the evidence speak for itself, and readers should not assume that I believe whatever I have let pass without comment. One thing I have not been prepared to do was to reject a story just because it was fantastic. If you do so, important evidence may be lost because it has never been allowed to accumulate. Some things are more probable than others, but even the fantastic deserves its day in court.

One aspect of my style I would like to explain. Australian education authorities have decreed that our children will no longer be taught imperial measures. That means they will not be able to understand anything published in Australia before metrication, or published today in Britain and America - and that is most of the books on the shelves. For these unfortunates, I have provided metric translations wherever necessary. No attempt has been made to give the metric translation a precision not found in the original, and for that reason the word, "yard" has been left unmetrified. For estimates of distance, a yard is as good as a metre.

It is traditional at this point for an author to provide a long list of those who assisted him, but which no-one ever reads. My method is different. Those whom I interviewed, either face to face, by telephone, or by mail, I have acknowledged in the text, and my sincere thanks are extended to them all. Those who provided me with material, or directed me to it, I have mentioned in the references, and I certainly hope you read the references, because on them rests the credibility of the book.

However, there are two people who warrant a blanket expression of gratitude. These are the two persons to whom the book is dedicated, Bernard Heuvelmans and Paul Cropper.

Dr. Heuvelmans is the father of cryptozoology. His books, *On the Track of Unknown Animals* and *In the Wake of the Sea-Serpents*, introduced me to the field, and I have used them as the starting point of my research. I have attempted to trace all the relevant references in both books, and when that has not been possible, I have cited him directly. Our correspondence over the years has also been of great assistance, both direct and indirect, in the compilation of the evidence.

Paul Cropper must be one of the most dedicated pursuers of unknown animals in this country, and one of the most generous. To mention his name every place where it deserves would be tedious. The amount of material with which he has supplied me is so vast that it is safe to say this book could not have been written without him.

Two other points need to be raised. As will soon become apparent, a number of other people have worked far more actively in the field than I have. If any of them feel that I have stolen their thunder, let me say that nothing would give me greater pleasure than that this book should inspire them to publish their own findings. But right now, that evidence is simply sitting in their files, lost to the world.

Secondly, I make no apology for being an armchair investigator. The compiler and analyser of data has an equal place in science with the original researcher. If anyone thinks it is a small thing, I invite him or her to try sifting through old newspapers and magazines, and see how time consuming it is.

Finally, I began this research without preconceptions. I felt, however, that even the most improbable stories were worth recording. Since then, I have been forced to change my mind on more than one occasion as to what was probable and what was not. I hope you enjoy the fruits of my enquiries. All I ask is that you approach them with an open mind.

INTRODUCTION TO THE SECOND EDITION

Australian cryptozoology made be said to have formally come of age a quarter of a century ago, with the publication of two comprehensive books. The first, *Out of the Shadows, mystery animals of Australia* by Tony Healy and Paul Cropper, came out in 1994, followed by the first edition of this book in 1996. That they shared about half of their respective contents should come as no surprise because, as mentioned, Paul provided me with an enormous quantity of material. The best comparison would be to say that the first book had more depth, and the second more breadth. In other words, Tony and Paul's volume provided more detail in the topics covered while, as you will see, mine covered a whole range of lesser cryptids, as unknown animals are called, in addition to the major ones.

Of course, a species would not be a mystery if it could be easily found, so it is not possible to cite any new discoveries in the intervening quarter century. Instead, there has been a succession of positive and negative developments.

On the negative side, *Cryptozoology*, the peer reviewed journal of the International Society of Cryptozoology (ISC), which would publish research in this field, ceased publication in 1998. On the positive side, a new journal, the *Journal of Cryptozoology* was inaugurated in 2012, but it is not the same.

Consequently, the conference planned by the ISC for Australia, referred to in Chapter 9, never eventuated. Nevertheless, a successful "Myths and Monsters" conference was held in Sydney in 2001, and you will can find a PDF of its reports by following the links at the end of this book.

Of the three founders of the Australia Rare Fauna Research Association (ARFRA), two have left the organization, and one has passed away. ARFRA still exists, and has its own website, but I gather its documents are not open to the public. On the plus side, a new organization, Australian Yowie Research has been created.

A number of relevant books have also been published, the most important and comprehensive being *The Yowie* by Tony Healy and Paul Cropper, and *Australian Big Cats* by Michael Williams and Rebecca Lang. Both are published "print on demand" (POD), and so never out of print. I shall be referring to a couple of other books in later chapters.

Of course, the biggest development this century has been the massive expansion of the internet, allowing ready access to cryptozoological news at everyone's fingertips. I have listed the most significant websites in Appendix 2. Even more important has been the instigation of Trove[i], the Australian National Library's program, admittedly still incomplete, of digitalising Australian newspapers up to the mid-1950s, as well as a great many important old documents. Such a vast treasury of material has allowed me, last year, to publish two books which I am certain will become the definitive works on their respective subjects: *The Truth About Bunyips* and *Australian Sea Serpents*. Both are published as POD paperbacks and as Kindle e-books.

With respect to this second edition, at the end of most chapters I have appended an addendum providing any corrections which may be necessary, and expanding on the new material which has arrived during the interval. As for the original chapters, I have made only marginal changes. In the original edition, I was frequently compelled to rely on secondary sources. Although I have since located many of the original sources, I have still, by and large, left the endnotes unchanged from the earlier edition.

Nevertheless, there are two major changed made in the text. The original editor insisted that all measurements be in metric, except where original texts were cited. I have now gone back to the the system in my original manuscript, of giving all measurements in both metric and imperial versions.

Furthermore, the editor made a number of minor stylistic alterations which, in may opinion, were not improvements. Editors are good at knowing what will sell, and proof readers can recognize where the text is ambiguous or misleading. However, they themselves are not authors. I have gone back to my original wording. Anything you don't like, you can blame on nobody but me.

The earlier reviewers sometimes commented on the racy style of the book. No doubt I would have written it differently if I were doing it today, but it is a bit late in day to change it. To quote Pontius Pilate, what I have written I have written.

Malcolm Smith, 2021

---

[i] https://trove.nla.gov.au/

ACKNOWLEDGEMENTS

This time around, I have decided I really will acknowledge everybody who assisted me. Anyone whom I have inadvertently overlooked will, I trust, accept my apologies.

Therefore, in addition to Paul Cropper and Bernard Heuvelmans, I would like to thank:

Victor A. Albert, Lucille Andelle, Chad Arment, L. O. Arnold, John Belcher, Neil Blyth, Carol Borck, Janet and Colin Bord, Gerry Bowles, Peter Chapple, Lois Cipalo, Nick Costello, Leonie Dennis, Christine Downie, Robert L. Downing, Robbie Fatt, Dr. Tim Flannery, David Fleay, Franz of Austria, Dan Guillespie, Peter Hansen, David Heppell, Don Hitchcock, Esther Ingram, Roy Jenkinson, William Kitson, Gerry (Geert) van Klinken, Meg Lloyd, Mrs. Lomond, Brian Lund, Fred McCue, Chris McLean, Kay Makeig, Kevin Maley, Phil Manning, Stellamary Matheson, Lance Mesh, Ralph Molnar, Kerry Morgan, Ken Raddunz, Roma Ravn, Norman Robertson, Karl Shuker, Edgar Skoda, Shannon Smith, Warren Smith, Christine Stiller, Roy Swaby, Simon Townsend, Bruce Thomson, Percy Tresize, Charles Tutt, Nigel Tutt, David Waldron, John Winter, Gerald Wood, and Joy Zeller - as well as several witnesses who asked not to be identified.

CHAPTER 1

THE PASSING OF THE BUNYIPS

It was just the year after the first settlement that the British ship, *Rover* put in at Botany Bay. While his crew went ashore to take on fresh water, Captain Lee watched through his spyglass, and was just as surprised as they when three huge, naked men came out of the bush. The crew fled for the boat, leaving the casks of rum on the shore.

Two of the savages, painted wildly with red circles, spots and stripes, were presumed to be youngsters, for they bore little in the way of beards. They tried the rum and immediately spat it out. But the third, presumed to be the father, drank heavily and fell unconscious. When he woke up 24 hours later, he was chained up aboard the *Rover*, and the crew took the precaution of keeping him chained for the rest of the voyage. He would eat human flesh if he could get it (one wonders how they found out), but was never seasick.

On 29 November 1789, the ship put in at Plymouth, and the giant immediately went on show, with thousands of people flocking to see him. In features he was like a black, by which I presume was meant a negro, but his skin was yellow. According to a contemporary account:

> He is much tamer, and not so savage in temper as might be expected. He is 9 feet 7 inches [292 cm] high, 4 feet 10 inches [147 cm] broad, a remarkable large head, broad face, frightful eyes, a broad nose and thick lips like a black, very broad teeth, heavy eye-brows, hair stronger than a horse's mane, a long beard strong as black wire, body and limbs covered with long black hair, the nails of his fingers and toes may be properly called talons, crookt like a hawk's bill, and as hard as horn.

You never heard of him? I'm not surprised. It's not in the history books. It was in a handbill published in England about that time, and unquestionably the type of tall story Australians would eventually become famous for[1]. Nevertheless, it illustrates a point. A new land is by definition a mystery, the fitting background for all sorts of rumours, hoaxes, and garbled tales. Nobody knows what may be hidden there, and often truth is stranger than fiction. After all, the platypus was originally thought to have been a hoax.

Liverpool might be contiguous with Sydney now, but in 1822 it was a separate town, and not a very big one. In was in that year that two men deposited an oath at the bench of magistrates about the snake they had met just 2½ miles [4 km] out of town. It was 45 feet [14 m] long and three times as thick as a human being. Thinking it was dead, one of them threw a missile at it. Much to their shock, it rose up 5 feet [1½ m] off the ground. A third witness also offered to confirm the event on oath[22].

Now, an oath is a very serious matter. It carries the penalty of perjury, not to mention damnation. So the local population gathered their servants, and presumably their weapons, and hastened to the site. There they found a large track, bearing the impression of scales, and a mark 14 inches [35 cm] long, which someone thought was made by the jaw of an alligator.

What was it? Crocodiles are never 45 feet long, and cannot raise themselves five feet off the ground. The giant python, *Montypythonoides* (yes, that really is its name) was nowhere near as large, and is supposed to have been extinct for quite a few million years. Also, it hasn't been back. So, despite the track, perhaps it was a simple case of perjury. After all, nobody could prove that they had lied - at least not in this life.

The year before, something strange was seen in Lake Bathurst, a very small body of water surrounded by a much larger stretch of marsh, situated not far from what is now the ACT. I shall let the witness, E. S. Hall describe it:

> One fine morning in November, 1821, I was walking by the side of the marsh which runs into Lake Bathurst, when my attention was attracted by a creature casting up the water and making a noise, in sound resembling a porpoise, but shorter and louder: the head only was out of the water. At the distance I stood (about 100 yards) it had the appearance of a bull-dog's head, but perfectly black; the head floated about as though the animal was recreating itself; it cut up the water behind, but the quantity thrown up evinced neither strength nor bulk; it remained about five minutes, and then disappeared. I saw it at a greater distance afterwards, when it wore the same appearances.
>
> One night my overseer placed a cart in the marsh, and in the morning got into it armed with a musket, very heavily charged with pieces of lead. The creature appeared at day-light, and the man fired; he saw the creature rise, and lie at full length on the reeds, about 5 feet [1½ m] long, but

his shoulder was in such excruciating pain, from the recoiling of the musket, that he involuntarily shut his eyes from the agony, and when he opened them, the creature had just turned over and disappeared. Numbers of them have since been seen, but never shot at[33].

That was written two years after the event, but we must presume that he told the explorer, Hamilton Hume right away, because on 19 December we find the Philosophical Society of Australasia resolving to reimburse Mr Hume any expenses he might incur in procuring a specimen of the head, skin or bones[4] of what they suspected was a manatee or dugong. Nothing ever came of the venture, though about 1930 - 32 Lieutenant W. H. Breton recorded that the natives believed that a devil resembling a seal dwelt in nearby Lake George[5].

But back to Mr Hall (who was later to become Coroner, and a founder of the Bank of New South Wales):

In December last [1822] Mr. Forbes and I were bathing at the East-end of the Lake, where an arm runs among the honey-suckles. As I was dressing, a creature, at the distance of about 130 or 150 yards, suddenly presented itself to my view; it had risen out of the water before I perceived it, and was then gliding on the smooth surface with the rapidity of a whale-boat, as it appeared to me at the time. Its neck was long, apparently about three feet [90 cm] out of the water, and about the thickness of a man's thigh; the colour a jet black; the head was rather smaller in circumference than the neck and appeared surrounded with black flaps, which seemed to hang down, and gave it a most novel and striking appearance. The body was not to be seen; but, from the rippling of the water, I judged it to be longer than the neck. After it had continued for about 300 yards, I turned round to ascertain if Mr. Forbes had also seen it, and, on looking again, it had dived, and was seen no more.

He decided it was not the same as the first one seen, because that one had no flaps around the head. One wonders if they were not something simple, like peeling, moulting or torn skin. He also mentioned that the natives would never go near the marsh, and claimed that the "devil-devil" had previously taken their children.

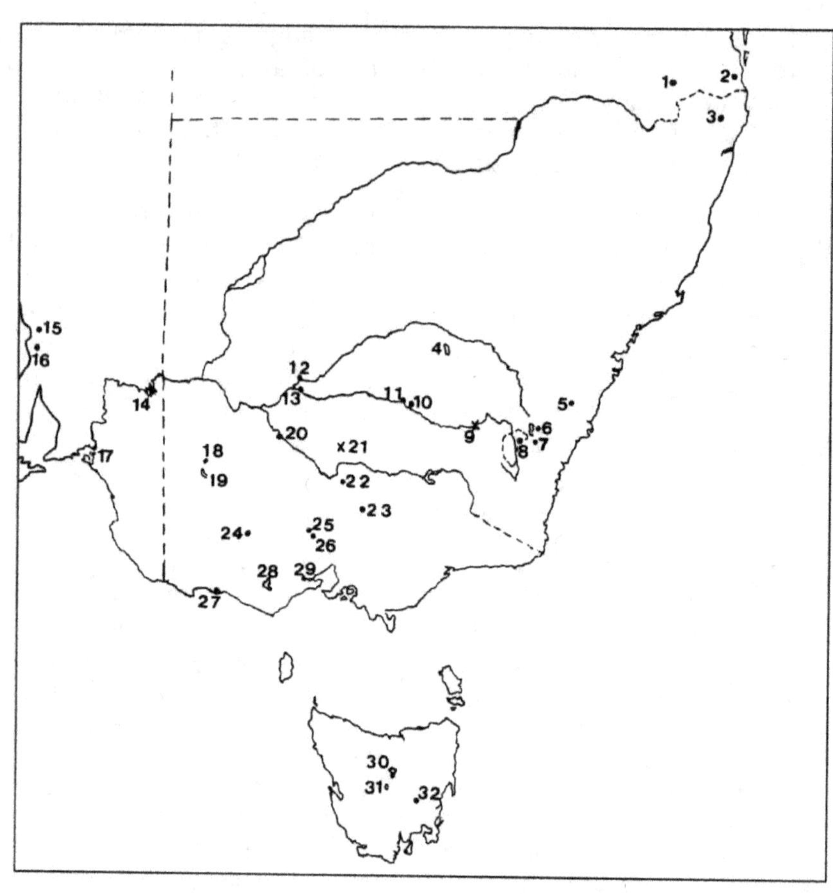

L. Albacuytya	18	L. Hindmarsh	19
L. Alexandrina (mulgewanke)	17	Kyneton	26
Barwon R.	29	Lismore	3
L. Bathurst	6	Malmsbury	25
Challicum	24	Midgeon Lagoon	10
Conargo (seal)	21	mochel mochel	1
L. Corangamite	28	Molonglo R.	7
Cowal Lake	4	Murray R. (seal)	14
Crystal Brook	15	Queanbeyan	8
L. Echo	31	Rocky River	16
Eumeralia	27	skull	13
Euroa	23	Swan Hill	20
Gilston	2	L. Tiberias	32
Goublurn R.	22	Tuckerbill Swamp	11
Great Lake	30	Tyson's sighting	12
Gundagai (seal)	9	Wingecarribee R.	5

Map 1.1 Locations of bunyip reports mentioned in the text.

At that time the creature had no name. It was not until settlers entered Victoria that word got out how the swamps, lagoons and billabongs of southern Australia were alleged to haunted by a mysterious something, huge and dangerous, with a loud, booming bellow or roar.

It is not certain just when the word, *bunyip* entered the English language. For that matter, no-one can be absolutely sure which language originated it. Most likely it moved from language to language in the same manner as "kangaroo" i.e. the whites used it thinking they were speaking "Aboriginal", and the Aborigines picked it up thinking they were speaking English. By then it had probably acquired the same sense as the English word, "monster".

The form, *bahnyip* appeared in a pamphlet published by the *Sydney Gazette* in 1812, and was described by James Ives as "a large black animal like a seal, with a terrible voice which creates terror among the blacks."[6] When Luise Hercus was seeking out the last speakers of Victorian languages in the 1960s, she recorded the word, *banib* [pronounced "bunnip"] from Wergaia[7]. A language of the northwest, it was originally spoken from Dimboola to Lake Albacuytya, and from Yanac to Warracknabeal. According to Wergaia lore, they were generally large and dark. One resembling a black pig was seen floating in Lake Hindmarsh.

Another term recorded by Hercus was *banib-ba-gunuwar*, or "bunyip and swan", a dark-coloured monster with a long neck once seen by an uncle of her informant in Lake Albacuytya. This is interesting, because one of the most common "sea serpent" and lake monster types reported from around the world is a creature with a bulky, often humped body and a long, slender neck like a swan's. If one actually arrived in Lake Albacuytya from the sea, it would have to have followed a long and extremely tortuous route along the Glenelg and Wimmera Rivers, with a waddle or slither overland in between.

The Western Port version of the bunyip was called the *toor-roo-don*[8]. A pool by that name existed, and probably still does, on the northern shore of Western Port. In the days of yore, it was said to be haunted by one of the monsters, and the Aborigines would never bathe there.

Belief in monsters lurking in the depths of lakes is, or was, rife throughout the continent. The background of these legends was seldom fully explained to the white man, but it is likely many of them had a religious basis i.e. the lurker was some form of that widespread creator spirit, the Rainbow Serpent. Other cases are less certain, and there has been a tendency for whites to assume they were all one and the same. Charles Barrett[9] listed the following terms: *toor-roo-don*, *kajanprati*, *katenpai*, *tunapatam*, *tumbata* and *bunyup* - all synonyms for *bunyip*. One could well ask how anyone could be so sure. Some of them could have been real animals, some imaginary. There might be more than one imaginary animal in the list. The collectors of these legends were not qualified anthropologists, but rank amateurs with little knowledge of Aboriginal languages and minimal understanding of their culture and thought patterns. A high degree of cultural confusion is likely to have resulted. The temptation is always to hear what one expects to hear and be told what one wants to be told. And that assumes good will on both sides. When the shoe is on the other foot- when the black man asks the white something about his culture - the latter often takes the view: "Tell the ignorant savage anything." He seldom suspects that he can be the victim of the same tactic. Let me assure you, it does happen.

People change, and traditions too, so enquiring of the modern descendants of the southern tribes is of little use. Largely detribalised, and of mixed descent, they still retain some traditions from the Aboriginal side of their ancestry. But a lot more have been lost, and mixed with ideas adopted from the white side of the blanket.

Nevertheless, I have noticed a certain social phenomenon. Whenever an unknown animal is reported, one of the local "Aborigines" will announce, "Oh, we knew all about it from the beginning." It makes them feel important. Then some white man will dip into the old literature and find a word or a legend which seems to fit. Considering how little is known of native languages and myths in the areas of greatest European impact, there will be plenty of ambiguous references to choose from.

Nevertheless, some of these references are rather interesting. The *tunatpan* of the Port Phillip district was described as:

> as big as a bullock, with an emu's head and neck, a horse's
> mane and tail, and seal's flippers, which laid turtle's eggs in
> a platypus's nest, and ate blackfellows when it was tired of
> a crayfish diet[10].

Certainly, the first half of the description sounds like one of the most common and cosmopolitan varieties of sea serpent, as the next chapter will explain.

Books and articles on bunyips frequently refer to the Mindi. However, this was a giant snake, and probably a form of the Rainbow

Serpent. The Mulgewanke of Lake Alexandrina, S.A. was believed to be half man and half fish, with a mop of reeds in place of hair. It is usually but, in my opinion, incorrectly, included with the bunyip legend because of his voice. The Ngarrindjeri people invoked him to explain a booming sound emanating from the region of the lake.

The Rev. George Taplin claimed to have heard it dozens of times [11]. It sounded like the boom of distant cannon, or the detonation of a blast, or even at times like the fall of a huge body into deep water. It was quite unlike the booming voice of the bittern. One peculiarity was that, no matter how loud it might be, it always appeared to come from a distance. At first he suspected people were blasting on the opposite of the lake, but convinced himself this was not so. He felt it was some unknown natural phenomenon. I would agree. It reminds me of other anomalous booming noises e.g. the Barisal guns of Bangladesh, the mist pouffers of the Belgian coast, and many other sites around the world[12]. To my knowledge, no-one has ever come up with a plausible explanation. However, the mystery belongs to the fields of meteorology or geology, rather than zoology.

In 1847 Governor La Trobe wrote of the existence of two types of bunyip, a northern and a southern, and managed to procure two drawings made by Aborigines. These he sent to Tasmania, where they have not been heard of since[13]. Fortunately, however, two other paintings have survived, by virtue of having been incorporated into Brough Smyth's tome, *The Aborigines of Victoria*[14].

Figure 1.1. Drawing of toor-roo-don by Kurruk

Now remember: the blackfellows were probably just humouring the whitefellows in the first place. Also, they probably had only a limited idea of what their subject was like. (Suppose you were asked to draw the Loch Ness monster?) So we should not be surprised that they varied somewhat in detail.

A native of Western Port named Kurruk was asked to draw a toor-roo-don under the direction of "a learned doctor" (i.e. a tribal elder), and came up with - would you believe? - an emu (Fig.1.1). To this Brough Smyth quotes a Mr. Stanbridge that the natives describe the bunyip as having a head and neck like an emu. In that case, you will be interested to know that the toor-roo-don/bunyip is not extinct. As will be seen in the next chapter, a sea serpent answering that description turned up not far away from there in 1973.

The other drawing (Fig. 1.2) was done by an unnamed Murray River Aborigine in 1848. Whether it was covered with scales or feathers something the artist could not say. Perhaps the northern bunyip really was different from the southern one. Or perhaps, as Gilbert Whitley suggested[15], it represented an Aboriginal view of the settlers' cattle, perhaps gone astray and grazing, bellowing and lowing in the swamps. He commented that Aborigines had been known to point out cattle bones as those of a bunyip, but were told that they couldn't be, as they came from cattle.

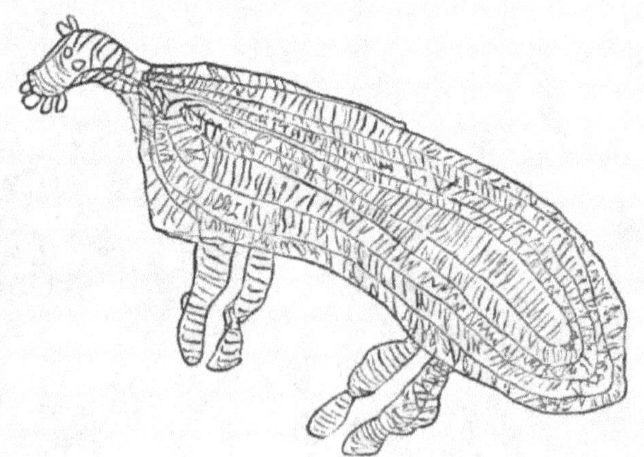

Figure 1.2. Drawing of bunyip by Murray River Aborigine, 1848

The fact that the bunyip never featured in Aboriginal art is surely significant. It means that it was not a dreamtime spirit. It was thought of as a flesh and blood animal too infrequently seen, and too terrible to approach, to allow its true shape to be determined.

There is an exception. Sometime perhaps in the early part of the nineteenth century, something huge and strange died, or was speared to death, on the banks of Fiery Creek, near Ararat[16], in Victoria. So overwhelmed by the experience was the local Tjapwurong people that they vowed they would never forget it. Digging their spears into the turf around the carcass, they preserved the outline of the monster for posterity, returning every so often to renew the figure, much in the same fashion as the chalk figures of southern England. It was there in 1840, when Challicum Station was built just a kilometre away, and presumably remained until the 1870s, when the Tjapwurong tribe itself faded into oblivion.

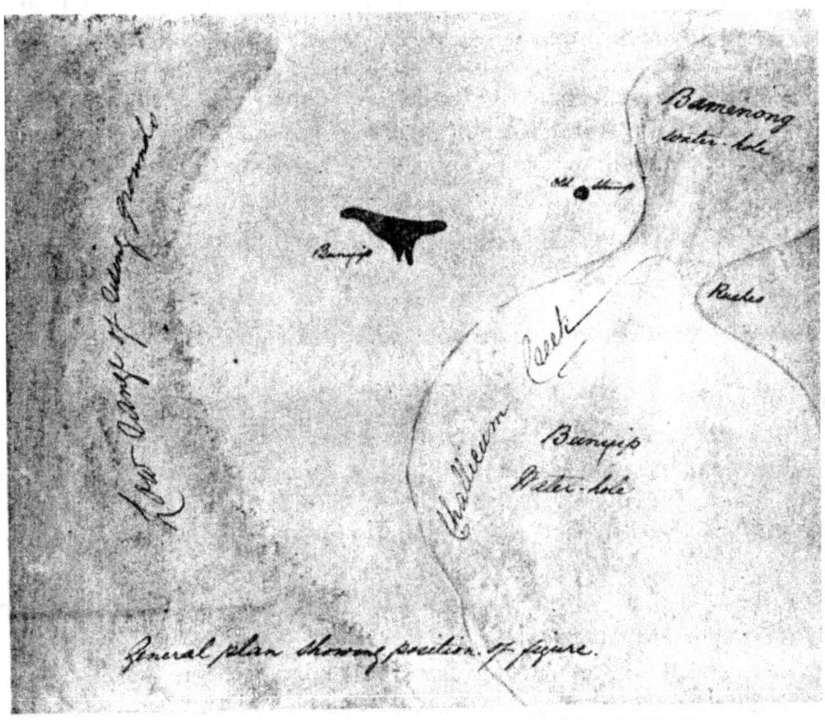

Figure 1.3. Challicum bunyip, sketched by J. W. Scott

And there it is (Fig. 1.3), as drawn by the Challicum overseer, Mr. I. W. Scott, in June 1867. Its length was 11 paces. A much later sketch makes it more elongated, and more like an emu. The original artist also commented that in 1867 the waterhole right next to it was still reputed to be haunted by a bunyip. An old shepherd there refused to leave his hut at night once he had seen it.

It is possible that E. S. Hall was not the first white man to see a bunyip. The first white settlers to arrive in Victoria in 1835 found not only stories of the bunyip, but something almost as fascinating: a wild white man. An abortive attempt at settlement had been made by Lieutenant-Colonel Collins in 1803. Less than four months later the site was abandoned, but that was too late for one William Buckley. With a group of other convicts, he made a bolt for freedom, fondly imagining it possible to walk from Port Phillip to Sydney, and thence to California. (Geography was not a strong point among convicts of that era.) Some of them died, others turned back, ready to face the lash for the sake of food. By the time Buckley had come to his senses, Collins and his men had decamped. The next 32 years of his life would be spent as an honorary member of the local tribe.

Buckley's life story was not put into print until 1852, by which time the bunyip had become a household word. The style of the book suggests that his ghost writer, John Morgan - for Buckley was illiterate - may have preferred a good story to strict accuracy. Besides, he had to rely on the word of a former criminal, of whom honesty may not have been a salient virtue.

Anyhow, according to this account, Buckley did see bunyips in Lake Modewarre. "It seemed to be about the size of a full-grown calf, and sometimes larger; the creatures only appear when the river is very calm and the water smooth[17]." However, he could never learn anything about its head or tail. All he ever saw was the back, which appeared to be covered with dusky grey feathers.

The Barwon River was also mentioned as a special site for bunyips. The natives believed that the large congregations of eels there were summoned by the monster for its sustenance. Buckley claimed to have several times attempted to spear a bunyip while on his own, but he suspected the Aborigines would have been highly displeased if they had found out.

An aquatic animal covered with feathers is too bizarre to be taken seriously without confirmation. But assuming that Buckley did observe bunyips of some description, he may not have been the only escaped convict to have the privilege. William Wilson claimed to have read papers in the Berrima Courthouse, N.S.W. dealing with bunyips encountered by escaped prisoners along the banks of the nearby Wingecarribee River. It is a pity he did not provide details on anything except how the reports were lost.[18]

> A few years ago, a number of "Bunyip" manuscripts were lodged, together with a large accumulation of Court correspondence, beneath the floor of the old Courthouse at Berrima where they could be readily examined by taking up a loose board and prospecting in the darkness with a long-handled rake until a likely-looking bundle was encountered. Unfortunately, nearly all these manuscripts were written on much softer paper than the correspondence, and the opossums of the neighbourhood, who drew regularly from this store, preferred the MSS. as a lining for their nest. Thus, doubtless, perished many precious documents which could have shed further light on the Bunyip and its ways.

Berrima Gaol was first occupied in 1839, which provides the earliest date at which these events can have occurred. However, discounting such undocumented sightings, it was a full generation after Mr. Hall's initial adventure before another white man encountered a bunyip. This time it was another explorer who brought to the attention of the world, Hamilton Hume's old companion, William Hovell[19]. In his travels along the Murrumbidgee he had heard the blacks refer to a mysterious and terrifying aquatic animal, by the name of *katenpai*, *kinepratia*, or *tanatbah*, according to the language. To be fair, it need not necessarily have been the same as the Victorian *bunyip*. Indeed, it might have been the type of the "northern bunyip" which LaTrobe was to describe the following year. From what Hovell could learn, it was as big as a bullock, with a head and neck like an emu's, a huge mane of hair from the head to the shoulders, the tail of a horse, and four legs, each with three toes, and webbed. In other words, if you don't know the answer, tell the ignorant whitefellow anything. Some of that is no doubt genuine native tradition, but one wonders what would have been the result if each informant had been interrogated in his own language, and individual descriptions had not been pooled.

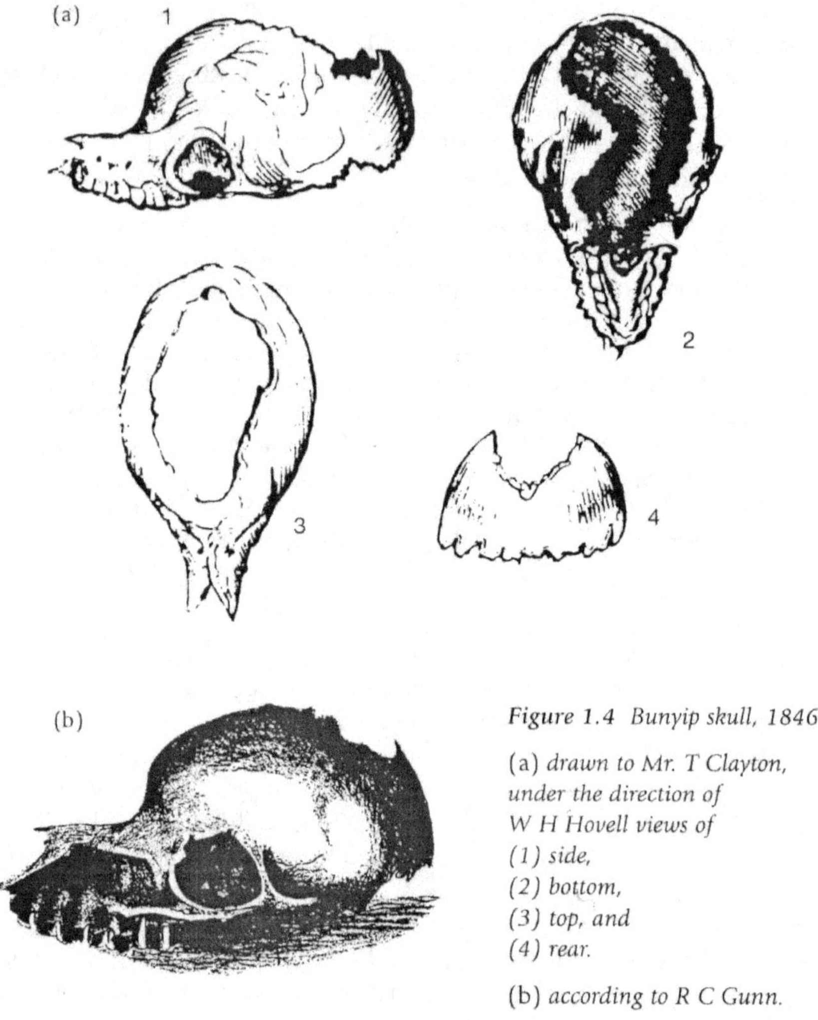

Figure 1.4 Bunyip skull, 1846

*(a) drawn to Mr. T Clayton,
under the direction of
W H Hovell views of
(1) side,
(2) bottom,
(3) top, and
(4) rear.*

(b) according to R C Gunn.

Nevertheless, although the *katenpai* was held in great dread by the blacks, they did manage to kill one by the banks of the lower Murrumbidgee. When a local settler, Atholl T. Fletcher heard about it, he visited the site and discovered a strange skull. No other bones were present, just a skull. Every tribesman to whom he showed it agreed that it belonged to a *katenpai*, though how many *katenpai* skulls they had seen was not asked. He took it with him on his next trip to Melbourne.

And there it is: depicted in Figure 1.4. The top of the cranium, the front of the snout, and the whole of the lower jaw was missing. According to Hovell, the cranium measured 9 inches [23 cm] in length, from point A to point B. To his untrained eye the molars looked similar to those of an ox, and he had heard from the Aborigines that the missing pieces of jaw would have sported enormous tusks. Dr. James Grant was able to examine the skull, and described it in the *Tasmanian Journal of Science* for January 1847. In his opinion, its original owner had been very young, possibly even foetal i.e. it might have been a stillborn or miscarried *katenpai*/bunyip. The arrangement of the head and teeth were unlike anything with which he was familiar, but it might have come from a young camel[20] - a few had been introduced about 1840.

The exact movements of the skull are hard to determine. A Mr. Edward Curr, of Port Phillip forwarded it to the Speaker of the Legislative Council in Sydney, and the latter placed it in the handed of William S. Macleay[21]. Macleay immediately saw that it was fresh. Marks of gnawing teeth were visible on the upper surface, and some membranes and ligaments were still attached. He had been told that it had been bloody when found. From the extreme fragility and lightness of the braincase, and the sharp crowns of the teeth, he could also tell that it was very young, if not foetal. The crowns of the molars, the form of the maxillary bone and the position of the infra-orbital foramen were exactly the same as in a horse. However, many of the other bones were totally different.

But Macleay had a trump card: the skull of the foetus of a mare found floating down the Hawkesbury River near Windsor in November 1841. The distinguishing features of the Murrumbidgee skull were even more pronounced in the one from the Hawkesbury. The major difference was that the eye sockets of the "bunyip" were stretched as far apart as possible, forcing the eyes virtually onto the lower jaw. The Hawkesbury freak, on the other hand, had only one eye. On this basis, Macleay decided that it was a deformed colt. However, when an illustration was sent to Professor Owen in London, he considered it to be a calf[22].

Although the "bunyip" skull was exhibited in the Colonial Museum (now the Australian Museum) of Sydney, according to Whitley[23], it appears to have been lost. But I can confirm that the less illustrious one-eyed horse skull is still around. Its home is the small Macleay Museum attached to Sydney University.

Three months after Hovell had released the skull to the world, he received word that a white man had seen a *kinepràtia*, or bunyip, on a cattle station owned by Mr. Tyson 12 miles [20 km] from the junction of the Lachlan and Murrumbidgee Rivers. At the time the area had been subject to extensive flooding.

> Well, some few weeks ago [i.e. in May 1847], an intelligent lad in Tyson's employ, who was in search of the milking cows on the edge, and just inside this reed bed, where there are occasionally patches of good grass, came suddenly, in one of these openings, upon an animal grazing, which he thus describes: it was about as big as a six months' old calf, of a dark brown colour, a long neck and long pointed head; it had large ears, which it pricked up when it perceived him; had a thick mane of hair from the head down the neck, and two large tusks; he turned to run away, and this creature equally alarmed ran off too, and from the glances he took of it, he describes it as having an awkward shambling gallop; the forequarters of the animal were very large in proportion to the hindquarters, and it had a large tail, but whether he compared it to that of a horse or a bullock I do not recollect; he took two men to the place next morning to look for its tracks, which they describe as broad and square, somewhat like what the spread hand of a man would make in soft muddy ground. The lad had never heard of the kinepràtia, and yet his descriptions in some respects tally with that of Aborigines[24].

According to Whitley[25], the following year a large, brown bunyip was reported from Eumeralla, Port Fairy, which also sported a head like a kangaroo's, a long neck, long shaggy mane, and enormous mouth. Since it was said to lure humans towards it by some form of mesmerism, I suspect the story originated with the Aborigines.

W. H. Jarrett told Dudley LeSouef, the Director of Melbourne Zoo, that when he was a boy, in the summer of 1849 or 1850, an animal referred to by the natives as a bunyip, appeared at Mooriling Station, on the Goulburn. Although terribly frightened, they were induced by the promises of gifts to wade into the water and shoot at it. It was hit several times, but the body was never recovered[26].

Some of the strangest bunyips ever reported by a white man were those seen by a Mr. Stocqueler while sailing down the Goulburn River in a canvas boat in early 1857. According to a report at the time,

Mr. Stocqueler informs us that the bunyip is a large freshwater seal, having two small paddles or fins attached to the shoulders, a long swan-like neck, a head like a dog, and a curious bag hanging under the jaw, resembling the pouch of the pelican. The animal is covered with hair like the platypus, and the colour is a glossy black. Mr. Stocqueler saw no less than six of the curious animals at different times; his boat as within thirty feet [9 m] of one, near M Guire's Point, on the Goulburn, and fired at the bunyip, but did not succeed in capturing him. The smallest appeared to be about five feet [1½ m] in length, and the largest exceeded fifteen feet [4½ m]. The head of the largest was the size of a bullock's head and three feet [90 cm] out of the water[27].

It is a little difficult to reconcile the quoted dimensions with a "swan-like" neck. Be that as it may, the animals were heading against the current at a speed of about 7 knots [13 kph]. He also mentioned that only the lack of a second barrel on his gun, the frailty of his boat, and the legendary ferocity of the bunyip deterred him from a serious attempt at killing one.

The farther west I've heard of a bunyip was the Rocky River, near Mt Remarkable, S.A. About 11 December 1853 a man heard a noise from the waterhole where he was camped, and in the moonlight saw a dark shape 15 to 18 feet [4½ - 5½ m] long heading for shore. The noise of his horse made it turn away, but not before he had noticed a large head, and a neck like a horse's, with thick, bristly hair[28].

The report farthest north comes from Thomas Hall. In the 1850s he had heard about the Darling Downs (Qld) version of the bunyip, known locally as the *mochel mochel*. As we have grown used to hearing, the natives were terrified of it, and would never swim in any waterhole believed to be haunted by it, or even camp in the vicinity. He and his brother, George were swimming in the Condamine River not far from Canning Downs station when "King Darby" ran down in great terror to call them out, because the mochel mochel lived in the hole and had eaten all the fish therein.

He got the impression that the animal was rather like an otter, and one day he saw it. According to his reminiscences, made 50 years after the event, he was bringing a herd of wild horses down from the head of Swan Creek, when they came to a place known as the junction of Gap Creek. Suddenly, he heard a piercing shriek like a woman in danger issue from the shallow end of the junction hole.

Much to my surprise I saw an animal in shape similar to a low set sheep dog, the colour of a platypus, head and whiskers resembling an otter, passing from the shallow water over a strip of dry land to the deep water. The back view of this creature's heard was exactly like the bald head of a blackfellow[29].

He also told a story, admittedly second or third hand, of a white man who went fishing in the Condamine near Lord John Swamp. What he saw gave him such a fright that he had to be taken to Warwick, where he died three days later. Swimming in the river had been an animal with the body of a horse and the bald head of a blackfellow.

If the Tasmanian Aborigines ever believed in a bunyip, I have yet to see the evidence. But the white settlers did. Charles Gould, son of the famous bird painter, John Gould, heard about them while acting as Government Geologist on the island, and eventually presented a paper on the subject to the Royal Society of Tasmania[30]. The centre of sightings was the Great Lake. The first one recorded occurred about 11 am on Monday 25 January 1863. Charles Headlam was in a boat in the middle of the lake with his son Anthony at the time.

The lake was very rough, and we were pulling our boat against a strong head sea, when my oar nearly came in contact with a large-looking beast, about the size of a fully-developed sheep dog. The animal immediately started off at great speed towards an island in the Great Lake known as Helen Island. It appeared to have two small flappers, or wings, which it made good use of, as I should think it went at the rate of 30 miles per hour [48 kmh]. We watched it as far as the eye could reach, and it appeared to keep on the face of the water, never appearing to dive.

We know the account is accurate, because it was recorded in his journal at the time. Although it was another nine years before he made it public, neither of them ever saw it again. In September 1870 Gould had a talk with Francis McPartland, the son of the constable at Picton. Several times in 1868 he had seen similar creatures in various parts of the lake, but particularly at Swan Bay. Once three or four of them were just a stone's throw from the shore, and he watched them at play, splashing water 7 or 8 feet [2.1 - 2.4 m] into the air. They were about three or four feet [90 - 120 cm] long, dark in colour, with round heads like a bulldog. Despite their splashing, they did not leap out of the water, but swam around, usually in pairs, with their heads, and occasionally their shoulders above the surface.

Chief Constable James Wilson made some enquiries on Gould's behalf, and discovered that quite a few shepherds had seen the animals, but never very clearly, and never more than one at a time. They were emphatic that they could not have been platypuses. They were twice as large and much darker, rather like a black sheepdog with only its head above water. Headlam's shepherd estimated that the one he saw measured four or five feet [120 - 150 cm], and was very black.

Gould next heard from a market gardener called Mr. Howe. On 17 July 1872 he went out hunting with six friends on Lake Tiberias. Being separated from the Great Lake by more than 70 km, and quite a few mountains and valleys, and not connected to either it or the sea, it is hardly the place where one would expect a bunyip to turn up. However, he had crept up on some swans by the bank, and no sooner had he fired a shot when there was a loud splash 100 metres away. A strange creature was making a dash for the nearby reeds. The only member of the party who saw it at all clearly thought it would have been 5 or 6 feet [150 - 180 cm] long and two feet [60 cm] wide. An hour later they saw the same (?) beast in the rushes, splashing water to a height of 10 or 12 feet [3 - 3.6 m]. Enquiries revealed that the locals had heard loud roarings at night.

Then John Butler reported how he and the Rev. H. D. Atkinson had visited Lake Echo (much closer to the Great Lake) "some years back". No strange animal had been sighted, but they could never account for the water being thrown 10 to 12 feet in the air. There were also rumours of an animal as big as a calf in the deep pools of the Jordan River.

A report on Gould's paper was published in the local press, which immediately brought a response from Joseph Barwick.

> In the autumn of 1852 I was lying in ambush near Lake Tiberias for wild ducks. It was a fine moonlight night, when my attention was attracted by a commotion in the water some 15 yards from me among the debris of a fallen tree. I noticed a large animal, which, after watching him for some time, I concluded must be a large devil. I fired at him, which caused him to flounder in the water. I saw he was seriously wounded and went in to secure him, but when I got within 3

yards of him I saw to my surprise it was quite unlike any animal I ever saw before, his length appeared to be about 4ft. of 4ft. 6 inches [122 - 137 cm], colour black, with a remarkable round bull dog like head, and what surprised me at the time was, instead of his making for the land he made for deep water[31].

His gun having only a single barrel, he was not able to prevent its escape with another shot. However, when he returned with a friend in the morning, they did find quantities of hair, torn off by the blast. Only 2 inches [5 cm] long, it was quite black and glossy, but lighter close to the skin. He also commented that the animal must have been extremely short-legged because, although the water there was only 15 inches [38 cm] deep, its back was not much above the surface.

It is a feature of these bunyip appearances that they run in cycles. A whole generation passed in New South Wales between the first sighting and the discovery of the Murrumbidgee skull, and another generation before a live animal turned up. All this time, the sightings were going on in Tasmania, but in 1872 the *Wagga Advertiser* carried a story just in time for Gould to include it in his survey. This time the name of the animal was *waa-wee*, and it had been seen many times in the Midgeon Lagoon, 16 miles [26km] north of Nerrandera. The journal printed the account of a man who had observed it for half an hour just a few days before (in April). Initially he had scoffed when a passing drover asked about it, but the next morning he went down between 6 and 7 o'clock. Suddenly, he heard the sound of something rushing through the water, making a noise like a North Shore steamer. The animal charged right up to 30 yards from the shore, when it caught sight of them, and halted abruptly. There it lay quietly for half an hour, before calmly swimming away.

The animal was about half as long again as an ordinary retriever dog, the hair all over its body was jet black and shining, its coat was very long - the hair spreading out on the surface of the water for about five inches [12 cm], and floating loosely as the creature rose and fell by its own motion. I could not detect any tail, and the hair about its head was too long and glossy to admit to my seeing its eyes; the ears were well marked.[32]

The following year, the same newspaper described what a boatload of surveyors had seen in Cowal Lake[33], a 10 by 30 km stretch of water, more swamp than lake, fed by the Manna and Yeo Yeo Creeks. At a distance of 150 yards, they saw something "like an old man blackfellow, with long dark-coloured hair", swimming in a straight line, rising to expose its shoulders at intervals of 6 to 8 yards, then diving as if to catch fish. Without showing any sign of fear, it managed to prevent them getting close. They heard that a white man and an Aborigine had seen the same thing a fortnight before.

I might add that the *waa-wee* is still talked about and believed in by the Wiradjuri people still in the area. The also use the term, bunyip as a synonym, and conceive of it as an animal the size of a calf. Some of the older people know people who have seen it[34].

About that time, Major Couchman, the Chief Mining Surveyor of Victoria, told how he and a companion had seen an animal like a water dog swimming in the Malmsbury Reservoir[35]. They were able to get close and watch it for some time before it dived and disappeared. It was large and very dark, and unlike any animal he had seem before. Its head was like a seal's.

In 1927 John Gale, just five years off the century in age, told of two events - one second hand - he remembered from who knows how many decades back[36]. He had been duck shooting on the banks of the Queanbeyan when he saw a big, dog-like creature rise out of the water 100 yards away. His friend, Captain Sam Southwell had seen an animal like a three months old calf basking on a sandbank near Cusack's Landing on the Murrumbidgee. As it slithered into the water, he noted that its rear end had fins or flippers, but not feet.

In 1896 Mr. D'Arcy, schoolmaster and passionate duck-hunter told of his experience at Lake Corangamite, Victoria back in 1872. He had shot a lot of ducks at the mouth of the Woordie Yallock Creek, but the current swept them into the lake. Just then, a man appeared with a little punt in a spring cart.

> I told him if he would go for them he could have half. He did so, but while I was looking at him I heard him scream out and presently he capsized the punt and swam for his life into shore. When he got in, he could hardly stand, and told me that just as he was taking up the last duck an animal like a big retriever dog, with a round head and hardly any ears, had come up close to the boat. He had such a fright he had

capsized it[37].

In the middle of February 1890, some 'extraordinary tales' issued from the vicinity of Euroa, Victoria about a strange animal or reptile in a swamp nearby. So, on Friday 21st of the month, a representative of the Melbourne Zoo arrived with an amateur photographer in tow, and with the object of capturing the animal in a net, formed a line across the swamp and beat every metre of the swamp. Alas! The monster had got away, leaving only 'several suspicious-looking tracks' (we are given no description) among the reeds as tokens of its passing.[38]

Gilbert Whitley has also made mention of some later cases which I have not been able to verify[39]. No doubt they were reported in various local papers. These include the Hairy Nondescript of Crystal Brook, S.A. of 1876. In 1886 some horsemen met a bunyip while fording the Molonglo River, just south of Lake George, and frightened it away with a shower of stones. In contrast to the normal black variety, it was "whitish in colour and about the size of a large dog. Its face was like the face of a child." But the all time classic must be the monster of Tuckerbil Swamp, near Leeton, N.S.W. in 1929/30. It could swim in either direction without turning around, because it had a head at both ends. Whitley also told how Charles Barrett, the naturalist, had investigated bunyip reports from the Haunted Hills near Melbourne in the mid-1920s. The inspiration for the reports was found to be - wait for it - koalas. Not many city slickers know that those little teddy bears bellow during the mating season.

That there are many other bunyip tales out there, I am quite certain. There are references to the seal-like bunyip of the Dynevor Lakes near Thargomindah, Qld, the Dalby bunyip of 1873, and the Warwick bunyip of the early days of this century, the last two being in mochel mochel territory. However, I know nothing about them except for a few brief sentences in second hand references[40].

Some of the modern stories can be weird indeed. On the night of 1st August 1947 three men, C.L. and J.S. Moser, and A. Rice happened to see something on the bank of the Little Murray River near Swan Hill. Being black, and only a metre long, it was assumed to be pig, and was ignored. However, a month later they saw it swimming against the current, with a head and neck about 9 inches [22 cm] thick protruding a foot [30 cm] out of the water. So far, so good. But it was also spouting water from its neck five feet [1½ m] into the air. When they turned a spotlight on it, it swam to the opposite back, lay in a shelter, and emitted a piercing whistle which "could be heard half a mile away"[41]. I wonder what it was.

Almost exactly two years later, the following story came in from Victoria.

> Kyneton has joined the open season for bunyips. Mr. and Mrs. L. Keegan reported to-day [8 September 1949] that several times in the past fortnight they had been astounded by what they described as an animal at least four feet [1.2 m] long, with long shaggy ears, in the new Lauriston reservoir, adjoining their property. They said it used its ears to propel itself through the water "at tremendous speed."
>
> "It dives and has remained under water for a considerable distance before surfacing," they said. "When it submerges the noise can be heard from about 20 yards away."
>
> The Keegans are unable to say if it has fur or feathers, because they have not been able to get a close-up view of it. But they are certain of two things - it is larger than a swan and has long ears.
>
> Mr. J. Beare, a school teacher on holidays, saw the creature twice and has confirmed the description given by the Keegans[42].

Just what were all these mysterious creatures which kept turning up in our inland waters at such wide, irregular intervals? E. J. Dunn had no doubt. In 1856 he was forced to camp on the banks of the flooded Murrumbidgee at Gundagai. Hearing a strange "moo-ing" like a group of calves, he and his party hurried to the river side. Much to his amazement, they saw a whole herd of bunyips swimming against the current. One man fired at then with a shotgun. The boys tried baited hooks, but all to no avail. According to Dunn,

> My recollection of these animals is that they had round heads, with no visible ears, but eyes that could be seen, dark-coloured fur, length of animals about five feet [1½ m]; while swimming the head and the top of the back were exposed above the water. Up to that time I had not seen seals, but since then many have come under observation, and I have no doubt the animals I saw in the Murrumbidgee were seals. Taking into account the windings of the Murray and Murrumbidgee Rivers, Gundagai would be about 2,000

miles [3,200 km] from the sea (estimated).[43]

Virtually every authority on the subject has come to the same conclusion. Seals, with which I include sea lions, were well known to the tribes of coastal Victoria, who hunted them. But the appearance of one inland, particularly with their accompanying barks and bellows, would have caused consternation and terror. To this must be added the presence of a bird, the brown bittern, *Botaurus poiciloptilus*. Skulking among the reeds and other swamp vegetation, it produces calls quite out of character for a bird: croaks and barks and a loud booming. Stray European cattle probably added to the legend.

However, the legends of emu-necked monsters may be based on sightings of genuine sea serpents cum lake monsters. If so, Mr Stocqeler's animals would be the only authenticated case of any being seen in Australian inland waters. (In coastal waters it is a different matter.) The reference to their being covered with sleek fur would then settle the controversy about whether such animals are mammals or not. Even so, in all my reading on sea serpents and lake monsters, I have never come across another with a pelican's pouch.

Although seals are really ocean dwellers, in the past they have turned up far inland[44]. Around 1850 a seal was shot at Conargo, N.S.W., 1500 km from the sea, and well away from the main water courses. For many years its stuffed remains held pride of place on the chimney piece of the Conargo Hotel. Had it not been for that lucky shot, it might have ended up as one more bunyip story. The chairman of the South Australian Pastoral Board saw and recognized a seal at Overland Corner, 400 km up the Murray. That was in 1890. In the early 1930s eyewitness accounts verified the presence of a seal in the riverine swamps of the Murray between Renmark and Loxton. It was stranded in a lagoon 500 km from the sea.

The Challicum bunyip was obviously a seal. The repetitious digging up of the diagram by the natives' spears appears to have at least doubled the original size, but it managed to keep its overall shape.

Ignoring the double-headed, ear-rowing, and whistling, spouting varieties, and allowing for exaggeration, faulty perception, and at times, problems in the transmission of second hand reports, all the bunyips sighted by white settlers can be explained as seals. The very dark colour attributed to many was no doubt a lighting effect on wet fur. I do not think references to long necks mean anything more than the normal extension of a seal's neck and body under certain circumstances. My only reservations concern the very high splashing recorded of a few in Tasmania.

How they got there is another matter. The Molonglo River is one of the headwaters of the Murrumbidgee. To get to Lake George or Lake Bathurst, the intrepid animals would have to have swum almost as far, and then humped, slithered or dragged themselves over a lot of solid ground - fairly high ground, too, which would not have been subject to much flooding. Floods, however, might have assisted the *waa-wee* into Lake Cowal, a similar distance from the Lachlan. I will not even attempt to comment on the single-mindedness, or sense of direction, of the *mochel mochel* of Queensland. Its only exit to the sea would have been in South Australia.

James Wilson, one of Gould's correspondents, thought that the Great Lake creatures must have been very large platypuses. The other sightings would tend to negate this theory. However, the reason he rejected the seal hypothesis was that the only route to the lake from the sea would have been via the Derwent and Shannon Rivers, and the latter is blocked by a large waterfall near its junction with the Ouse. It was not just a solitary wanderer, either; you will remember that McPartland several times saw more than one together. But a waterfall would have been child's play to whatever got into Lake Tiberias, as explained earlier. I might add that as late as 1943, when Charles Barrett visited the Great Lake, he heard stories of a bunyip rising into full view, and found that many of the local still believed it was haunted by a mysterious monster[45]. Perhaps it was.

The situation is different in the Murray-Murrumbidgee-Lachlan basins. Since the heady days of early settlement, the inland rivers have been invaded by fleets of noisy shipping, and their banks infested with noisy, polluting civilized man. It is not surprising that the bunyips have not been back. A chapter of history has closed, and the bunyips have departed forever.

Or have they? In 1971 Jack Evans of the Tweed Heads Pet Porpoise Pool heard of a lagoon in northern New South Wales where dwelt a creature "several feet long with a head like a dog, but with small ears close to its head, [and] had been seen to take white swan"[46]. In some parts the lagoon was reputed to be 60 feet [18 m] deep. According to the owner of the property, at least six people had seen it over the years, and described it as being as thick as a small oil drum. He suspected that a missing cow of his had fallen prey to it, and remembered a story of two

Aboriginal stockmen who went missing when camped by a nearby pool 70 years before.

Feeling it would make a useful addition to his Porpoise Pool, Mr. Evans kept the site secret. Later it transpired that it lay about 20 miles [32 km] north of Lismore. Like any respectable bunyip, it had vanished by the time the investigators had arrived - and that included a team led by Dr. Robert Endean, a Reader in Zoology at Queensland University. Dr. Endean believed it to be a platypus. They normally appear at dusk and sunrise, when the sightings were made, and refraction in the water would produce an impression of size. Readers, however, will immediately note the similarity to other sightings, and a glance at the map will reveal that the route from Lismore to the sea, though circuitous, is not over long.

It was interesting that the word "bunyip" was never raised during that investigation. Back in 1965 there had been a veritable bunyip flurry on Queensland's Gold Coast. It began with a booklet written to mark the jubilee of Mudgeeraba State School. In it, Duncan Campbell mentioned the bunyip which had allegedly haunted the 2000 acres [800 ha] of lagoons and swamps from Mudgeeraba to the back of Burleigh 80 years before. None of the search parties dispatched from Burleigh during the daylight hours ever saw it, but at night it would call. "The sound was a roar similar to, but distinct from, that of a bull and coming at some five seconds intervals." Explanations raised at the time included crocodiles, a large bird, or air blowing through the swamp by pressure from the sea. The *Gold Coast Bulletin* picked up the story and casually asked if anyone had seen or heard of bunyips recently[47].

Well, I don't know if these things are always going on, or whether it was just an incredible coincidence, but a bunyip had actually been calling over the past two weeks[48]. A weird barking roar had been emanating from a river just 200 yards from Tommy Hinde's dairy farm at Gilston. His neighbour, Billy Hill, 3 km away , had also heard it. So on 30 April, just in time for the next edition of the *Bulletin*, they both went to the river. It was all churned up, with mud splashed high up on the bank, but they knew cattle could not have been responsible, for the water was 6 to 8 feet [1.8 - 2.4 m] deep.

Tommy's daughter, Virginia had seen disturbed patches of the river. One big patch of weeds and mud was swirling as if by the thrashing of a large animal. Mud had been splattered all over the bank. Mrs A. Kavanagh, also of Gilston, told how she and her husband had both witnessed churned up mud, and although they had not heard any roaring, it was frightening the local children.

That set the cat among the pigeons. As far as I could discover nobody made any attempt to find out what was responsible, but old timers came forth to tell of their experiences in the past. Mrs Valmai Natlock claimed that when she first settled in Burleigh 40 years before, hardly a night went by without the bunyips calling from the swamp. She was sure there were two. The call was a barking kind of hollow roar, given three to five times in succession, but never just once or twice. About the time their bunyip disappeared, a seal was found dead near Miami, and she thought another one had been found dead just before. An old lady told her she had seen a creature with shaggy black hair attack a dog and throw it out of the river[49].

Carl Lentz remembered searching for bunyips in the Merrimac Swamp back in 1887. He knew there were two, because they could been heard calling, half a mile [0.8 m] apart, at the same time[50]. He also knew what they were: crocodiles, because he had actually seen and stalked them in 1934. However, that is another story, which we shall leave for Chapter 8.

The affair ended on a note of farce, when the Nerang Crocodile Club, allegedly 240 strong, burned the bunyip in effigy because it was taking credit for their animal's activities[51]. Personally, although I do not know what produced the calls in bygone years, I am sure a mundane explanation can be found. However, I fail to see how either seals or crocodiles - or pigs, or eels, which were two other suggestions - would have been responsible for the Gilston phenomena. That is, unless the barking roars and the churning, splashing mud were quite independent.

Little by little strange stories keep leaking out of the Gold Coast hinterland. Eight years later, the sighting of a much stranger monster (see Chapter 6) elicited responses from two old timers[52]. F. Hougonin told of working on the new bitumen road between Currumbin and Burleigh Heads "many years ago".

> I was boarding at the Palm Beach Hotel at the time and every Saturday night I would go by push bike to Burleigh. One night on my way home I got to the top of Burleigh Hill when suddenly there was a terrible roar close by. I peddled until I got to the hotel scared out of my wits. During this winter no female would be seen on the streets after 10pm. And the story goes about a local resident taking his boat (per horse and sledge) down to the water, passing by the

old swamp in those days, there was this terrible roar. The horse bolted, smashing boat and sledge.

W. Robin Smith scoffed at all talk of bunyips, which he had first heard in the 1920s.

The original story told of the bunyip somewhat resembling a horse was claimed to have been seen on the Nerang-Camira Road about 70 years ago [written in 1973] when the countryside was in a state of deluge. It was a shy creature and plunged into the Nerang River and was not heard of again for many years. Not until it was supposed to have been seen in the reputed "Bunyip Hole" at the lower end of the Merrimac Estate.

Obviously, there is some marvellous folklore out there, if we could only access it, but I greatly fear that all those who knew the old stories have passed away.

ADDENDUM

You will have noted I listed a number of cases of which I had no knowledge at all, and if he check through the references, you will see that I was heavily reliant on secondary sources. Also, in the final chapter, I stated that I wanted more information on the early history of the bunyip.

These problems have since been rectified by the widespread digitalisation of old newspapers and other old documents by the National Library of Australia. By this means, I was able to record practically all the information in my book, *The Truth About Bunyips* which, like this present book, is permanently available as a print-on-demand (POD) paperback and e-book. Since it is almost three times as long as the present chapter, it is not possible to include the full details in this addendum. Instead, I shall elaborate on some of the matters raised in the chapter.

Firstly, the 1812 reference to the term, *bahnyip* by James Ives cannot be confirmed. Healy and Cropper apparently obtained it from some secondary source, but later researchers, like David Waldron, Peter Ravenscroft, and I have been unable to locate it.

Rather, it is now established that the word, *bunyip* originated from the Wathaurung language to the south and west of Geelong - incidentally, precisely the area where Buckley had lived. The first written citation was in 1845, when some settlers discovered a huge fossilised bone, which the Aborigines immediately attributed to a bunyip, which they described in fanciful terms.[53] I was able to establish that, although the variety of names indicated that the legend was of long standing, it was limited to the Riverina, and to the central part of Victoria south to the central coast ie around Port Phillip Bay and Western Port. Anything outside of those areas represented a separate myth, or was picked up from the white man.

It is unlikely that the place called Toor-roo-dun by Western Port Bay exists any more, because the swamp to which it belonged has since been drained for asparagus cultivation.

I was wrong to say that Lake Tiberias has no outlet to the sea, although it is true that the route any seal would have to follow in order to reach it is very convoluted. I was also wrong to claim that seals and "bunyips" had ceased to enter the Murray-Murrumbidgee-Lachlan river system. Their numbers have been much reduced, but Peter Ravenscroft managed to locate references to several such instances, as well as in the heartland of Tasmania[54]. I myself also managed to locate references to many "bunyips" not recorded by earlier authorities, including a very humorous occasion when citizens of a small South Australian town unsuccessfully attempted to flush out their local bunyip with dynamite[55]. However, I shall limit myself here to two cases mentioned in this chapter.

The Eumeralla bunyip of 1848 was reported, not by Aborigines, but by white settlers[56]. With regard to Mr. Stocqueler's remarkable encounter of 1857, he later claimed to have been misinterpreted, and that their necks were not like a swan's, nor did they have a pouch[57]. Finally, I am reasonably certain that the weird 1947 bunyip of Swan Hill was not an out of place seal, but an out of place dolphin or beaked whale. The position of its blow-hole would lead to the appearance of spouting from the neck and, although it is not well known, these animals tend to whistle loudly when under stress.

But I still have no idea what sort of thing rowed with its ears at Kyneton two years later.[58]

REFERENCES

[1] The full text can be found in 'The monſtrouſ ſavage from Botany' in the *Sydney Morning Herald* 1st Sept.1987, p17

[2] Roderick Flanagan (1862) *The History of New South Wales*, vol.1, London: Sampson Low, p 233

[3] E.S.Hall (1823) Letter to *Sydney Gazette and New South Wales Advertiser* 27 March1823

[4] Gilbert Whitley (1940) Mystery animals of Australia. *Aust. Mus. Mag.* 7: 132 - 9 (1st March 1940)

[5] R. Brough Smyth (1878) *The Aborigines of Victoria: with notes relating to the habits of the natives of other parts of Australia and Tasmania.*   Vict. Govt. Printer

[6] Cited by Tony Healy and Paul Cropper (1994) in *Out of the Shadows, mystery animals of Australia*, Ironbark Press, p 161

[7] Luise A. Hercus (1969) The languages of Victoria: a late survey. Part II. *Aust. Abor. Studies* No. 17: p 279

[8] Brough Smyth (ref. 5), p 436

[9] Charles Barrett (1946) *The Bunyip and Other Mythical Monsters and Legends.* Melbourne

[10] Whitley (ref. 4) p 135

[11] George Taplin (1878) *The Narrinyeri Tribe*, quoted by Barrett (ref 9).

[12] William R. Corliss (1974) *Strange Phenomena* vol. G1 pp 207 - 232. (Corliss's "Fortean sourcebooks" are a veritable mine of information on anomalies, mostly published in the scientific press, but overlooked.

[13] Whitley (ref. 4) p 134

[14] Brough Smyth (ref. 5) pp 436 -7

[15] Whitley (ref. 4) p 135

[16] A. Massola (1957) The Challicum bun-yip. *Vict. Nat.* 74: 76 - 83

[17] John Morgan(1852) *Life and Adventures of William Buckley*, A. MacDougall, Hobart, pp 48, 108-9 (republished in 1980 by Australian National University Press, Canberra, pp 55-6, 114-15)

[18] William Hardy Wilson (1920) *The Cow Pasture Road*, p 19 (70pp, edition limited to 600 copies)

[19] William H. Hovell (1847) 'The apocryphal animal of the interior of New South Wales'. *Sydney Morning Herald* 9 Feb. 1847

[20] Barrett (ref. 9) , p 11

[21] William Sharp Macleay (1847) 'On the skull now exhibited at the Colonial Museum of Sydney, as that of "the bunyip"'. *Sydney Morning Herald* 14 July 1847

[22] Whitley (ref. 4), p 134, Barrett(ref. 9), p 11

[23] Whitley (ref. 4), p 134

[24] George Hobler (1847) letter to William H. Hovell dated 6 May 1847, published in the *Sydney Morning Herald* 16 June 1847

[25] Whitley (ref. 4), p 134

[26] W. H. Dudley LeSouef (1907) *Wild Life in Australia*, Whitcombe and Tombs, Melbourne, pp 118-9

[27] 'The bunyip.' *Moreton Bay Free Press* 15 April 1857

[28] 'The bunyip of South Australia.' *Argus* 19 Dec. 1853

[29] Thomas Hall. *A Short History of the Downs Blacks, known as "The Blucher Tribe"*. Warwick, published by Warwick Newspaper Co., 36 pp (A carbon copy of this booklet, which was apparently typed rather than printed in the early 1900s, was consulted in the Fryer Library, University of Queensland.)

[30] Charles Gould (1872) Large aquatic animals. *Pap. & Proc. Roy. Soc. Tasm.* 1872 pp 32 -38.

[31] Joseph Barwick (1872) letter published in *Pap. & Proc. Roy. Soc. Tasm.* 1872 pp 40 - 41

[32] *The Mercury* 26 April 1872. (Gould [ref. 30] actually quoted the report from *The Mercury*, which repeated the *Wagga Wagga Advertiser*'s report verbatim.)

[33] Brough Smyth (ref. 5) p. 438

[34] Frank Povah (1990) *You Kids Count Your Shadows, Hairymen and other Aboriginal folklore in New South Wales*, published by the author

35 Brough Smyth (ref. 5), pp 438-9

36 John Gale (1927) *Canberra: History of and legends relating to the Federal Capital Territory of the Commonwealth of Australia*, A. M. Fallick and Sons, Queanbeayan, cited by Tony Healy and Paul Cropper (1994) in *Out of the Shadows, mystery animals of Australia*, Ironbark Press, pp 167-8

37 Quoted in 'Is there a bunyip?' *Bank Notes* December 1958. (Peter Hansen of *The Sunday Mail* supplied me with this information. According to Barrett (ref. 9), the original appeared in the *Geelong Naturalist* in 1896.

38 'A search for a mysterious animal', *Argus* (Melbourne), 28 Feb. 1890, p 6

39 Whitley (ref. 4), p 135

40 Pam Shilton (1980) 'Mythical monsters of Australia', unidentified Brisbane newspaper of 27 April 1980, clipping provided by Peter Hansen of *The Sunday Mail*.

41 'It swims, whistles and spouts. What is it?' *Argus* (Melbourne) 19 Sept. 1947

42 'Weird animal "uses ears as paddles"' *Sydney Morning Herald* 9 Sept. 1949

43 E. J. Dunn (1923) The bunyip. *Vict. Nat.* 40 p93

44 Charles Fenner, D.Sc. (1933) *Bunyips and Billabongs. An Australian out of doors.* Angus and Robertson, pp 5-6

45 Barrett (ref. 9), p 24

46 'Monster search in NSW lagoon.' *Telegraph* (Brisbane) 24 Sept 1971, 'They'll hunt 'lagoon monster' unidentified Brisbane newspaper 18 Sept 1972

47 'Has the bunyip been smoked out by the smog?' *Gold Coast Bulletin* 28 April 1965

48 'Stalking the Gilston Bunyip.' *Gold Coast Bulletin* 30 April 1965

49 letter to the editor, *Gold Coast Bulletin* 7 May 1965

50   'Pioneer claims that "bunyips are crocs"'. *Gold Coast Bulletin* 12 May 1965

51   'Ban on bunyip'! *Gold Coast Bulletin* 14 May 1965

52   letters to the editor, *The Sunday Mail* (Brisbane) 12 Aug. 1973

53   'Wonderful discovery of a new animal', *Geelong Advertiser and Squatters' Advocate*, 2 July 1845, p 2

54   Ravenscroft, Peter (11.11.09), 'Seals observed inland', http://pandora.nla.gov.au/pan/97461/20100202-1526/www.pool.org.au/text/peter_ravenscroft/seals_observed_inland.html

55   However, I did publish the entire amusing newspaper reports in https://malcolmscryptids.blogspot.com/2019/06/the-great-koolunga-bunyip-hunt-of-1883.html

56   'The bunyip again', *The Melbourne Argus*, Tues. 18 July 1848, page 2

57   Stocqueler, Edwin, 'The bunyip', *Bendigo Advertiser*, Fri. 3 July 1857, page 3

CHAPTER 2

YES, VIRGINIA, THERE ARE SEA SERPENTS

Fraser Island is being virtually overrun with tourists these days, but not many of them make it right to the northernmost point, Sandy Cape. If you do, you might pause to gaze out at the beach and imagine what it must have been like in June 1890 when the *moha-moha* appeared. The moha-moha is Queensland's - nay, Australia's - most celebrated "sea serpent", and the only one with an official scientific name: *Chelosauria lovelli*, or Miss Lovell's tortoise-lizard. I shall begin the story with an extract of a letter from Miss S. Lovell, the local schoolteacher, being published in the English journal, *Land and Water*[1].

> We have had a visit from a monster turtle fish. I send a sketch of it. It let me stand for half an hour within five feet [1.5 m] of it. When tired of my looking at it, it put its large neck and head into the water and swept around seaward, raising its dome-shaped body about five feet out of water, and put its twelve feet [3.66 m] of fish-like tail over the dry land, elevating it at an angle. Then, giving its tail a half twist, it shot off like a flash of lightning, and I saw its tail in the air about a quarter of a mile off [400 m] where the steamers anchor.
>
> It has either teeth or serrated jaw-bones. Native blacks call it 'Moka, moka,' and say they like to eat it, and that it has legs and fingers. I did not see its legs, as they were in the water. What I saw of it was about 27 ft. or 28 ft. [8.2 - 8.5 m], but I think it must be 30 ft. [9.1 m] in all. Whilst its head was out of water it kept its mouth open, and, as I could not see any nostrils, I fancy it breathes through its mouth. The jaws are about 18 in. [46 cm] in length; the head greenish white, with large white spots on the neck, and a band of white round a very black eye and round upper and lower jaws.
>
> The body was dome-shaped, about 8 ft. [2.4 m] across and 5 ft.[1.5 m] high, smooth, and slate-grey in colour. Tail about 12 ft. [3.66 m], the fish part wedge-shaped, and fin of chocolate-brown. Then beautiful silver shading to white scales size of thumb nail.

Miss Lovell, and nearly everybody else who has commented on it, assumed that the animal was half fish and half tortoise, but she never actually said that its body was covered by a carapace. However, when the editor suggested she was mistaken about the length of the tail, she replied:

> The tail was over the dry shore for half an hour, so close to me, that five footsteps would have enabled me to put my hand on it.[2]

She also added:

> The blacks, who had not seen it on the day I did, named it at once from my sketch, which must, therefore, be pretty accurate, and called it 'Moha, Moha,' and laughed and said 'Saucy Fellow, Meebee,' in English, 'dangerous turtle.'
>
> It is eight years since it attacked the black's camp. It can stand upright, and it put its legs on the shoulders of a powerful black, 6ft. [183 cm] high, and knocked him down. That year it invaded their camp, and nearly caught one man by the leg. For months after the blacks camped inland.

The tale caught the attention of William Saville-Kent, the assistant curator of the London Natural History Museum, who obtained a fuller account from Miss Lovell for his book, *The Great Barrier Reef of Australia*[3] and it was he gave it its scientific name. Here, then, is her second version of the event:

> I was (while walking on the Sandy Island beach) admiring the stillness of the sea, it being a dead calm, when my eye caught sight of the head and neck of a creature I had never seen before. I went to the edge of the water and saw a huge animal, lying at full length, which was not at all disturbed by my close proximity to it, enabling me to observe the glossy skin of the head and neck, smooth and shiny as satin. Its great mouth was wide open all the time it was out of the water. In about a quarter of an hour or so it put its head and neck slowly into the sea, closing its jaws as it did so. I then saw what a long neck it had, as it moved round in a half circle, and also perceived that the head and neck were moving under a carapace. When the head was pointing out to sea it rose up putting a long wedge-shaped fish-like tail out of the water over the dry shore, parallel to myself, and not more than five feet from me, not touching

the sand, but elevated. I could have stood under the 'flukes of its tail.'

The only part of the body that had marks like joints (like in size and shape to a common brick) was also on the dry shore, but *resting* on the sand; the great dome-shaped carapace, dull slate-grey, was standing quite five feet high, and so hid its long neck and head from my view, which before it rose I could see as a long shadow in the water. The carapace was smooth and without marks of any sort. The fish-like part of the tail was as glossy and shiny as the head and neck, but of a beautiful silver-grey, shading to white with either markings or large scales, each bordered with a ridge of white, but if scales, not like those of a fish in position, as the fishes' scales lie horizontally, whilst the Moha's, if scales, lie perpendicularly, each the size of a man's thumb-nail. It had a thick fleshy fin near the end, about three feet from the flukes, and, like them, chocolate-brown. The flukes were semi-transparent: I could see the sun shining through them, showing all the bones very forked. One of the girls asked me if a shark had bitten a piece out of its tail, and the other one wanted to know it I thought it was an alligator! The fish-like part was quite twelve feet long.

All the time the animal was on shore it was perfectly motionless; at last it gave a curious half-twist to the fluke part of its tail, the movement only reaching just beyond the fleshy fin, and, without disturbing the water in the slightest degree, vanished. I seemed only to have taken one breath when I saw its tail out of the water about the place where the steamer anchors, sending a quantity of fish into the air. I then saw it give a twist to its tail and it disappeared altogether. The black boy saw it on shore the previous Monday, the 9th inst. As I was so close to it for at least half an hour, I was able to study its shape and colouring. In moving about, head and tail were seen alternatively above water, but not even the shadow of its great body, and, from the length of that a spectator could not guess that the head and tail belonged to the same creature, particularly as the colouring is so different. The parts I did not see were the legs. I stooped down and tried, but in vain, to see them, although the Moha was only sanding in a foot [30 cm] of water, but the Black described them as being like an

alligator. I wrote to Dr. Ramsay (Sydney) to ask if the Moha
was the same creature as the great turtle of New Guinea, of
which the Sydney Museum possesses a skeleton, but he
said in reply that it was quite unlike, and calls the Moha a
tortoise, which I think is correct. Dr. Gunther (of the British,
Natural History, Museum) would give £100 for the entire
animal, £50 for part, and a fair price for head and neck
sun-dried.

This account came with a couple of sketches (Fig. 2. 1) and a signed
testimonial:

We, the undersigned, saw the Moha-Moha (as described by
Miss Lovell) making for the shore of Sandy Cape on June
8th, 1890:
James Alsbury, 1st assistant, Sandy Cape Lighthouse.
William H. Lees, 3rd assistant, Sandy Cape Lighthouse.
Mrs. Lees,
Donald Henderson.
Jemima Alsbury) daughters of James Alsbury.
Jessie Alsbury   )
Robert, the black boy, set his "mark" against it, it having
been seen by him on the shore on the previous Monday.
The two girls, Jemima and Jessie Alsbury, were present on
the shore, having gone down there previously, when Miss
Lovell interviewed the monster.

Figure 2.1: Moha-moha, as drawn by Miss Lovell.
A. The animal lying prone in shallow water.
B. The animal with head reared above the water, the body and tail
submerged.
C. The tail raised above water, its action scattering a shoal of fish.

Did you catch all that? I'll run it past you again, slowly. On 8th June

1890, which I've confirmed was a Sunday, a group of white residents saw the moha-moha heading for shore. The previous Monday, which, oddly enough, was the 9th, it was seen on shore by Robert, a remarkably clever Aboriginal boy who, though he lived on Fraser Island and couldn't read or write, knew what the feet of an "alligator" (i.e. crocodile) looked like.

When Miss Lovell and two of the girls were walking on the sandy beach they saw the animal's head and neck protruding from water so deep that it completely hid a carapace five feet high, although it was right next to shore. (You might like to look for this spot when you visit Sandy Cape. I haven't been there, but my experience is that the island's beaches slope very gently.) After a quarter of an hour it swung around, so that the junction between tail and carapace, which had marks like joints, rested on the dry sand. Its hind legs were in a foot of water and its forelegs presumably dangling in very deep water. It then performed the remarkable action of holding its tail high above the sand for half an hour, although the entire sighting lasted only half an hour. Miss Lovell was standing only five feet, or five paces, away, but could not be certain if she was looking at scales or marks on the tail.

Suddenly, it gave a quick flick of its tail and vanished, making only a single reappearance, but this was enough for her to see that it swam by bobbing its head and tail alternately out of the water - a remarkable motion for something with a vertical fluke on its tail. Although the moha-moha has never been seen since, it was not uncommon then, for the Aborigines liked to eat it and it, in turn, liked to eat Aborigines. Miss Lovell was very lucky it wasn't hungry when she saw it.

Originally, the name was written "moka-moka". Only in her second letter did it turn to "moha-moha", a word hard to pronounce in English and impossible in any Aboriginal language, as they lack the sound of "h". I presume the second spelling resulted from a misreading of Miss Lovell's handwriting, and she decided to retain it.

As for the animal itself, we might assume that the "carapace" was merely a bulbous, but unarmoured body. But even so, it would be extraordinarily unlikely to find the tail of a fish attached to the body and head of a reptile, especially one without nostrils. (Even fish have nostrils - in order to smell, rather than breathe.) Moreover, as Heuvelmans[4] correctly points out, a vertical fluke presumes that the tail flexes horizontally while swimming, and that therefore the scales must slide over one another. They cannot overlap vertically. And if that is not enough, the fact is that such a creature has never been reported anywhere else at any time.

In short, I have to agree with Heuvelmans that this is an outrageous hoax. The wild story of the creature coming ashore and attacking the blacks was the last straw on an already over-burdened imagination. Pity. I always liked the moha-moha.

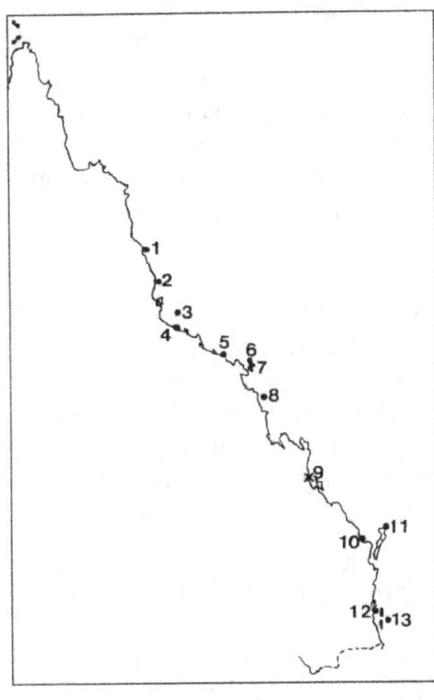

Bawean (ship)	13
Bowen	5
Bribie Island	12
Burrum Heads	10
Deception Bay	12
Fraser I. (moha moha)	11
Green I.	1
Hayman I.	6
Hook I.	7
Mackay	8
Mourilyan Harbour	2
Orpheus I.	3
Rockhampton (stranding)	9
Townsville	4

Map 2.1 Sea serpent reports from Queensland

Well, so much for the fun and games. Let's get on to the serious business. For the fact is, there are such things as sea serpents - not true snakes, of course - not necessarily even reptiles, but various types of large, elongated sea creatures unknown to science. Should anyone doubt then, I should refer them to that encylcopaedic work, *In the Wake of the Sea-Serpents*, in which Dr Bernard Heuvelmans has catalogued 587 reports for the period 1636 to 1966. After eliminating obvious hoaxes, mistakes and vague reports, he was still left with 358[5]. That is more than one a year, or considerably more often than such well known monsters as the giant squid. Furthermore, he was able to tentatively classify them into nine separate categories. (And you always thought there was only one type of sea serpent!) So pay attention, for some of Australia's visitors are so amazing they defy even Heuvelmans' classification.

1849. The good ship *Alpha* was cruising somewhere south of Australia on Wednesday 30 May when, at about 1.15 pm, it began to shake. According to the log of Captain Edwards[6], he and a number of others ran on deck to see a monster about 20 feet [6m] wide swimming nearby. It was a light fawn in colour with large brown spots about the shoulder, with large, glossy eyes and a pointed head, but no fins or broad tail. It tapered from the shoulders down to the tail, which was about 24 inches [61 cm] wide. Finally, it departed at about 30 m.p.h. [48 k.p.h.]. Heuvelmans suggests that it was a giant ray, its two horns twisted into a point, as is often the case. The spots on the back might indicate that it belonged to an unknown species.

1870. Nepean Island is a tiny islet off the coast of Norfolk Island, and John Adams was an inhabitant of the latter, a grandson of one of the *Bounty* mutineers and, according to Captain Marcus Lowther, "a man incapable of telling an untruth"[7]. On 15 October 1870 he and his crew spotted what they thought was a young whale a couple of kilometres off the said Nepean Island, so they hurried over to it. But when they got to within a few metres the look-out exclaimed: "Look! it is a Sea Serpent!"

> The boat shot within a yard of it, and there it was, a veritable Sea Serpent... When first seen it must have been asleep, for its head was lying flat on the surface of the sea, and its body coiled up. The tail of the monster I saw plainly, hanging some three or four fathoms [5.5 - 7.3 m] below the surface. When we came near it, the beast, if I may call it so, raised its head out of the water, looked at us, then slowly straightening himself, he very leisurely moved off. I cannot tell you with any certainty the length of it, for it was not lying with its whole length on the surface, but, as far as I could judge, it must have been thirty or forty feet [9 - 12 m]. It was of a reddish colour, and about a foot or eighteen inches [30 - 46 cm] in diameter.[8]

Unlike other sea serpents, this might really have been a serpent - a sea-snake four or five times the largest recorded species. However, if Mr Adams meant "looped" rather than "coiled', it might be a gigantic eel. In either case, it belonged to a species unknown to science.

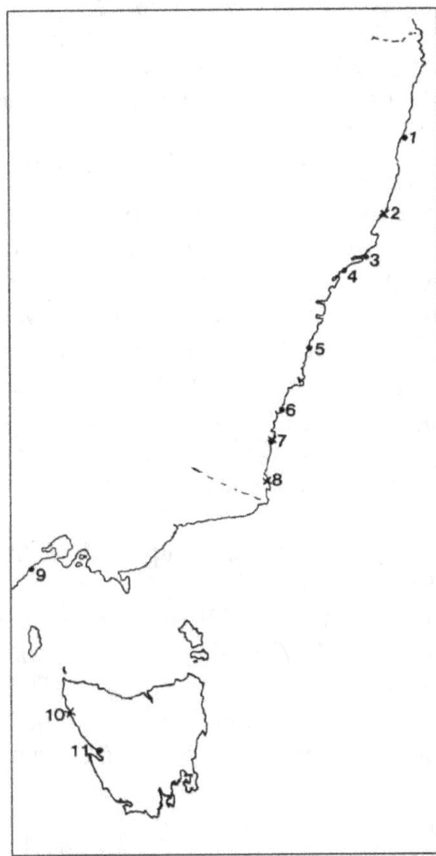

Aireys Inlet	9
Bellambi Beach	5
Broughton I. (shark)	3
Coff's Harbour	1
Macquarie Harbour	11
Manning R. (stranding)	2
Narooma (stranding)	7
Newcastle	4
Sandy Cape (globster)	10
Scarborough	5
St. François-Xavier (ship)	3
Tabourie Lakes	6
Twofold Bay (stranding)	8

Map 2.2 Sea serpent reports from south-eastern Australia

1871. When a sea serpent was witnessed by the crew of the *Granada* off California in 1879, the second officer mentioned that he had also seen one off Australia in 1871. No details are available except that it was "several yards long".[9]

1877. This was the year of the following report[10] :

The chief officer of the *Maid of Judah* sends us the following memorandum: - "Tuesday, November 20th, 1877. - Longitude 121.26 E., latitude 40.2 S., at 11 a.m., while some of the hands were aloft they saw a very large serpent on the weather bow. The vessel passed close to it about forty yards off, and it appeared to be about the length of the vessel: the head of this object appeared to be sunk down out of sight, while a good part of the body and tail was to be seen quite plainly. It was of a browny green colour, and did not appear to have any motion at the time of the vessel passing. There was a fresh gale blowing at the time and a good deal of sea on, yet the thing was broadside on to the sea in curves, as if it was swimming, but the vessel was going faster and so I could not see if it had any motion."

My best guess is that it was a giant salp chain. Salps, or tunicates, are extremely primitive precursors to the vertebrates, and tend to grow in elongated colonies, which tend to pulse in unison to produce a sort of lethargic, undirected swimming motion. Mackal[11] has devoted a whole chapter on them in his book on mystery animals, because in cold waters such as these such colonies tend to grow quite large indeed. Needless to say, it would be extraordinarily unlikely that science has captured the largest chain ever grown, and he made the plausible suggestion that they would explain sightings such as that of the *Maid of Judah*.

1878. A number of rotting carcasses found washed up on shore have from time to time been mistaken for sea serpents. According to Heuvelmans, one such case from Tasmania in 1878 was probably an oarfish (*Regalecus glesne*), a ribbon-like fish of the deep sea, and another one from Queensland in March 1883 was must likely a whale. (This, I presume, was the one found near Rockhampton which was described as being 40 feet [12 m] long, with a snout 8 feet [2½ m] long, an enormous hip bone, and no respiratory tract.[12])

1879. The sun was going down after an oppressively hot afternoon on Sunday, 30 March, when the Rev. H. W. Brown, for 27 years a Colonial Chaplain was riding home along the beach at Geographe Bay, Western Australia. The air was still, the sea as smooth as glass. Just a stone's throw from shore he saw a black log, almost end-on to him, when suddenly he noticed it was moving, leaving a long, narrow wake. Keeping abreast of it, he coo-eed to his friend M'Guire, only to notice that the sound had caused the animal to head seawards underwater. It then doubled back in-shore with the speed of a sword-fish, leaving the sudden change of direction plainly visible in the wake. Just as he caught up with M'Guire, the creature surfaced.

> ... when he was almost at rest, and all apparently was in view, I estimated the length to be 60 feet [18 m], straight and taper, like a long spar with the butt-end, his head and

shoulders, showing well above the surface.

I can only describe the head as like the end of a log, bluff, about two feet [60 cm] diameter; on the back we noticed, showing very distinctly above water, several square-topped fins.[13]

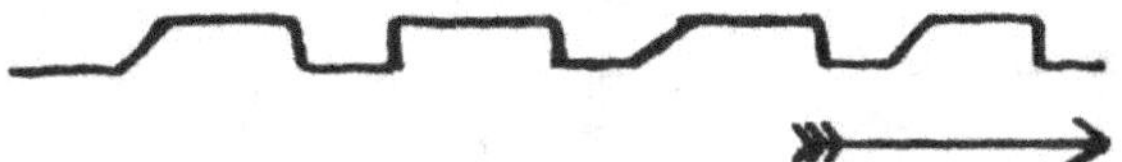

Figure 2.2 *Geographe Bay monster*

The head, he claimed bore little resemblance to a snake's, and he saw no lateral or tail fins. The men and the monster parted company when it became too dark to observe. However, next day a fisherman called M'Mullan told him he had seen it 50 yards from the jetty, and considered it to be only 20 feet [6 m] long. What the creature was is anybody's guess. Mr Brown's drawing (Fig. 2.2) shows how wise he was to take up holy orders rather than art as a career.

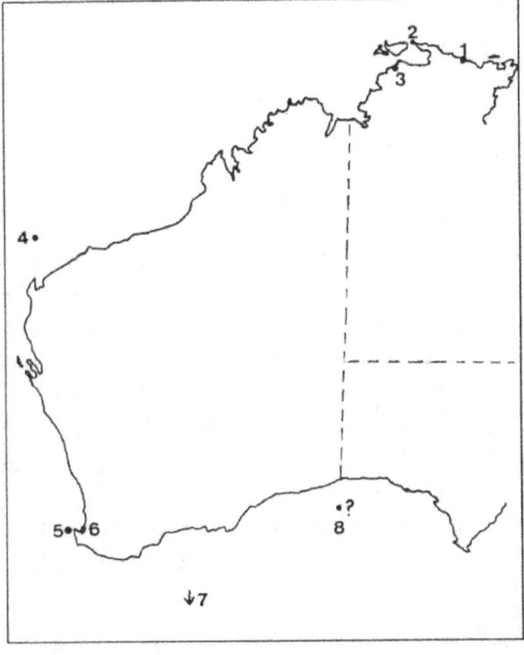

Cape Naturaliste	5
Darwin	3
Geographe Bay	6
Great Australia Bight	8
Kurumba (ship)	4
Larrekeyah	3
Maid of Judah (ship)	7
Maningrida	1
Melville I.	2

Map 2.3 *Sea serpent reports from the western half of the continent.*

1890, of course, was the year of the moha-moha.

1891. There was a moment of high drama in Newcastle harbour on 17 November. A Government diver was working at the moorings in about 30 feet [9 m] of water when it seemed a dark cloud passed overhead.

> As it came closer he perceived a huge sea monster fully 30ft long, with a bulldog-shaped head, sharp piercing eyes, and a savage mouth. It seemed to be extremely flat, with two large fins flapping, and swam along quietly, but determinedly.[14]

He wasted no time in getting out of that water, and refused to go back in that day. While he was relating his adventure, the monster rose from the water near the pontoon. Two boats gave chase, and the animal was stabbed several times with boat-hooks, but to no avail.

It was not until 5 December that the monster (allegedly the same one) appeared again. This time two men called Brinkworth and Emslie managed to spear it with a joiner's adze and drag it ashore, where they earned a tidy sum exhibiting it at the market wharf. It turned out to be a male sunfish, whose dimensions were quoted as: diameter 12 feet [3.65 m], length 9 feet [2.74 m], thickness 3 feet [91 cm] and weight approximately 1½ tons.[15] A sunfish, as the newspaper article pointed out, is a fish of quite extraordinary shape, being short and very high, as if it consisted merely of a head and nothing more. Whether this agrees with the description by the panic-stricken diver I shall leave up to you. Three days later a female was also caught.

1900. On 13 July the good ship *Chillagoe* was sailing off Victoria when, according to Captain W. Firth, he and the crew saw an extraordinary creature 30 to 35 feet long [9.1 - 10.7 m] long, with a seal-like head 2 feet [60 cm] wide. It had four angular fins, each 4 to 5 feet [1.2 - 1.5 m] high and 6 feet [1.8 m] apart. Then they got to within 100 yards of it, it raised its head, stared at the ship, and vanished[16].

The next story is even more extraordinary and considerably more dubious. Captain Laurence Thomson of the *Nemesis* claimed that in October of the same year he saw a very unusual sea serpent off Cape Naturaliste, Western Australia. Heuvelmans couldn't take it seriously, and neither can I.

> It was a rubbery worm-like animal some 300 feet [90 m]

long and 3 feet [91 cm] in diameter, which rose out of the water in three huge arches in a way that was both mechanically and dynamically utterly impossible. In front of these arches a head rose on the end of a long neck, and on the spine was a sort of high soft fin that could fold up like a parasol.[17]

1913. On 6 July two Tasmanians, called Oscar Davies and W. Harris saw something strange at Macquarie Harbour.

The animal was about fifteen feet [4½ m] long. It had a very small head, only about the size of the head of a kangaroo dog. It had a thick, arched neck, passing gradually into the barrel of the body. It had no definite tail and no fins. It was of chestnut colour, well-groomed and shining. It had four distinct legs. It travelled by bounding - i.e., by arching its back and gathering up its body, so that the footprints of the forefeet were level with those of the hind feet. It made definite footprints. These showed circular impressions, with a diameter (measured) of 9 inches [23 cm], and the marks of claws, about 7 inches [18 cm] long, extending outward from the body. There was no evidence for or against webbing.[18]

Here I should point out that one of the most common "sea serpent" types, reported all over the world, is a beast with a bulbous, often humped body and a long, swan-like neck. (We shall meet a few later on.) Heuvelmans[19] considers that Macquarie Harbour is one of the few sites where it has been reported on land, and he quotes it as evidence that the "long-necked" sea serpent has no tail, and moves like a sea lion, with its hind flippers pointed forward. I beg to differ. There is nothing in the above report to suggest that the neck was long and thin - rather the reverse - nor that its feet were in fact flippers. The footprints would tend to deny that. All we can say is that this monster was a true unknown.

1916. It was not until he read reports of the Loch Ness Monster that Mr W. S. Arthur was game to describe the encounter he had on the King's Birthday long weekend in June 1916. At that time he was employed constructing lighthouses at Darwin and Cape Don, so he and seven other men decided to sail the 18 miles [29 km] from Cape Don to Melville Island.

We started about 3pm on the Saturday afternoon in a 27ft [8¼ m] surf boat, with a long sail and long sweep oar for steering purposes. We also carried 4 spare oars in case of need, with rifles and ammunition and a good supply of stores and fresh water. After leaving the bay we got a steady breeze, favourable to carry us over, doing about 4 knots [7½ kph] against strong tide part of the way. About 6.30pm, most of the men were laid out in the boat in thwarts, and in the bottom of the boat. Baxter was sitting in the bow keeping a lookout for the reef marked on our chart called Elphinstone Reef...

Ned Baxter, he had already mentioned, was an old time skipper of a Grimsby trawler. These details are not important in themselves, but they suggest that the story is genuine. A hoaxer would more likely go straight for the monster punch line.

I was steering with the big sweep oar, when Baxter shouted out to me "What's that just astern there?" I turned sharply, thinking it was rocks when to my surprise, and not more than 30 feet [9m] from me, appeared a huge head about 6ft [1.8m] out of the water, with 5 or 6 large parts of its body in a straight line with a division between each of them, reaching in all about 40 feet [12m]. As it came nearer I lifted the blade of my oar as high out of the water as I could and tried to hit it on the head, which by this time was only a foot [30 cm] above the water.
I missed hitting it, but felt a hard sudden jerk on my blade which nearly knocked me over the side. I grabbed the sheet of the sail, or I must have gone over. I looked around again, but could only see its wake windward to our boat. I found 4 teeth, 3 on 1 side and 1 on the other broken off deeply into the ash oar. We extracted them from the oar and kept them as souvenirs, 2 of which are still in my possession.[20]

Apparently, nobody of any scientific background ever read that account, or asked to examine the teeth. I wonder if his heirs still have them, or recognize their significance. They must be the only relics of a sea serpent in existence.

1918. The crayfish men of Port Stephens had seen whales; they'd seen sharks; they thought they'd seen them all. But what they saw that day in 1918 sent them scurrying, panic stricken back to port, and for several days nothing would persuade them to go back to sea. They had been out near Broughton Island, quietly minding their own business, handling their crayfish pots - which were each 3 foot 6 inches [107 cm] across and often filled with 20 or 30 kg of crayfish - when out of the water rose a gigantic shark. The sea boiled into a fury as the ghostly white monster charged into their midst, gulping down 'pots, mooring lines and all' as if they were snacks.

Along came the noted fish expert, David Stead, with the Fisheries Inspector, Mr Paton. Now, these fishermen were stolid, prosaic men who seldom even discussed their catches, and they knew that the two officials had heard all the fish stories before. But they were terrified beyond the bounds of reason. How big was the shark? Oh, it was as long as they wharf: 35 metres. No, it was "three hundred feet [90 m] long at least". Its head! It was "at least as large as the roof of the wharf shed at Nelson's Bay."[21]

Stead had no doubt that they had seen a surviving specimen of the supposedly extinct *Carcharodon megalodon*, a giant version of our own white pointer, reputed to have reached 25 metres. Gerald Wood[22], on the other hand, suggested it might have been a genuine Moby Dick, an albino sperm whale. His argument was that the huge head was more appropriate to a sperm whale than a shark. Agreed. But it seems to me that the fishermen's terror, and their consequent exaggerations, was produced by the sheer ferocity of the attack, which is more reminiscent of a shark's feeding frenzy, especially one which would have to raise its head out of water to swallow the pots.

However, we are right to ask: just how big should we expect a shark to grow? The largest of all are the whale shark and the slightly smaller basking shark, both of which are inclined to top 15 metres, the size of a humpback whale. And like a humpback whale, they eat nothing but plankton. For the real maneaters we must turn to the genus *Carcharodon*. A successful breed, this genus has been around for about 100 million years. Its present representative is *C. carcharias*, the white pointer, the white death, the great white shark, "Jaws", but in bygone days, for 20 or so million years, its big brother, *C. megalodon* roamed the seas, dropping its huge jagged teeth on the sea floor when it passed away. Some of them are no more than 11,000 years old[23].

Its size has also been greatly exaggerated. When you read of Jaws being 30 feet [9m] long, or see a reference book state : "It reaches 30 feet in length", you assume this is the norm. Wrong. In the first place, there are freakishly large fish, as with everything else. (After all, human beings "reach 272 cm in height".) In the second, unlike us, these things continue growing, albeit slowly, throughout life, so all of those caught will be under the maximum size.

John Randall[24] decided to investigate the sources of these stories. They related back to Günther's 1870 *Catalogue of Fishes in the British Museum,* in which was listed the jaws of two specimens caught off Port Fairy in Victoria 36½ feet [11 m] long. No-one knows where that figure came from, but it is strongly suspected that it was a misprint for 16½ feet [5 m]. The largest actually measured was a 21 foot [6.4 m] brute taken off Cuba. However, the tooth marks measured on a whale of Western Australia in 1972 suggested a length of 25 - 26 feet [7.8 m], and an even larger bite was seen, but not measured, in 1968. Judging from the size of its teeth, *C. megalodon* would have come to 43 feet [13 m], which is quite a fall in reputation, but still enough to put the fear of hell into any prudent fisherman.

While we're talking about sharks, lets go to back to David Stead[25]. In May 1939 Captain J. S. Elkington wrote to him about what he saw outside the Townsville Breakwater in 1894 when his launch was broken down for half an hour. He knew sharks, and he was positive the monster which lay just 3 metres from the boat was not a basking shark, but a great white. Presumably, he did nothing to arouse it, for it protruded a couple of feet beyond each end of his launch. And the launch was 35 feet [10.7 m] long. Wood himself quoted a rumour of a 43 footer [13 m] which was caught at False Bay, South Africa[26].

Then there is the story of the *Rachel Cohen*[27]. Allegedly, while riding out a storm off Timor the captain felt a violent shock and assumed they had hit a floating log. But when they got back to dry dock in Adelaide (this was March 1954) they found seventeen shark teeth embedded in the keel next to the twisted screw. They were an average of 8 cm wide and 10 cm long, and the semicircle of tooth marks was almost a metre across. From the spread of the jaws we must assume that it was the largest teeth which were wrenched free. Based on Randall's figures, this little beauty would have measured somewhere between 11 and 13 metres.

If any of these anecdotes were to be accurate, the message is clear: old Super-Jaws, *C. megalodon,* is still prowling the seven seas. And you thought it was safe to go back to the water!

1924. Sharks at least make comfortable monsters. We know them. We can identify them. Not the thing that rose out of the sea at Green Island, off the coast of Cairns in the winter of 1924. Although its friends and relatives turn up in every sea in the world, not to mention quite a few fresh water lakes, nobody has an inkling what it was. After the Bellambi Beach sighting in 1930 (see below) an anonymous writer came clean about what he saw.

> It was only a few oars' length from the launch, and about 9 feet [2.74 m] of an arched neck was exposed. With a diameter about 15 inches [38 cm], its color was a mottled brown and yellow. The whole body must have been of great length. It was assuredly a member of the serpent order, and not a porpoise, seal, dugong, or tortoise, with all of which I am familiar. Others saw the animal. It was no optical illusion, and there was no liquor on board!"[28]

Funny, isn't it, how people who report something strange have to defend their sobriety? But can you really imagine anyone who had been drinking reporting his DTs? In fact, since strange things are bound to happen to drunks as well as sober citizens, I'm inclined to think a lot of things go unreported because the witness thought he was "seeing things".

1925. Two very different sightings were recorded from the east coast this year. The first was, in fact, was reported shortly after the event by the captain of the *Saint-François-Xavier* in the private letter to the Director of the Oceanographic Institute of Indo-China. It was not published for another twelve years[29].

Haiphong, 18 March 1925

> Sir, I am sending you a little sketch drawn at sea several minutes from the appearance of the famous sea-serpent. The second captain, the second lieutenant, the radio officer and the third engineer are unanimous in confirming the following lines:
>
> On 2 February 1925 while on passage from Nouméa to Newcastle, the ship making 10 knots [18½ k.p.h.], at 18.30 hours abeam of Port Stephens on the east coast of Australia, two masses like turtles' shells were seen floating 30 feet [9 m] from the ship on the starboard bow.
>
> Abeam of the engines there rose a big head like a camel's head, on a long flexible neck having a great similarity to a swan's neck. The height of the neck was about eight feet [2½ m]. The body, as thick as the big Bordeaux barrels, formed a chain of five loops; on the fourth loop, an aileron as on sharks of great dimensions,

measuring 5 feet [1½ m] in height and in width at the base. The aileron seemed to be black in colour; the colour of the animal was dirty yellow, the skin smooth without appearance of scales.

As it passed astern of the ship and was abeam of the starboard screw, the animal's head began to move backwards and forwards, which led us to think it had been touched by a blade of the screw; its movements seemed hindered and was not at all like that of the little snakes seen near the coast.

The animal was visible for fifteen minutes, no optical illusion is possible. For, besides the testimony of the Europeans, the Blacks from New Caledonia serving as seamen on board, the Annamite boys and Chinese stokers all gave one cry: 'There's the Dragon!' The Chinese even made an offering to it.

As night falls very quickly at that time we could not give other details, being one and all fairly taken aback by this fantastic apparition...

Raoul Jaillard

Figure 2.3 Saint-François-Xavier *monster*

The thing that turned up six months later a bit further north it not quite as strange, though you mightn't think so at first sight. It was 23 July, and the *Bawean* had just dropped its Brisbane pilot and was heading for Sydney when, according to the Dutch Captain P. de Haan:

We were suddenly aware of a violent disturbance in the water to starboard. A little later a long black body, estimated at 8 metres [26 ft] long, emerged at an angle of 45°, then fell back into the water with a loud splash, making the sort of waves we had already seen. It reappeared again, closer to us four times; the body, sticking out obliquely, which was about 1½ metres [5 ft] thick and was more or less cylindrical, seemed to have a long head, with a beak and eye, and rounded at the end. When the animal fell back, a fin about 4 metres [13 ft] long rose at an angle on the right side behind the head, and the body curved to this side when it fell. At the same time there rose out of the water, several feet away, a sort of tail, much thinner than the front part. On the top of the head the skin was black and pimpled, while underneath it was lighter and smooth. The erected 'fin' was much lighter still: almost white with black patches. Its breath was very clearly seen and heard. To my great regret nobody had a camera handy, and it was very difficult to focus glasses on the animal, as we did not know exactly where it would appear next. The shortest distance at which it appeared was about 350 metres.[30]

The officer of the watch thought that the 'fin' was an open jaw, but Captain de Haan insisted that he saw the animal head on, and it was definitely attached to the side. However, not many sea creatures possess a right pectoral fin half the length of the body, especially not one which could be mistaken for a jaw. I suspect that "4 metres" may have been a misprint for " 0.4 metres". This would make it rather small, I agree, but at least it would explain how the left fin was overlooked. The reference to a beak and a clearly visible breath suggests that we are dealing with an unknown species of dolphin, perhaps one of the Ziphiidae, or beaked whales. Quite a few of these species are known only from a handful of strandings, or even by sightings alone, but because they are not serpentine in shape their existence is not disputed.

1926/27. It was in either of these years that the *City of Manila* was sailing from Melbourne to Fremantle. It was crossing the Great Australian Bight about six bells (7 am) on a Sunday morning when the third mate, Alec J. Gracie, happened to see something about a mile [1½ km] away. It was in view for about half a minute while he, and then the quartermaster, gazed at it through binoculars. Unfortunately, Mr Gracie did not tell the story until 1953, by which time he had mislaid his notes. It was described as a series of six to eight undulating arches without a head being visible[31].

1930. I find the next two sightings particularly frustrating, but I cannot locate the original reports. My friend, Paul Cropper suggests they first appeared in some Wollongong newspaper, but all I have are some secondary references. The most detailed is this one, also sent to me by Paul himself:

Wollongong, Thursday. [i.e. 10 June] - Four men fishing off Bellambi claim that they came in contact with a sea serpent 30 feet [9 m] long, and with a mouth large enough to take in their boat and its occupants! The party comprised J. Lin, A. Gray, R. Wiley, and G. Richardson. One of the number noticed what he took to be a piece of wreckage, and gave the order to pull closer to it. When within about twenty feet [6 m] the monster raised its neck and head about six feet [1.8 m] out of the water, they say, and roared something like a seal. The party pulled away, and the monster followed for half a mile [0.8 km]. Then they made for the beach and safety[32].

David Stead (the fish expert, remember?) said it was a giant squid. However, when he heard that the monster's head was six feet [1.8 m] across, that it opened its mouth eight feet [2.4 m] wide, and that said mouth looked like a pelican's, he changed his identification to the piked rorqual, *Balaenoptera rostrata*. He might be right, though I'd be inclined to choose a larger whale. The piked rorqual only reaches 9 metres, but like other baleen whales, it has an enormous gape, and the underside of its jaws is a grooved pouch somewhat like a pelican's. Also, there are no other reports of such a head attached to a sea serpent.

However, two days later, while three people were standing on a cliff at Scarborough they were able to watch a new monster undulate lazily in the direction of Bellambi Reef. It was described as "about 80 or 90 feet [24 - 27 m] long, of dark greyish color and with a frightfully ugly head" which was held in the air at the end of a long snakelike neck.

This, said Mr Stead, was definitely a giant squid. Now, giant squids, like sharks, are something we know and can relate to. They are described in text books, and make their appearance in lurid novels. But they fact is, they are creatures of the deep seen much more often in print than in real life, and certainly much less often than sea serpents. In fact, if they didn't have the bad luck to be washed ashore dead every now and then, they would still be as mysterious and as controversial as the sea serpent. They propel themselves by a jet funnel with their tentacles trailing behind Under such circumstances they might appear to undulate. In a trice, they might even speed off with their tentacles in front. But if there is one thing that is out of the question, it is for one to do so with a tentacle waving in the air like a snake or swan.

On 9 November the same year a Mr George Morris was admitted to Hobart Hospital with deep bite wounds on his leg. He and his companion said they'd been happily fishing off East Risdon when a sea monster rose up, placed its forepaws on his boat, grabbed him by the overcoat and dragged him overboard. Once in the sea, it took him by the leg, and only let go when his free leg kicked it in the eye. The newspaper suggested he was attacked by a sea lion, and I agree. But why it would behave like that is anybody's guess.[33]

1931. A Goulburn man, Walter Roots had heard about the South Coast Sea Serpent, but it did not stop him from holidaying there in early February or late January 1931. There he was, fishing off the rocks at Tabourie Lakes (I presume the town was meant, not the lake of the same name) when he saw something swimming in the deep water immediately below him.

> The animal, Mr. Roots said, was of a reddish brown colour and was from 25 to 30 feet [8 - 9 m] long. It had a head resembling a pig and just behind the head were two floppy arms. The body was similar to a huge barrel and the tail was vertical, like a ship's rudder.
>
> Most surprising features were the creature's eyes, which were protruding and appeared to be as large as saucers, and its teeth, which were sabre-like, were fully six inches [15 cm] long.
>
> Mr. Roots says that the animal dived into the water and rose with a fish in its jaws. The fore part of its body was lifted about five feet [1½ m] from the water and, swaying from side to side, the animal bit the fish in half and after chewing the portion, dived after the other, bringing it to the surface and eating it also.[34]

What he found truly alarming was the way it roared at intervals "like the loud grunt of a pig". Yet although it passed within a few feet of him, he watched it for fully 25 minutes before it headed for the open sea. He was in poor health, and his two companions confirmed that when he rejoined them he was most upset.

I presume that the tail was in fact a pair of flippers which only appeared vertical because of their movement at the time. Apart from that, there are lot of animals which look and act like Mr Roots' monster. They're called seals. The only trouble is, they tend to be only half or a third of the length of this one. Admittedly, startled witnesses do have a tendency to exaggerate (remember the Broughton Island shark?) but Walter Roots had this thing in view for 25 minutes, much of it at point blank range. The only seal that comes anywhere near that size - and only really outsized specimens at that - is the male elephant seal. Unfortunately, it possesses a large, bulbous proboscis which could not be overlooked, and which would tend to flop around hiding its teeth while it was feeding. Also, it has little piggy eyes, not protruding saucer-like ones. Finally, it would have been a long way from home. I can only presume that what Mr Roots saw that day in 1931 was a member of a unknown species of giant seal. It must be exceedingly rare, but somewhere, in some little visited corner of the world, there must be a beach where it comes ashore to breed.

1932. Boyd Lee was a professional shark fisherman. He took Norman Caldwell for a shark fishing expedition in 1933, and the latter wrote a book about it. According to Caldwell, Boyd told him about the time, eight months before, he had been fishing in very deep water 27 km northeast of Hayman Island. Out of the depths rose the biggest turtle he'd ever seen: at least 4 feet [1.2 m] long and weighing an estimated 500 pounds [227 kg]. Before the turtle had time to know what had happened, a mighty head, a head that resembled the head of a giant snake, came out of the water, and struck once, only once, at the turtle. Then the turtle and the vast sinister head that had engulfed it, disappeared. I repeat, that turtle must have weighed over five hundred pounds... Boyd and his companion went for their lives.[35]

According to Caldwell, Boyd Lee was "not above a leg-pull" but fishing was far, far too serious an activity to be the subject of such a hoax. He was convinced that Boyd was telling the truth. Now, at this distance I am in no position to judge the character of Mr Lee. But I have myself become a minor connoisseur of sea serpent tales. And the fact is that nothing the size and voracity of this creature has been reported before - unless you count the dubious photograph of le Serrec, of which more later. Also, I know that most people take the term "sea serpent" far too literally, and when spinning a yarn are likely to describe a snake-like head - something which rarely appears in the more plausible stories.

1934 was a very good year for sea serpents. The previous year the beastie from Loch Ness had made his début, so now people were no longer afraid to mention it when his Australian cousins made a call. (Which makes one wonder how many are seen and not reported in normal years.) In that year a wave of sea serpent sightings spread southwards down the east coast. And here I am almost as frustrated as with the Bellambi sightings. The primary reports all appeared in North Queensland newspapers, which are not accessible to me, and I have had to rely on secondary sources. (That's a hint for all my North Queensland readers.) I have never, for instance, been able to find anything on the monster than visited Mourilyan Harbour, except that it was seen a week before the following sighting.[36]

> A sea monster appeared in the Bowen Harbour this week.
>
> Mr H. Hurst, a very well-known local fisherman, was making his way towards Bowen when he saw a dark object floating on the surface of the water, about two hundred yards away. The sea was dead calm at the time. He pointed it out to his two mates, C. Hunt and J. Ayles. At first they thought it was a whale as these have been fairly plentiful in these waters lately, but whilst they were approaching it suddenly lifted its head about eight feet [2.4 m] out of the water, and the launch party called a halt. Mr Hurst said he did not like the look of it at all. It appeared to be about thirty feet [9 m] long and had a head like a large turtle just as has been described farther north, and a body like a huge armoured hose. So they decided not to stop any longer, as they had no rifle on board, but went on to town.
>
> Mr Hurst did not mention the incident at first, for fear of being disbelieved.
>
> When first seen the monster was between Sinclair Bay and Gloucester Passage, and was heading in the direction of Sinclair Bay.

This must have been only a few days before the events of Sunday 18 August, off Townsville.

> At a quarter to seven in the morning a party aboard a yacht sighted it between Cockle and Bolger's Bay just off Magnetic Island. It lifted its tail out of the water several

times and dropped it. The tail was not the fluke tail of a whale, but more that of a huge eel.[37]

About the middle of the day a 14 foot [4¼ m] launch set out with a fishing party: William Quinn, Oscar Swanson and the latter's nine-year-old son, Harold. The sea was as smooth as glass. Swanson had told his son to keep an eye out for whales, because he himself had seen four the previous day. Sure enough, the lad noticed four objects three miles [5 km] away and close to the Fairway Beacon, at the end of Platypus Channel. They turned out to be the head and humps of a sea monster - a monster which sank slowly like a submarine once they got to within 150 yards.

They headed for the beacon. After five minutes the animal rose again - once more like a submarine. They climbed the ladder for a better look. Except for a slight swaying of the head, it never moved. So after half an hour they headed back to shore, deposited the boy, and fetched the press. But by then the noise of another boat, the S.S. *Marella*, scared the monster into diving. However, the press photographer, Mr Ellis, did see two dark shapes in the deep about 6 metres apart.

About 3.30 the monster stuck up its head next to a small fishing dinghy, whose occupants took off for shore.

Oscar Swanson himself wrote a full description for the *Victorian Naturalist*[38]:

The head rose about 8 feet [2.4 m] out of the water, and resembled a huge turtle's head; the mouth remained closed. The head was about 8 feet from the back of the head to the front of the mouth, and the neck was arched. The colour was greyish-green. The eye (we could see only one, being side on) was small in comparison to the rest of the monster. The other part in view was three curved humps about 20 feet [6 m] apart, and each one rose from 6 feet [1.8 m] in the front to a little less at the rear. They were covered in barnacles. We could not get a glimpse of the tail, as it was under water.

The article continued :

Mr. Swanson further stated that there was no sign of fins and that there was a dark line along the back, but as the monster was motionless he could not discern what power it used to swim. It had no mane or sign of legs, as far as he could make out. The scales were shiny in the sun and

seemed to be butted and perpendicular. There were many
barnacles on the body, some the size of soup plates, whilst
the scales were the size of saucers.

Pretty darn big barnacles! They don't normally come wider than 5
cm, and since Mr Swanson was never closer than 150 yards [137 m] I
suspect he was really looking at special body markings or protuberances.
His sketch is reproduced as Figure. 2.4 but, judging from the description,
the head should be longer. I'm not certain what he meant by saying that
the scales were "butted and perpendicular". However, it should be noted
that he has the scales pointing vertically on both the neck and the humps,
which is more likely to indicate amateurish drawing skills than biological
reality. If not, then its body must flex vertically, like a mammals, rather
than horizontally like a reptile or fish, because scales must overlap in the
direction of flexure.

Figure. 2.4. Swanson's sketch of the Townsville sea serpent

Oscar Swanson continued:

A week before, a monster was seen at Mourilyan Harbour
by a fishing party in a large launch, and the description
given by them tallied with what we saw, only the creature
made a loud noise as it swam around their boat, about 50
yards away. A week later, it was seen again around Bowen,
and the account in the North Queensland Register
describes what was seen there. A week later, the M.V.
Trentbank, on her way to Canada with a shipment of sugar,
sent a wireless to Townsville that they had sighted the sea
monster off Mackay. Some weeks later, when a motor boat,
the *Rahata*, was coming north from Brisbane (to fish for the
kingfish season off Palm Islands), one of the crew, a man
named Mills, was on deck, when he saw the monster a few
feet off the boat. This was further south, near the Barrier
Reef. He described in our paper that he saw two big humps
about 25 feet [7.6 m] apart, of a grey-greenish colour,
covered with scales the size of saucers. He did not see the

The full reports were no doubt published in various north Queensland newspapers now buried deep in some north Queensland archive.

The Townsville monster is really peculiar. String-of-humps type sea serpents are rather common around the world, but this is the only one I know of which was covered with large scales. And what about the others? People blithely assume that there is only one species of sea serpent, and when several reports occur together they automatically notice similarities in the descriptions. Nevertheless, it must be admitted that these descriptions do sound similar. At least, brief as they are, the all mention something with humps and scales.

But look at the time and distance factor. The Townsville sightings occurred on 18 August. The Bowen sighting must have been around the same time, because the report dated 21 August said "this week". The visit to Mourilyan Harbour was a week previous. Yet Townsville is 170 km northwest of Bowen and 200 km southeast of Mourilyan Harbour - as the crow flies, and considerably farther as the sea serpent swims. If the same individual were involved, those brief stopovers must have been the only rests it had. Either that, or this rare species had suddenly decided to put North Queensland on its migration route. It's a pity they haven't come back.

I presume that the following sighting took place later in the year. Robert F. Steele was a producer and Pierce Mack a co-director for Australia Travel Pictures. They had been shooting scenes for a documentary called "Australian Today" at Orpheus Island, 72 km north of Townsville and travelling away from the island when the creature appeared. It came quite close to the boat, following it effortlessly for a quarter of a mile [400 m], occasionally raising its head three or four feet [about a metre] out of the water. Would you believe? Their cameras were in another boat. Mr Julian, the chief medical officer at Fantome Island also claimed to have seen it. Robert Steele described it as:

tinged with brown about the fins.[39]

In other words, it was nothing like the earlier monsters. It sounds like a green version of the Nepean Island monster of 1870, and the fins identify it as a giant eel rather than a giant snake. Mr Steele drew a picture of it, but my source has not reproduced it.

If this happened in September, and likewise the Mackay sighting, September must have been a memorable month. Another monster showed up in New South Wales.

> Charles Blanche and Alfred Jackson, of Coff's harbour, two well-known deep-sea fishermen, report that about four miles [6½ km] from the entrance to Coff's harbour they saw from their launch yesterday [i.e. 13 September] what they first took to be a log. Then they saw two legs which were about a foot [30 cm] in diameter, and were about 20 feet [6 m] apart. They turned their craft about to make a closer inspection, but when nearing the object, they saw it roll over and a head, which both men declare resembled that of a horse, appeared. With a snort the creature plunged down to the depths, disappearing in a cloud of spray.
>
> Blanche and Jackson declare that the monster was up to 40 feet [6 m] in length, and that in all their years of the sea they had never seen before such a weird-looking sea dweller[40].

It's a pity they weren't more explicit. How long were the two legs, and what did they look like? Was the animal lying on its side? How close did they get? Why don't newspaper reporters ask such questions?

David Stead said it was a giant squid. The horse-like head was one of the long tentacles lifting out of the water. The suckers looked like a mane (the witnesses did not mention a mane) and the snort the sound of the squid's water jet with which it propels itself.

And so ended a most amazing year.

1935. The east coast was still in "sea monster" mode when, on the 15 April, two boys, Keith and Joseph Thomson, discovered a body washed ashore 3km from Narooma.

> The animal was about eight feet [2.4m] long. It had a long, tapering, bony head. The lower jaw was studded with about 48 teeth, which were separated by half-inch [13mm] gaps. Most of the teeth were missing from the top jaw. The eyes

were set just behind the gape of the large mouth. There
were two fins just behind the head, a large dorsal fin, and
two horizontal fins at the end of the tail. The whole animal
was covered with a smooth, leathery skin.[41]

Mr Stead said it was probably a dolphin, and for once I agree. It's a
pity no scientist thought to preserve it and identify the species. It might
have been rare, or even new to science.

Less than three weeks later came another report:

Mr. Michael Fourter, of Shadrach's Creek, near Eden,
reports that some days ago he saw on the Boyd Town
Beach, on the western side of Twofold Bay, the carcass of a
marine animal, unlike any he had previously seen or heard
of. It was, he said, about 8 feet long, and the head
resembled that of a horse. The neck was arched. On the
body were five fins, which were split so as to appear to
consist of seven segments. On the inner side of the fins
was a very hard bristle, white in colour. The flesh that was
left was much like that of a fish. At the tail were two long
bones, protruding in the shape of a cow's horns, and the
ribs were about the size of a calf's ribs. The description
resembles, in some respects, that of the strange beast
found recently on a beach near Narooma, but whether the
two animals were of the same species is not known.[42]

Whew! The reporter couldn't have read his own newspaper if he
thought there was any resemblance between the two other than length.
Over the centuries there have been quite a few carcasses like this, and
they have almost invariably turned out to have be belonged to badly
decomposed sharks[43]. However, the mention of ribs might suggest a
dolphin, unless the witness was confusing the bones supporting the gills
and fins for ribs.

While we're on the subject of carcases, in 1952 something was
found washed ashore at Old Bar entrance to the Manning River, near
Taree. It was described as having "a head like a calf, an elongated
duck-shaped bill, two small flaps on either side, and a fan-shaped tail."[44]
Its length was estimated at 15 feet [4.6m] and its circumference 9 feet
[2.7m]. There was nothing to say whether it was fresh or rotten. The
locals suspected it might be a dugong, but Dr Troughton, the curator of
mammals at the Australian Museum, pointed out that it was far too big.

He suggested it might be "some unusual form of whale", but made no efforts to investigate for himself.

1939. It was the middle of October, and the Empire had just gone to war. Seaman Cecil W. Walters was on anti-submarine watch when he saw a quite remarkable sea serpent. Mind you, he didn't mention it at the time. But when he read a review of Heuvelmans' book in 1969, he made notes of the episode, with sketches, for his own record. In late 1980 he sent a brief note to the *Sun-Herald*. This in turn allowed Paul Cropper to find and interview him more than eight years later. Here, then, is the full story.[45]

He was on a naval oil tanker, the HMAFA *Kurumba* two days out from Darwin, and now northwest of King Sound, W.A., at what he estimated to be 114°E, 20°S, heading south-southwest at 10 knots [18½ kph]. It was 2 bells, or 1 pm, and the weather was fine and hazy, but not enough to prevent a clear view. He and Jack Mack (later killed in action) were manning the telescopes at either side of the stern gun. It is important to understand that these telescopes, which were automatically co-ordinated to focus on the same point, were calibrated for distance and very powerful.

Mr Walters saw it first - a huge animal 4 miles [6½ km] away to starboard on a somewhat divergent course from that of the ship. There was a bow wave in front of it; it must have been doing at least 10 knots, and probably 15 because it was gaining on the ship. They watched it for the next half hour in between watching for submarines, until it got so far in front it was beyond the maximum angle for the telescopes.

Figure. 2.5 will give you an idea of what it was like. The neck and body was easily as thick as a man, with the front end an estimated 10 feet [3 m] out of the water and 30 feet [9 m] from loop to loop. Remember, the telescopes were calibrated for distance; he knew it was a long way off. The size of the monster is unlikely to have been underestimated. Yet if his estimates are correct, the visible parts alone must have totalled 90 feet [27½ m] - a veritable sea dinosaur, bigger than the biggest whale. Yet, it will be recalled that the Townsville monster was larger than most whales. The loops stayed motionless. Seaman Walters could see no tail, no fins, and no paddles, but underneath that vast bulk something must have been paddling furiously. But the most extraordinary feature was its colour pattern. The background was brownish yellow, like a withered leaf, with a matt rather than a shiny texture. But all over it were blotches of pale blue, green and yellow, like a multi-coloured giraffe. As I said before, string-of-humps sea serpents are rather common, but never anything like this.

Figure 2.5 Karumba *monster, as drawn by Cecil Walters. (A) original sketch 1969. (B) preliminary sketches of head. (C) final sketch, 1989*

The head merged into the neck without a break, and did not move. The mouth remained shut, but the jaws were constantly "working" and the tongue flicking in and out. There were dark greenish patches over the eye and nostrils, and Mr Walters distinctly remembers a dainty little ear tucked back behind the eye. In fact, his memory was pretty vivid considering a lapse of fifty years. If he was correct on this point, the animal must have been a mammal.

In his own personal notes he mentioned that he took a photograph through the telescope and sent it to his brother-in-law after the war. But the latter could not remember what became of it.

1941. In November two fishermen in a boat off Mooloolaba saw a serpentine creature 60 feet [18 m] long, marked with red and with a red beard. On this basis, naturalist Charles Barrett identified it as an oarfish[46]. He was probably right. This mysterious denizen of the middle depths is as thin as a ribbon, with a tall crest of its head. The largest reliably measured was 6.4 m long. There are no doubt longer ones, and the fishermen may have exaggerated.

1942. According to Rex Gilroy[47], in 1942 some strange tracks, 60 cm wide came out of the sea onto the beach between Lambs Point and Huskinson, near Jervis Bay, turned around, and went back into the sea. Mr Gilroy is an interesting character who appears on the scene whenever strange animals are reported. We shall meet him again later. For various reasons, I regard him as quite uncritical and unreliable, but I think it only fair to alert you to this story. I know nothing else about it personally, but somebody might be able to provide details.

Late 1940s. A precise date cannot be given, because the witness, Mr. R. M. Richardson, did not speak out until 1980, but it was in the incumbency of Mick Driver, the Northern Territory Administrator from 1946 to 1950. At that time Mr Richardson was a resident of Larrekeyah Barracks, Darwin, and was walking along the cliff near the barracks when he saw them. In the water off Larrekeyah Point were three black objects, each about eight metres [26 feet] long. At first took them for logs, but then he saw they were alive and swimming. He hurried down to the old jetty for a better look, and one of them raised its head. It was serpent-like, reminding him of a tiger snake ready to strike. A couple of days later he mentioned them to Mr Driver. The Administrator told him he knew of such creatures, and that he was very lucky to see them, because they rarely visited the Top End.[48]

1955. Would you believe a sea monster so fast that it crossed Darwin Harbour in just ten minutes? Two women, one a nursing sister, are said to have seen it in 1955. It was at least 100 feet [30 m] long, and consisted of a string of humps rising and falling[49]. Unfortunately, I have not been able to trace the original story.

1959. What became known as the Mandorah monster was actually the subject of a naval search of Darwin Harbour in October of this year. It was originally prompted by a report by Allan Carter, manager of the Mandorah holiday resort.

> Mr Carter saw the object late one evening. He reported by radio that it was "a long black shallow object travelling just above or close to the surface" of the sea between Mandorah and Doctor's Gully. He thought it was moving at 80 to 90 mph [130 - 145 kph]. When it was moving towards Delissaville a green light shot into the sky. The next morning Mr Carter saw the strange object again and it headed towards one of the creeks on his side of the harbor[50].

Ten days later a Mr. J. G. Slaggert also saw something near Mandorah.

> "It was either some kind of low flying object or monster" he said. He could not hear anything which sounded like a motor "only a queer swooshing noise like giant wings or a new type of jet."[51]

Needless to say, the newspaper omitted such trivial details as distance, length of sightings, lighting and visibility, but did state that both men estimated the length as 80 to 100 feet [24 - 30 m].

Enter Ted Maloney, who'd been fishing the waters of Tasmania, the Barrier Reef and the Northern Territory for 18 years. He'd seen the monster plenty of times, he said. It was a giant ray, the biggest he'd ever seen, but friendly and harmless. It was 25 feet [7.6 m] across, and at least 40 feet [12.3 m] long, including its tail. However, it was easy to overestimate its size, he added (not without reason, for he himself had obviously just done so). Seen in clear water, at a distance, with its shadow behind it could easily appear the reported length of the Mandorah monster. (Of course, there wouldn't have been any shadow at night, when Mr Carter saw it.) Its top speed was 40 mph [65 kph - another exaggeration] but appeared faster[52].

Next came Mrs Dorothy de Fraine, who claimed to have seen it in 1955, when she was managing the Seabreeze Hotel at Seabreeze Point. This ray, however, was only 12 to 14 feet [3.7 - 4.3 m] across[53]. It was stranded in shallow water, rolling and flapping its huge wings, but fortunately, it managed to get away before one of her friends could shoot it. However, she also mentioned that in 1954 security police had investigated a strange green light which rose out of the ocean off the hotel, just like the light of the Mandorah monster[54]. Curiouser and curiouser.

Then a fisherman called Ian Harper sighted a huge black object in the water[55]. It turned out to be a ray 20 to 25 feet [6 - 7½7m] across, a "huge, black shallow object", as Mr Carter would have put it. Mr Harper also told how "something went through his 350 lb [159kg] breaking strain nylon net and left a hole big enough for a car to drive through".

That ought to have settled the matter, but Allan Carter came back and stated categorically that what he saw was not an animal[56]. This thing seemed to have a superstructure, and was definitely mechanically driven, although it left no wake and there was no sound of engines. He also mentioned that on that first day a woman had seen it through a pair of binoculars and her description tallied with his. (By the time I contacted him, Mr Carter was a very old man, and could hardly remember the episode.)

So there you have it. There definitely was a huge, but not abnormal, ray in the area during the period of the sighting. It is also certain that unskilled witnesses can grossly overestimate an object's size and speed. You will have to decide for yourself whether two independent witnesses, one of whom (Allan Carter) had been a test pilot during the war, had been guilty of such a mistake. It is quite certain that no marine animal can travel as fast as described. Neither can any boat, at least not without making something more than a "queer swooshing noise". But not even phosphorescence on the water could make a green light shoot up into the sky. It is noteworthy that both witnesses describe the object moving on or just above the surface, and I wonder whether this story does not really belong in a book on UFOs.

1959/60. Deception Bay is the section of Moreton Bay between Redcliffe and Bribie Island. It is not far from my home, and I can never hear the name without immediately recalling the friendly monster which turned up there when I was a boy - just after the Mandorah monster episode, in fact. It is also the best documented sea serpent in Australian waters.

Twenty-two year old year old Ron Spencer had been fishing the area for eight years. He had seen dugongs, dolphins and turtles, but never anything like the frightening thing he saw five times in 1959. It used to pop its head two or three feet [60 - 90 cm] out of the water, look around for a few seconds, and submerge with a tremendous splash. His wife, Jeanette told how she'd been with him when it appeared in the early part of the year, and she was so scared he had brought her to shore. Then a family friend, John Belcher, told how he had seen it with Ron in the middle of December. The description was the same in all cases: a brown, neckless head, 18 inches to two feet [40 - 60 cm] wide, with strange, staring eyes.[57]

After that, at least ten people contacted the newspaper to say they had seen it too, but only one testimony was published, that of Nigel Tutt, who saw the monster close up on New Year's Day, 1960, along with his daughter, Carol, and her friend, Joy Zeller.

Months later, the *Sunday Truth* decided to run a tongue-in-cheek contest for the best Queensland "monster" story. Out came all the tall tale spinners with yarns about talking bunyips, corkscrew-shaped sea serpents and things that go screech in the night. If nothing else, they effectively highlighted the difference between bush tales and the genuine articles. So when Nigel Tutt told the full story of his encounter on New Year's Day, he won first prize hands down: 20 guineas ($42) and a 30 cm baby crocodile called Huey which, perhaps fortunately, died before it became a monster in its own right. Twenty-nine years later I was able to contact all three witnesses separately. Although Joy could remember nothing more of the incident, Nigel's memory was remarkable, and correlated well with what Carol said. Here, then, is the full story[58].

It was a clear, sunny day, the sea as smooth as a millpond. ("Otherwise I wouldn't have gone out," said Carol). They headed to the mouth of the Caboolture River to see the huge flocks of swans there, then moved off a couple of miles to the edge of the shipping channel. The time was now about 12.15 and the tide at its peak. Nigel throttled the engine back and handed the tiller to Carol while he went up to the bow.

Suddenly, about 20 metres in front of the bow, a huge, square-shaped head rose almost vertically 4 feet [1.2 m] out of the water and side on to the boat. The girls let out a shriek, and Carol turned the tiller so had it nearly tied the boat in knots. With a loud "plop!", the head disappeared. Disappointed at not getting a clear view, Nigel decided to run the launch in a couple of circles in the hope it would surface again. Sure enough, it came up three more times, each one closer to the boat and with its head at a lower angle to the water. The creature was inquisitive, and quite unaggressive, but Carol was terrified it would capsize the boat. When its great mouth opened, her first thoughts were: "Thank goodness it's not a whale, otherwise with a mouth like that I might end up like Jonah and the whale."

Nigel then decided to head for shore and get a camera. After 10 minutes, when they thought they'd left the monster behind, up came the monster "curving and gliding calmly along beside the boat and only about 8 ft. [2.4 m] away". Its head and tail protruded beyond the boat at either side.

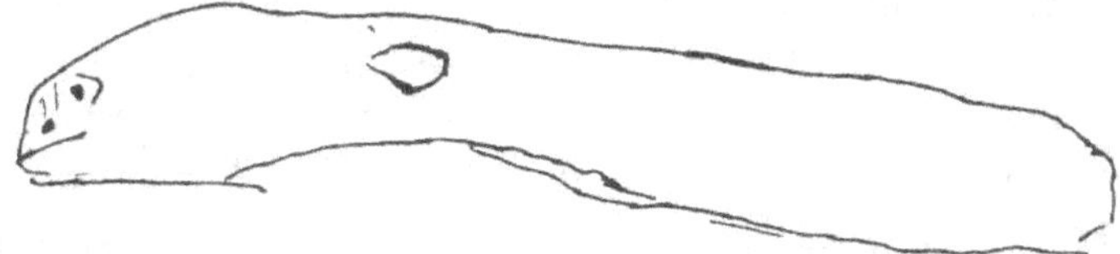

Figure 2.6 Deception Bay monster drawn by Nigel Tutt, 1989

The whole sighting lasted about 20 minutes. What they saw has been crudely reproduced as Figure. 2.6. The monster was about 22 feet [6.7 m] long. Nigel remembered wondering if it could have been a giant eel, but then he remembered that an eel swims with lateral undulations and this one's undulations were vertical. In other words, it must have been a mammal. There might have been half a dozen undulations, each as long as a man's arm and 30 cm out of the water (he was very uncertain about this), but he didn't think there were any humps. The tail was not seen clearly, but he suspects it was tapered rather than lobed. I wouldn't be so sure. The skin was lumpy and mottled, like a huge cane toad's, even slimy or wet, but not scaly, and definitely not furred. It was brown in colour, with the underside lighter. There was a definite neck, though it was almost as thick as the head, and a little longer. The head itself was square, like the boot of a Mayflower car, about two feet [60 cm] wide, with a truncated muzzle. The mouth was wide, like a fresh water catfish's, and yellow inside. Neither of them remember any teeth or tongue, but there were a pair of nostrils widely spaced above the mouth and just a few inches about it. The eyes were well forward, and neither could remember any whiskers.

One unusual feature was a pair of fins about 6 to 8 feet [1.8 - 2.4 m] back from the head. Nigel later told me that they were on the body rather than the neck, and placed rather high. They were rounded, with a definite bone-and-muscle structure like a paddle rather than a fish's fins, and despite the size of the owner, they were only about a foot [30 cm] long.

Needless to say, by the time Mr Tutt returned with the camera, they monster was gone. And although he built himself a special dinghy made unsinkable by means of air tanks, and with a special waterproof compartment for the camera, he never saw the monster again. This isn't, however, the last we'll hear of Nigel Tutt, as a later chapter will reveal.

Nor was it the last sighting of the monster. Sometime later, I suspect September, it appeared to 26 year old Dave Manners and his mother. They were quietly fishing at Woody Bay, on the southern tip of Bribie Island, at 7.20 am when it surfaced 20 yards off shore. Dave dropped his rod with amazement. The monster was clearly visible in the shallow water, and they followed it along the beach for 1½ miles [2½ km] before going for breakfast. According to Dave it was 25 feet [7.6 m] long and

> The head is round, something like a man's, at least 2ft. 6 in. [76 cm] across and 2 ft. [60 cm] long, with a flat nose and sort of semi-detached to the body. ... It was a dirty brown color and appeared to have a body about 2ft. across and a queer-looking fin 18ft. from the head. It kept surfacing about every 50 yards."[59]

Presumably he meant the fin was 18 inches [46 cm] from the head, and was including the neck with the head. In that case, we have the same animal the Tutts saw, right down to the curiosity. What was it? Its method of swimming reveals it to be a mammal. The lack of fur rules out a seal, and the placement of the nostrils rules out any modern whale or dolphin. My guess is that it was a relic archaeocete: one of a group of primitive whales with a serpentine shape and nostrils placed forward. It's nice to know they are still around. There might be more around than we know. Indeed, Dr Roy Mackal suggests that the monsters reported from a great many Canadian lakes fit the description of archaeocetes very well.[60]

Bribie Island must rate high in the sea serpent travel guide. As I said before, the entries in the *Truth* "monster" contest were mostly outrageous, but a couple would pass muster. A runner-up prize was given to Mrs M. L. Carr who referred to something she once saw in the water on a reef near Bribie Island "with a big body and neck poised as if staring up at me." In other words, not like the 1959/60 monster, but the long-necked variety such as appeared at Green Island in 1924 or Loch Ness in 1933.

Or turned up off Russell Island in Moreton Bay[61]. Mr E. J. Bailey claimed it was "like a horse or hippopotamus, with an arched neck, a short back, that moved through the water with great speed and power." That story also turned up in the *Truth* contest, but monsters like that have been reported from every ocean in the world. What is infuriating is that the witness appears to have lived within a kilometre or two of my home, but it is too late to interview him now.

1962. The deep hides many huge animals, most of them known, others perhaps not. Have you ever wondered what happens to them when they die? Then sit back and follow the story of the Tasmanian "Globster"[62].

The story began in August 1960, when Ben Fenton and two of his stockmen, Ray Anthony and Jack Boote (!), were rounding up cattle south of Sandy Cape, near the Interview River. There on the beach lay a blob of - whatever. It measured 18 by 20 feet (5½ x 6 m) and weighed between 5 and 10 tons. (One wonders how they estimated that.) As the months passed the tide gradually moved it northward, but the thing still has no smell or sign of decay, and the skin was still hard. It took a year and a half for the story to reach Hobart. A team of two zoologists and two naturalists, led by Bruce Mollison of the C.S.I.R.O., hiked to the site. What they found on March 7 was beyond their scientific expertise to interpret. The horses and dogs kept their distance. A smell like strong battery acid rose from a blob covered with creamy, rubbery, hairy skin, but without eyes, head or bones. Instead, there were:

> ... five gill-like, hairless slits on each side of the front. There were also four large hanging lobes in front, with a smooth gulletlike orifice between the center pair. The rim of the hind part of the creature had many cushiony flanges, each, carrying a single row of sharp, pencil like spines.[63]

The ivory-colored flesh was too tough to cut with a hunting knife. He brought his team back to Hobart, then returned to the monster with an axe and a cameraman. While the latter rolled off hundreds of feet of film (where is that film now?) he was chopping off great chunks of monster meat for analysis. Meanwhile, the world press was running wild.

That was obviously not good enough. What's the use of having scientists if they don't explain things? Questions were asked in Parliament. On 16 March out went a new team - this time by helicopter - consisting of some of the top names in Australian zoology : John Calaby, A. M. Olsen, Eric Guiler and William Bryden. They didn't waste time. Three days later a report was not only submitted to the Minister, John

Gorton (later Prime Minister) but published in the *Hobart Mercury*. Obviously quite a bit of the blob had rotted away since it had been first discovered, but it had left a large stain a few centimetres under the sand consistent with the original reported size. As for what was left:

> When laid out flat, the material was eight feet long, three feet wide, and ten inches thick [2.4m x 90cm x 25 cm] . . . It consists throughout of tough, fibrous material loaded with fatty or oily substances . . . The material did not contain any bones, spines, or other hard structures . . . the hair-like material of the exposed surfaces was merely a consequence of desiccation and leaching of fat-filled fibrous material.[64]

They thought the material was blubber. Tests later revealed the samples to consist mostly of collagen, the chief component of connective tissue. After all that investigation, the Globster was officially identified as "a decomposing portion of a large marine animal". Fancy that! No-one can say our scientists are not on the ball. Mind you, Bruce Mollison, perhaps miffed at the way he had been pushed aside, did have the temerity to ask exactly what kind of marine animal. He was adamant that he could rule out "a whale, seal, sea elephant, or squid."

So there the mystery rests. If it were blubber, then, from what I've read about whaling, it should not have been so hard to slice through. The original size is also a problem, because no whale is 5½ metres wide. The blubber would have to have come free in a single sheet. And what about the meat and the skin? There is also the matter of the pencil-thick bristles around the edges, which are not as easy to explain as the "hair".

Without further evidence I am not prepared to conclude that the globster was anything new to science. But I sure hope some of those samples are still preserved somewhere.

To make matters more interesting, at the height of the hullabaloo a Perth resident, Mr. R. H. Timberly, announced that he and his father had found an identical blob washed ashore at Henrietta Rocks, Rottnest Island, W.A. in 1934. He had photos and cuttings to prove it. It had been 18 feet [5½ m] long, roughly stingray-shaped, with a long tail and vaguely formed flippers. It was coated with the same strange wool, and its creamy flesh had the consistency of tough tripe. However, it was believed to have had frontal bones and a toothless mouth[65]. Unlike the Tasmanian carcass, I'm inclined to think this was a giant ray.

It seems anomalies like to appear in twos and threes, because six years later another Globster was washed up on Muriwai Beach in New Zealand. This one was 30 feet [9 m] long and 8 feet [2.4 m] high, and it was covered by hair 4 to 6 inches [10 - 15 cm] long. Beneath that was a centimetre of hide, a layer of fat, and finally, solid meat. However, it was eventually identified as the remains of a whale, the "hair" being strands of connective tissue, all that was left after the outer tissues had been chewed, frayed, or eroded away[66].

Speaking of anomalies coming in clusters, September 1962 also saw the appearance of something three kilometres off Woorim, Bribie Island. That's just next to Deception Bay, but it was different from the 1960 visitor. According to the witness, Robert Duncan:

> It was whitish-grey in colour, about 12 feet [3.7 m] long, and seemed to have a swan's neck, a whale's body, and a fish's tail and fins. It repeatedly raised its neck out of the water, and then flipped its strange tail[67].

He had watched it for four minutes through field glasses. Two weeks later, when he sighted it again 10 km off the north point of Bribie Island, he added:

> Its snout, instead of being pointed, is flat like a pig's. It has two little holes near the centre. They'd be nostrils, I suppose[68].

This time he estimated its length as 20 feet [6 m], and saw a fin on its swan-like neck. For the next couple of months Mr Duncan walked the beach every day hoping to see it. Although he never saw it again, it was recorded that, about the same time, an amateur fisherman called James Kentworth saw a "strange animal" playing in shallow water between Scarborough and the village of Deception Bay[69].

1964. The year was almost over when an actual photograph was produced (Figure. 2.7); the place: Stonehaven Bay, Hook Island, just 3 km from the more famous Hayman Island. In the course of a voyage around the world, Breton yachtsman, Robert le Serrec, his wife and three children were staying on Hook Island with a Sydney skindiver, Henk de Jong. About 9 a.m. on 12 December they were crossing the bay in an 18 foot [5½ m] motor launch when they saw it. Clearly visible in the clear water, a dark shape lay motionless on the bottom. Its estimated length was 70 feet [21.3 m] or, according to a later account, 22 to 24 metres[70]. It had apparently sought shelter in the bay to recuperate from a wound,

Figure 2.7. Hook Island monster, photograph by Robert le Serrec

which appeared as a white mark about 5 feet [1½ m] long on its side. Later in fact, they theorized that the monster had crept into the sheltered waters of the bay to recuperate. Only when the word, "snake" was mentioned did the children get frightened, so the adults decided to take them ashore - which also conveniently kept them from telling their side of the story.

Back on the scene again, they decided, with some trepidation, to get into the water, de Jong with an anti-shark powerhead containing a 12-gauge cartridge, le Serrec with a movie camera. From a range of 6 metres they could see the head clearly. It was 4 feet [1.2 m] high, the jaws 4 feet wide. The skin was brownish-black, smooth and scaleless, the eyes pale green, almost white, and pointing upwards. Neither fins nor nostrils were visible, but the lower jaw was flat, the interior white, and the teeth small. A brown fragment of food hung from the upper teeth.

The body itself was black with brownish rings a foot [30cm] wide every five feet. And the shape itself was quite incredible. The broadest section was the head. For the next 25 feet [7.6 m] the body remained a uniform 2 foot 4 inches [71 cm] in diameter, after which it tapered to a whip-like tail. The wound seemed almost to reach the spine. As the camera started to roll, the great head rose slowly from the sand, and began to turn towards them. The photographer's wife was frantic. Racing back to the boat, they started up the engine, while the monster twisted sluggishly and dragged itself away. They never saw it again[71].

Only when the still photos had been developed did they tell their story - and attempt to get the best price for them. The movie film eventually turned out hazy, and showed none of the movement reported at the time[72]. Then, when le Serrec finally returned to France he was arrested. Apparently, he had left the country without paying for his supplies, and without the companions who had aided in the finances. He had even mentioned to them he had plans to make money out of a sea serpent[73].

Heuvelmans, and his fellow cryptozoologist, Ivan Sanderson, suspect the film shows a carefully prepared roll of cloth, and I am not inclined to dispute it. Apart from everything else, a deep sea monster shaped like a giant sperm, but without stabilising fins, and with eyes pointed upwards is not exactly biologically plausible. And nobody else has seen one.

1970. I told you strange things come in threes. In November, up jumped Ben Fenton (remember him?) to announce the discovery of - would you believe? - another globster, not very far from the site of the original discovery ten years before. Only this time he was careful not to get too involved. He would only say that it had not been there when he last visited the site seven weeks before, and that it was humped, with a tough, leathery hide. And it was comparatively fresh, and could probably still be identified[74]. So two pressmen flew in and found, on a beach about 30 miles [50 km] south of Temma, a humped blob 10 feet long and 4 wide [3m x 1.2m], which looked and smelled like a rotting whale, and the same wool-like growths of the 1962 globster[75].

And now, fellow taxpayers, you will be glad to know that your science allocations are not being wasted. Your scientists are all being kept very busy at their allotted tasks. Because not a single one had time to visit Sandy Cape and find out what it was.

1972. Two men from Maningrida, in Arnhem Land happened to be fishing when a tremendous disturbance occurred three quarters of a mile [1.2 km] out to sea. The fabled Maningrida Monster had returned. For 15 to 20 minutes they watched the sea boil and foam from the writhings of a great, serpentine monster while water birds of every description rose panic stricken into the air. The whole spectacle was accompanied by a high pitched moaning, a cross between the howl of a dingo and a bellowing elephant. The minimum length they could estimate for the monster was 50 to 60 feet [15 - 18 m]. They could see the sun glint on its incredibly large, metallic looking scales. But the most amazing feature was the way the creature's head was split into three sections, like a propeller. Well, that's the account given in the community's now defunct newsletter[76]. However, a man who was there at the time told me it was a practical joke by a school teacher[77]. Can you doubt it?

1973. A sea serpent popped its head out of the ocean off Victoria for just three seconds on Sunday 3 June, but it was well reported at the time[78]. Moreover, the witnesses had good memories, and independently provided me with extra details when I contacted them 14½ years later[79]. They were a 25 year old architect, Neil Blyth, and his father-in-law, Norman Robertson. The latter was used to estimating distances and size from his wartime work with the R.A.A.F.

It was 3.30 p.m., and they were fishing about half a mile [0.8 km]

Figure 2.8 Original sketch of Airey's Inlet sea serpent by Norman Robertson

off Eastern View, roughly 4 km southwest of Aireys Inlet, and 100 km southwest of Melbourne. It was a very dull winter's day, with little wind, but with a large swell running. The waves were higher than the boat and the troughs twice as long. Just before a swell breaks, a distinct hissing noise is audible. However, they were now a long way from the breaking surf when a similar hiss occurred, and up popped a serpentine head and neck. What they saw, at a range of 50 or 60 yards, was a graceful, black periscope held at an angle to the water. Mr Robertson estimated it as 9 feet [2.7m] high and 12 inches [30 cm] thick. Mr Blyth, who thought the animal closer, guessed 6 feet and 9 inches respectively. Both agreed that the neck merged into the head without a constriction. Mr Robertson remembered the head as being blunt (Fig. 2. 8), but his son-in-law considered it tapered like a dog's. In the dull light neither could see any eyes or scales.It stood upright for just three seconds, then slid back into the water without a splash, like a periscope at an angle. It did not dive.

Nothing in that scene would have been out of place at Loch Ness. They remained fishing for another 15 minutes, then rowed ashore and phoned the press. A woman at the Aireys Inlet store, 400 yards inland, observed a dark object moving along the surface parallel to the shore. Meantime, down at the beach, Mr Robertson's wife watched as a large number of fish began tossing themselves onto the shore. I should like to add that when the press reported this incident, they referred to previous sea monster sightings off Gabo Island. I know nothing about this, and would appreciate any information.

1976. According to Rex Gilroy[80], a typical sea serpent appeared in the Brisbane Waters, near the mouth of the Hawkesbury River in May. A married couple fishing 200 yards from shore saw the body of a long-necked animal swim close to their boat, but a metre under water. When it raised its head a metre out of the water and continued to the open sea, they headed for shore. A few weeks later something similar was seen near Ettalong. A woman living near the headwaters of river watched for 15 minutes through binoculars as a dark shape moved upstream. It then raised its head at least 4 feet [1.2 m] out of the water, and part of its back appeared. I have no other information on these sightings, and am not happy about their source, but have included them for the sake of completeness.

1977/78. I occasionally wonder how many sea serpents would be reported from northern Australia if more people lived outside of Darwin. In 1980 the local newspaper[81] carried a sensational front page story about plesiosaurs living in Bynoe Harbor, just southwest of Port Darwin. Burge Brown, a beach sands prospector of 20 years, told how, sometime in 1977 he and his son, Geoffrey were searching for a shipwreck when a loud bellow terrified their dogs. A quarter of an hour later they watched through their field glasses as three monsters appeared 800 yards away. The biggest he estimated to be 30 metres long. A year later he was with a fishing party in deep water off Rankin Point when suddenly fish and sea snakes started leaping out of the water. (This was confirmed by a friend in another boat around the corner.) Heading down the harbour like a submarine came a thing with a tail and front like an elephant's head and pairs of fins running down the length of its back. Much to his amazement, the fins were not rigid, but floppy.

One of his companions, Police Sergeant Kevin Maley described the creature as "black, about 30m long with a head the size of a football", and told how it kept within 20 metres of their boat for 20 minutes. The testimony of the police officer made me suspect this was not just a wild fisherman's yarn. When I contacted him years later he obviously wasn't keen on publicity, but he confirmed most of the report. The monster's length was more like 25 feet [7.6 m] rather than 30 metres, and had no obvious humps. The neck was 8 to 10 feet [2.4 to 3 m] long, with a vertical S bend. The triangular serrations along its back - there were three rows rather than two - were not unlike those of a crocodile's, but 6 inches [15 cm] long and floppy. He was adamant that it was not a crocodile, dugong, turtle or shark.

Or, for that matter, anything else known to science or legend.

1980. Now, how's this for a coincidence? One day the local paper publishes Burge Brown's story. Two weeks later Mr Richardson comes forth with his story from the 1940s, and just five days after that a sea serpent appears in Darwin Harbor right in front of the journalist who wrote the previous reports. Nine years later Paul Cropper was able to contact the first witnesses, Terry Annesley, and obtain further information[82].

Mr Annersley was working on the 3rd floor of the Hooker Building, overlooking the harbour. About 11 am he saw something moving from the direction of Bynoe Harbor towards the shore at about the same speed as a whale. After a couple of minutes he alerted a friend, John Hamilton. When it was about half a kilometre away (the newspaper report said a kilometre - how did they estimate it?) he called the *Northern Territory News* office across the road, and up came a reporter and a photographer. The journalists were virtually in a state of shock, the photographer angry because the lens he had brought was too small. For about half an hour the four of them took turns watching it through binoculars from the roof of the building. The animal was black, and about 20 metres long which, if their estimates were in any way accurate, would make it as big as a whale. A series of loops like half-tyres stood high out of the water, their number constantly changing, once as few as three, at other times as many as five or six. The length of each loop seemed to be the same as the distance between loops, which suggests that it was really an elongated animal flexing. A series of dorsal fins rose from the loops, but the viewers were certain it was not a school of dolphins. It would have been impossible for them to have kept perfectly in line for such a length of time.

1995. By now there had been a prolonged "drought" of sea serpent stories. Then, suddenly, an unsigned letter was thrust under the door of the weekly *Isis Town & Country* in Childers. It read:

> During the first week of September a friend and myself were fishing from a tinnie.
>
> It was about three in the afternoon and we were near the junction of the Isis and Burrum Rivers, when I spotted something unusual. [The site is at the head of an arm of the sea, halfway between Bundaberg and Maryborough.]
>
> I called my companion's attention to it and for what

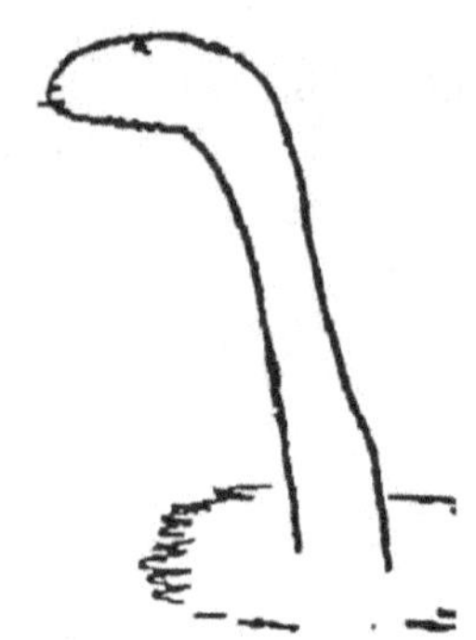

Figure 2.9 Anonymous sketch of the Burrum Beast

seemed about a minute we watched what appeared to be an enormous snake with a bulbous head. I really do mean enormous; the neck/body was upright out of the water and was topped by a head the size of a Labrador dog, while the neck seemed about half the girth of a timber power pole.

It was very dark grey, almost black and neither of us noticed any teeth, tongue, ears, fur or scales. There did seem to be a small wash as it moved slowly upstream but neither of us became aware of any swimming motion. After a while it just slipped under the water and that was it, we didn't see it again. It definitely did not dive, it slid away.

Has anyone else seen anything similar or can offer an explanation? I can say it wasn't a snake or an eel (too big), dead stock, vegetation or birds (familiar with Darters, Cormorants etc.). It wasn't a dog, roo or mirage. We weren't drunk, smoking dope or aren't seeking money or fame. In fact this account is anonymous because of the ridicule that usually goes with anything out of the ordinary. My friend says we should forget it and just put it down as an unexpected incident, and that if we came forward we would end up as the Forrest Gumps' of the Isis. Me, I'm full of curiosity and just want to know[83].

So do I, but readers will immediately compare the description, and the sketch provided by the witness (Figure 2.9) with the virtually identical sightings at Airey's Inlet and Green Island.

So there you have it. What can be made of this bizarre assortment of sightings? If we eliminate probable hoaxes and known species, we have a giant salp chain (1877), a giant, prehistoric shark (1918 et.al.), a giant seal (1931), perhaps a smaller species of seal (1913), a beaked whale (*Bawean*, 1925), a giant sea snake or eel (1874, Orpheus Island, 1934), and a primitive, prehistoric whale (1959/60). After that, we move into very murky waters.

At this point, it is useful to understand what's been happening in the wider world. The most common sea serpent sightings - recorded from every ocean, not to mention many fresh water lakes - consist of a number of humps attached to a long neck and a small head. Heuvelmans dubbed them the long-necked and the merhorse, the difference being that the eyes of the first are very small, those of the second very large. God only knows what they are. You might immediately think of the extinct (?) plesiosaurs. However, plesiosaurs didn't have humps, and they certainly breathed air. The long-necked apparently doesn't. At least, sonar recordings of its representatives in Loch Ness reveal it to be a creature of the bottom, which rises occasionally to the middle depths, but very rarely to the surface (hence the rarity of sightings)[84].

You will immediately recall quiet a few of our own visitors which fit this description e.g. 1916, 1924, 1930, 1934 (Coff's Harbour), Darwin in the 1940s, 1962, 1973, 1995. But even here we have anomalies. None of these creatures has ever been seen with an enormous dorsal fin, except for the beast seen off Port Stephens in 1925. The giraffe-like pattern of the 1939 monster has never been seen elsewhere, nor the bizarre pattern (? armour) of the 1934 visitors to north Queensland.

Again, Heuvelmans was able to chronicle a number of animals with rows of fins down the back. But what a variety we have in Australia: square fins (1879), tall, pointed fins (1900), low, pointed fins (1980), and - the *pièce de résistance* - a triple row of floppy fins and a long neck (1977/78). (All the other many-fins have short necks.) What they are is anybody's guess.

By now you're probably thinking that the ocean is a vast menagerie of weird and wonderful unknown monsters. And you'd be right. Let's not forget that the giant squid, which everyone thinks they know, was only proved to exist last century [written in 1996]. It is several orders of magnitude bigger than the common squid, as much a freak of nature as an elephant-sized rat. And it has only ever been taken alive once.

The sea covers three quarters of the globe. It has three dimensions, not just two. And it is not our home. We cross its surface in noisy ships on very narrow sea lanes. We seek its citizens with the crudest methods of hunting: by casting nets where we think they will be, and throwing baits which we hope they will like. Rare creatures, huge creatures, creatures of the middle depths, creatures whose behaviour keeps them away from our nets, and whose anatomy prevents them from being trapped in the shallows - what makes you think they will cross our paths except by chance?

ADDENDUM

Just a few corrections to the material already published in this chapter.

Firstly, a bit of trivia about the scientific name of the moha-moha, *Chelosauria lovelli*. Of course, it isn't valid, because there is no physical specimen held for reference, as the rules require. Apart from that, what most people have overlooked is that Saville-Kent got the Latin gender wrong in the specific name. Because Selina Lovell was a woman, it should have been *lovellae*.

Secondly, although the account of the 1849 encounter by the *Alpha* is accurate, the location was not. The shipping notes in the Melbourne newspapers record that it arrived at that city on 30 June. Since the encounter took place exactly a month beforehand, it almost certainly occurred in the Indian Ocean in a latitude comparable to that of Melbourne.

Next, I have to admit that I was rather uncritical in my discussion of the survival of the megalodon shark. Ben S. Roesch, who is both a shark expert and a cryptozoologist, or student of mystery animals, has published an article effectively demolishing these claims[85]. He points out that *C. megalodon* would have haunted shallow seas, where it would hardly have gone unnoticed, and that the alleged sightings are either undocumented, or more easily explainable as whale sharks, which are much larger than great whites, but eat only plankton.

Nevertheless, there was one account which he considered so fantastic he simply did not believe it, and that was the one recorded in this chapter: the 1918 attack on the lobster pots at Broughton Island, off Port Stephens. However, we can't simply dismiss a story because it sound unbelievable, especially since it was actually reported in the newspapers of 30 January of that year.[86] I think we must accept the report as genuine, even if the interpretation may be a matter for debate.

With respect to the Tabourie Lakes monster of 1931, which I interpreted as a huge seal of an unknown species, I have come around to the suggestion made to me by my friend, Paul Cropper, that it was really a leopard seal whose size was exaggerated by the terror it inspired. In point of fact, about six months later a female leopard seal, outsized at 15 feet [4½ m] was washed ashore at nearly Batemans Bay.[87]

The Manning River carcass was dated incorrectly at 1952. In fact, it was discovered in 1947[88]. (That's the problem you have with undated clippings.)

The remains hacked off the 1962 "globster" have, in fact, been preserved, and are on display in the Tasmanian Museum. Not only that, but they have been analysed, along with several other "globsters" from around the world, and they have all been proved conclusively to be whale blubber[89]. What a disappointment!

The best investigated Australian "sea monster" remains the strange creature encountered up close and personal on multiple occasions by multiple witnesses in Deception Bay in the years 1959 and 1960. It is only fair to add, however, that when I telephoned John Belcher in 1996, he said he was indignant at the newspaper report, and what he had seen was a sea cow, or dugong, of which there are quite a few in Moreton Bay.

In 1996 I also phoned the journalist who witnessed and reported the many-humped creature in Darwin harbour in 1980. He told me that he wrote the article on orders from his editor, but had reservations about it. Nevertheless, he was unable to provide an explanation of what they saw.

You will note from this chapter a number of cases known only from secondary sources, and not described in detail. I have since searched Trove's digitalised archive of Australian newspapers for the phrase, "sea serpent", and managed to locate nearly all of them. I was even able to ascertain that the *Saint-François-Xavier* sea serpent of 1925 had been reported in local newspapers at the time, and that a different captain had been in command.

What was extraordinary was how many *new* cases came to light - more than doubling the tally of Australian cases, and allowing me to produce a new book, *Australian Sea Serpents*. (I also unearthed a large number of *foreign* cases overlooked by previous researchers, resulting in a separate book, *Forgotten Sea Serpents*.)

Since *Australian Sea Serpents* is three times the length of this already lengthy chapter, it would not be feasible to include the new material here. Instead, I shall make a couple of observations.

- Typically, reports were picked up and ran in a great many newspapers all around the country. However, they reported only the information volunteered by the witness(es), which meant that a tremendous lot of useful data went missing. If you happen to be a journalist, and someone claims to have witnessed a sea serpent (or a yowie, a flying saucer, or a ghost), then it means either you are on to something extraordinary, or you are on to something ridiculous. You owe it to your readers to dig deeper. (I have included a number of relevant questions in the last chapter of this book.)

- Only a quarter of the Australian cases, and just a couple of the foreign cases, date from after the Second World War. I refuse to believe that all these remarkable creatures have suffered a catastrophic population decline. It is far more likely that, having their minds preoccupied with that terrible conflict, people forgot that it was once acceptable to see sea serpents, and for newspapers to take them seriously. In fact, back in 1996, when I was commissioned to locate witnesses for a British television station, the only ones willing to speak about it were those with no professional reputation to lose.

Ironically, it is now respectable to see and report lake monsters.

REFERENCES

[1] *Land and Water*, London, 3 Jan. 1891. (I have not been able to access this reference, or the following, and am quoting from Bernard Heuvelmans (1968) *In the Wake of the Sea-Serpents*, who apparently quoted from *The Great Sea-Serpent* by Antoon C. Oudemans (1892). This sort of successive quoting is not uncommon in cryptozoology, but as long as the passages are retained verbatim, not much harm is done.)

[2] Selina Lovell (1891) *Land and Water,* 25 April 1891, quoted by Heuvelmans, pp 295-8

[3] William Saville-Kent (1893) *The Great Barrier Reef of Australia,* W. H. Allen, London, pp 324-6

[4] Bernard Heuvelmans (1968), *In the Wake of the Sea-Serpents*, Rupert Hart-Davis, London, p. 301 (Originally published in French by Librarie Plon, 1965)

[5] Heuvelmans (ref.4), pp 537- 585

[6] *Melbourne Daily News* 1st July 1849 and *Illustrated London News* 19 Jan. 1850, quoted by Antoon Oudemans (1892) *The Great Sea-Serpent,* and in turn by Heuvelmans (ref. 4).

[7] From a letter quoted by Heuvelmans (ref. 4), p 251

[8] John Adams (1877) Account of a supposed sea-serpent seen off Nepean Island. *Proceedings of the Literary and Philosophical Society of Liverpool* 31, p 68 , quoted by Heuvelmans (ref.4), pp 250-251

[9] Heuvelmans (ref. 4), p 283

[10] 'A sea serpent near the Australian coast'. *Sydney Morning Herald* (undated clipping)

[11] Roy P Mackal (1980) *Searching for Hidden Animals.* London: Cadogan, pp 181-192

[12] *New Zealand Times*, 19 March 1883, quoted by Charles Fort (1931) in *Lo!*

[13] H. C. Barnett (1879) The Sea-Serpent. *Nature* 24 July1879, pp 289-290

[14] 'Sea monster in the harbour. Escape of a diver.' *Newcastle Herald* 18 Nov. 1891

[15] 'Another sea monster in the harbour. Captured and on exhibition.' *Newcastle Herald* 7 Dec. 1891.
'The sea monster's mate captured. Together in life and death.' *ibid.* 8 Dec. 1891

[16] *St. James Gazette*, London 19 Aug. 1902 and *Irish News*, Belfast 28 Aug. 1902, both quoted by Heuvelmans (ref. 4), p 367

[17] Heuvelmans (ref. 4), p 366, summarising Laurence Thomson: 'How We Saw the "Sea-Serpent"' *Wide World Magazine*, London, March 1901. (The illustrations provide even further grounds for Heuvelmans' disbelief.)

[18] London newspapers of 6 July 1913, quoted by Charles Fort (1931) in *Lo!*, chapter 9.

[19] Heuvelmans (ref. 4), pp 391-2

[20] *Sydney Morning Herald* 28 April 1934

[21] David George Stead (1963) *Sharks and Rays of Australian Seas*, Angus & Robertson, pp 45 - 46

22 Gerald L Wood (1972) *The Guinness Book of Animal Facts and Feats*, Guinness Superlatives, Enfield, pp 220 -221. (I am grateful to Wood for bringing the previous story to my attention.)

23 W. Tschernezky (1959) Age of *Carcarodon megalodon*? *Nature* 184 (4695): pp 1331 - 1332 (24 Oct 1959)

24 John E. Randall (1973) Size of the great white Shark (*Carcharodon*). *Science* 181 (4095): pp 169 - 170 (13 July 1973)

25 Stead (ref. 21), p 45

26 Wood (ref. 22), p 220

27 Pierre Closterman (1969) *Des Poissons si Grands*. Paris, Flammarion, pp 247 - 249. (Michel Raynal supplied me with this reference. The ultimate source is unknown.)

28 'Sea serpents do exist! "Saw one . . . no liquor aboard"' *Daily Pictorial* (now Sydney *Daily Telegraph*) 16 June 1930

29 P. Chevey (1937) Observation inédite sur un animal marin de grande taille observé sur la côte de l'Australie, en 1925. *Bull. Soc. zool. Fr.* 62, quoted in Heuvelmans (ref. 4), p 427

30 P. de Haan (1925) Een Zeeslang? *De Zee,* Den Helder 48 (23 July 1925), quoted by Heuvelmans (ref. 4), pp 410-411, who also provided me with a French translation.

31 Heuvelmans (ref. 4), p 432

32 'Would You Believe It! Fishermen say they saw serpent.' *Daily Pictorial* (Sydney) 13.6.1930. The later references are: 'Sea Serpent Off East Coast. There are such things. Evidence of authentic reports collected.' (press cutting, journal and date unknown), and "Monsters - real or ...?" by J Crockett, *The Argus Week-End Magazine*, 9 Feb. 1946, p24 of supplement. Heuvelmans (ref. 4) quotes *Giants and Pigmies of the Deep* by David George Stead (1933) p83

33 'Fisherman attacked by sea monster.' *Sydney Morning Herald* 10 Nov.1930

34 'Sea Serpent ? Queer marine animal. Fisherman's story.' *The Moss Vale Post*, 6 Feb.1931. Also: 'Fisherman's story. South Coast "Sea

Serpent."' *Sydney Morning Herald* 4 Feb.1931.

[35]   Norman Caldwell (1936) *Fangs of the Sea* (in collaboration with Norman Ellis), Angus & Robertson, pp 112-113

[36]   'The sea monster seen at Bowen. Fisherman's report.'   unidentified newspaper, almost certainly the *North Queensland Register* of 21 Aug. 1934, quoted by Caldwell (ref. 35).

[37]   'Monster of the sea.' unidentified newspaper, almost certainly the *Townsville Bulletin* of 22 Aug. 1934, quoted by Caldwell (ref. 35), p 115.

[38]   A. H. E. Mattingley (1935) 'The Sea serpent? Strange creature observed off coast of Queensland.' *Vict. Nat.* 52: 74-75. (A shorter version was published by Caldwell (ref. 34) pp 114-115. This version was quoted verbatim by Jim Oram, who was in turn quoted by Tim Dinsdale. By the time Heuvelmans finally picked it up, he assumed that it was different from Swanson's account. In fact, they refer to the same event.)

[39]   'Northern sea monster. Eye witness's description', undated and unreferenced newspaper article copied by Caldwell (ref. 35), pp 115-116 after the Bowen and Townsville reports.

[40]   'Sea creature reported by fishermen. 40 feet in length.' *Sydney Morning Herald* 14 Sept. 1934

[41]   'Unknown animal washed ashore on beach'. *Sydney Morning Herald,* 16.4.35

[42]   'Strange marine animal found on beach.'   *Sydney Morning Herald,* 4.5.35

[43]   Heuvelmans (ref. 4), pp 114-142

[44]   undated clipping from the *Sydney Morning Herald* supplied to me by Paul Cropper who also found another, unreferenced clipping. This latter mentioned the settlement of the Charlie Chaplin plagiarism suit, which sets the date at 1952. [But see Addendum.]

[45]   Paul Cropper and Malcolm Smith (1992) Some unpublicized Australasian "sea serpent" reports.   *Cryptozoology* 11: 51 - 69

[46] Charles Barrett (1947) *The Sunlit Land, Wanderings in Queensland*, p 240 , quoted by Heuvelmans (ref. 4) pp 469-70, also *The Bunyip and other mythical monsters and legends*, Reed and Harris, Melbourne, 1946, p 103

[47] Rex Gilroy (1977) 'Australia's marine colossus'. *Psychic Australian* Feb. 1977 pp 6-9, 28-30   (Much of the other information in this article is distorted.)

[48] Fred McCue (1980) 'More to monsters than meets the eye.' *The Northern Territory News* 15 Feb. 1980

[49] Marine mystery: Sea serpents still puzzle mariners. *Daily News*, Perth 8 Oct. 1959, in a general article on sea serpents.

[50] 'Is a sea 'thing' lurking in harbor?' *The Northern Territory News* 13 Oct 1959

[51] As per ref. 50

[52] 'Is that friendly ray the great Mandorah Monster?' *ibid.* 16 Oct 1959

[53] 'Mandorah Monster nearly ends it's career on beach'. *ibid.* 20 Oct 1959

[54] 'Security and the monster.' *ibid.* 23 Oct. 1959

[55] 'Did fisherman spot the Mandorah monster?' *ibid.* 27 Oct. 1959

[56] 'Monster 'not fish' - Carter.' *ibid.* 6 Nov. 1959

[57] 'Loch Ness Monster in Our Bay.' *Sunday Truth* (Brisbane) 3 Jan.1960 (This, and all the other press clippings are courtesy of Nigel Tutt.)

[58] 'They saw the monster.' *Sunday Truth* 10 Jan. 1960. 'Here's our monster in-chief'. *ibid.* 16 Oct. 1960.   Further details in Cropper and Smith (ref. 45), pp 57-61

[59] '"Monster" seen in bay again.' Unidentified Brisbane newspaper. (I suspect this sighting prompted the Truth "monster" contest.)

[60] Mackal (ref. 11), pp 222-246

[61] *Sunday Truth* (Brisbane) 9 Oct. 1960

[62]   'Bermuda blob remains unidentified.'   *The ISC Newsletter* 7(3) Autumn 1988 (newsletter of the International Society of Cryptozoology). The section on the Globster was abstracted from the newspaper files of the late Dr Ivan Sanderson. See also the front pages of the *Hobart Mercury* for the second and third weeks of March 1962.

[63]   '"Sea Monster" find may become world topic.' *Hobart Mercury* 8 March 1962

[64]   '"Monster' to get thorough check'.   *ibid.* 19 March 1962

[65]   'Identical to 1934 W.A. find?'   *ibid.* 12 March 1962

[66]   Tim Dinsdale (1976). *The Leviathans,* revised edition by Futura Publications, pp 163-4, quoting the *Townsville Bulletin*, 24 March 1965, and private correspondence.

[67]   Duncan, Robert (1962) '"Monster" seen off Bribie Island.'   *Courier Mail* (Brisbane) 26 Sept. 1962

[68]   Duncan, Robert (1962) That monster came again. unidentified Queensland newspaper quoted in Heuvelmans (ref. 4).

[69]   '"The Thing" bobs up again up North.'   *Australasian Post* 6 Dec 1962, p 27

[70]   'Ils ont vu le monstre'. *Paris-Match* 5 Nov. 1966 , pp93-95

[71]   Robert le Serrec (1965). 'The Barrier Reef Monster.' *Everybody's* 31 March 65 , pp 9-10.

[72]   'Nous ne sommes pas les seuls a avoir douté du "Monstre du Pacifique" aperçu par M. Robert Le Serrec : la preuve ...' *Le Journal Calédonien* (Noumea) 6-13.12.66

[73]   Heuvelmans (ref. 4) pp 533-5

[74]   Kerry Pink (1962) 'Unidentified "object" on beach.' *The Advocate* (Burnie) 12 Nov. 1970.

[75]   Kerry Pink (1962)' That 'monster' - is it a whale?' *ibid.* 13 Nov. 1970

[76]   'Monster at Maningrida'. *Maningrida Mirage* 23 June 1972 (vol.142).

[77]   Cropper and Smith (ref. 45), pp 61-63

[78] 'Has Aireys its own Loch Ness?' *Geelong Advertiser* 4 June 1973. Jeff Wells, 'What was the thing that rose from the ocean?' *Melbourne Truth* 16 June 1973

[79] For full details see Cropper and Smith (ref. 45), pp 61-63

[80] Gilroy (ref. 47), p 29

[81] 'Dinosaur found in NT harbor'. *The Northern Territory News* (Darwin) 2 Feb.1 980. See also *Sunday Mail* (Brisbane) 3 Feb. 1980. Full details in Cropper and Smith (ref. 45), pp 61-63.

[82] Fred McCue (1980). 'Unexplained Sighting in Darwin Harbor.' *The Northern Territory News* (Darwin) 20 Feb. 1980. Further details in Cropper and Smith (ref. 45), pp 65-66.

[83] 'Something strange in the water?' *Isis Town & Country* (Childers) 14 Sept. 1995

[84] Roy P Mackal (1976). *The Monsters of Loch Ness*. Swallow Press and Futura, pp 123-32

[85] Roesch, Ben S. (1998). A critical evaluation of the supposed contemporary existence of *Carcharodon megalodon*. *The Cryptozoology Review* 3(2): 14-24, also online as http://web.ncf.ca/bz050/megalodon accessed 22 June 2018

[86] ' "White Death" Startling shark story. Is it 115 feet long? Mystery at Port Stephens', *The Sun* (Sydney) Wed 30 Jan. 1918, page 5, 'Very like a whale. Shark that eats lobster pots. Queer story from Port Stephens', *Evening News* (Sydney) Wed 30 Jan. 1918, page 4

[87] 'Sea leopard captured. Now in aquarium.' *Northern Miner* (Charters Towers, Qld), Mon 3 Aug. 1931, page 4

[88] 'Strange mammal ashore at Manning River', *Sydney Morning Herald*, Sat. 3 May 1947, p 3 (and others)

[89] Pierce, Sidney K. Steven E. Massey, Nicholas E. Curtis, Gerald N. Smith Jr., Carlos Olavarría, and Timothy K. Maugel (2004), 'Microscopic, biochemical, and molecular characteristics of the Chilean Blob and a comparison with the remains of other sea monsters: nothing but whales', *The Biological Bulletin* 206: 125-133

CHAPTER 3

A LEGEND STALKS NORTH QUEENSLAND

If you visit Carnarvon Gorge, Central Queensland, as thousands do, you will come to a cliff face where the Aborigines have carved the footprints of numerous animals, perhaps as a blackboard for their children. Only a sign erected by the National Parks and Wildlife Service will alert you to the fact that one of them is not referable to any known animal. However, a keen cryptozoologist will immediately recognize its similarity to a footprint found in 1871 north of Cardwell, nearly 900 km away.

The North Queensland tiger has a semi-official position in the Australian fauna. No scientist has every examined or named it, but it has appeared in two of the classic (but now outdated) Australian mammal guides: *The Wild Animals of Australasia*, by LeSouef and Burrell[1], whose information was copied by Ellis Troughton, the long-time Curator of Mammals in the Australian Museum, in *Furred Animals of Australia*[2].

Now, a few words of warning are in order. People have a habit of seeing "tigers" on the slightest pretext. The most famous was the "Tantanoola tiger", which terrorised a farming community around the South Australian town of that name. It began in autumn 1885 when a youth returning home from a dance saw a beast leap a fence with a sheep in its mouth, and promptly announced that he had seen a tiger. Next morning the paddock was found littered with the torn carcasses of sheep, and since a couple of tigers had been reported escaped from a circus two years before, the legend was born[3].

For ten years the slaughter and the sightings mounted. Farmers roamed in pairs with rifles. Rewards were set. Posses were formed. Two Afghans, who claimed to have hunted tigers in India, joined the hunt, but failed. At last, on 21 August 1895, a Victorian bushman called Tom Donovan saw the beast savaging a sheep and downed it with a single shot. Unfortunately, he didn't get the reward, as the monster was not a tiger, but a huge dog. Somebody identified it as an Assyrian wolf. However, the killings started again, and it wasn't till 1910 that it was discovered that a sheep-stealing gang was using the "tiger" legend as a cover. Then, in 1957, 90-year-old Alf Warman, of Adelaide, walked into the Tiger Hotel at Tantanoola, saw the stuffed "tiger" and announced,

"That's my dog." It was the offspring of a bloodhound and a European deerhound bitch imported by a German chemist living in Adelaide. When working as a surveyor at Norwood, he had received the pup from his brother, Ted. When the dog became too large, he gave it to relatives of the mayor of Norwood to help in killing wild dogs. Instead, it went wild itself. His story was apparently verified from early records[4].

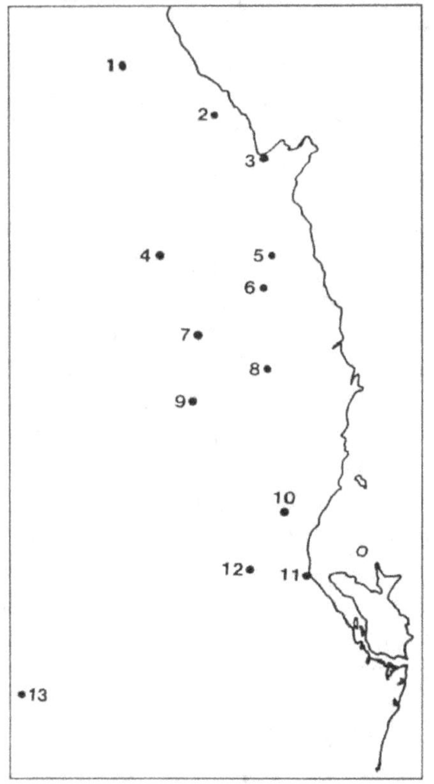

Atherton	4
Bellenden Ker Range	5
Cairns	3
Cardwell	11
Cardwell footprint (Murray River)	10
Kuranda	2
Millaa Millaa	7
Mt. Bartle Frere	6
Mt. Molloy	1
Palmerston National Park	8
Rockingham Range	12
Tully R. (George Sharp)	9
Valley of Lagoons Station	13

Eungella and Sarina are well to the south of the map limits.

Map 3A *Approximate sites of North Queensland reports*

In 1972 it was reported that a local trucking company proprietor, Roy Jenkinson and two companions saw a Tasmanian tiger in their headlights near Cannibal Creek, North Queensland[5]. However, I was able to contact Mr Jenkinson and one of the other witnesses, and received the following information: the sighting took place at 9pm on either 30 July or 6 August 10 miles [16km] along the Cannibal Creek Road, off the Mareeba to Cooktown Road. The sighting lasted 10 - 15 seconds, at a distance of either 25 feet [7.5m] or 100 feet [30.5m]. The creature was about the size of a sheep or Alsatian dog, the colour of a blue cattle dog, heavily built, with thick hindquarters and thick fur, and no obvious tail. It had a black, squarish, dog-like head, and crossed the road with a goat-like trot, jumping onto a nearby bank with ease. Obviously, this is some sort of dog, and a good indication of the unreliability of short newspaper articles.

In 1972 a Steve Knowles rang the police to report a lion he had seen crossing the Kingston Road near Beenleigh. It was about 4 feet [1.2m] long, with a round head, small ears and a white tip to its tail. It was a pity that the tracks beside the road looked suspiciously like those of a dog[6].

Canids (dogs, foxes, dingoes) often possess unusual coat patterns or strange, hybrid features which easily lend them to mystery animal reports. The creature killed by Strud Campbell while attacking his hens near the town of Craignish, northwest of Maryborough, was described as having a "[b]road head, sharp pointed nose, long teeth and abnormally thin ribs"[7]. However, when Michael Archer was able to examine its skull at the Queensland Museum he positively identified it as a fox. True, the photo shows something with a long, thin tail and rounded ears, quite unlike a fox, but Mr (now Prof) Archer is probably Australia's leading expert on skulls and teeth, and is not likely to be wrong.

But the false trail to beat all false trails must have been the Killarney beast. Shot in 1967, it was described as having the skin of a pig, the teeth and mane of a lion, the gait of a kangaroo, and the external attributes of both sexes. This remarkable entity was identified as a big mangy, male dog. The only fur it had left was around its neck, and the mange mites had entered its rudimentary nipples, making them swell like those of a bitch. As for the "gait of a kangaroo", perhaps it was tacked on to add flavour[8].

So when you read the following statement, often quoted in respect of the North Queensland tiger, you may be reasonably sure it is aberrant canids which are being discussed:

> ...it is the lion-like and tiger-like brutes that almost swamp the records in the manner of their appearances....
>
> There are records from Pipers Creek, Mansfield, Lockwood, Chiltern, Briagolong, and other places in Victoria; from Harden, Tantawonglo, Gouldburn. Gloucester, Wellington, Jamberoo, Orange and other places in New South Wales; from the Three-Mile Scrub, Brisbane, the St George district, and Normanton in Queensland.[9]

Yes, but without any further details, they must all be discounted.

The second fact to remember is that Australia has a genus of marsupial predators called *Dasyurus*, which are the size of cats and are generally of a fawn or grey colour, with white spots. They shouldn't come into the discussion at all, except that the largest, *D. maculatus* (it has a head-body length of about 60cm, a tail about 45-50cm, and is the only member of the genus to have the spots extend to its tail) is popularly known as the "tiger cat". Such usage can easily confuse the situation. Take, for example, the following statement:

> Yesterday Mr.G. W. Williams, of Springbrook Mountain, brought to this office the skin or one of these "tiger cats," which he shot on his farm on May 14 [1923]. It measured 3ft. 5in. [104cm] from the nose to the tip of the tail, and was 17½ in. [44½ cm] round at the smallest part, just behind the forepaws. Mr. Williams shot the beast with a heavy rifle while it was feeding on the carcass of a cow which had been recently killed. When disturbed it sprang on to a log and behaved just as a tiger might, swishing its tail from side to side and crouching in the same menacing manner as a "real" tiger. It showed no sign of fear. Mr. Williams stated that he killed a much larger specimen, about eight months ago, but took no measures to preserve the skin, as he was not aware of its scientific interest, his only object being to get rid of a destructive marauder. The recent discussion of the marsupial tiger, however, led to his taking the skin of his last victim. He says that these great cats are afraid of nothing, and will not hesitate to attack any animal. Dogs will not face them. They not only kill fowls, but many of the smaller animals. They have huge fangs, and sharp teeth, and instead of gnawing their prey as other animals of the cat species do they bite off lumps of the meat at a single snap. Their paws do not resemble those of the ordinary cat, but are shaped somewhat like the hand of a monkey, with a separate "thumb," and claws like those of a dog. Thus they are particularly adapted for climbing trees. Both the specimens shot by Mr. Williams were males[10].

Pretty strong stuff, eh? But remember, the quoted length includes a long tail, and is perfectly acceptable for *D. maculatus*. There was also no suggestion that the animal had actually killed the cow. The description of the paws could also, with some exaggeration, be applicable to *D. maculatus*. However, the behaviour suggests that, in this case, the predator might have been a simple feral cat. If you have a large cat or a lap dog, take a tape measure to it. You will be surprised at the dimensions of even a small animal.

Finally, many of the stories recounted later in this chapter, which were collected in the early 1970s, contain strong dramatic elements. Many of them are also based on memories 30, 40, even 50 or 60 years old. Now, it is a well-known fact that the adventures of one's youth tend to grow more dramatic with the years

> Till their own dreams at length deceive 'em,
> And oft repeating, they believe 'em.[11]

Though it is somewhat off the subject, I had an amusing experience of this myself when I was studying koala behaviour. There is a peculiar legend that these witless marsupials spank their babies. A middle-aged woman in fact told me how she had gone out one night to investigate a terrible screaming. Up in a tree sat two koalas: Mummy Bear and Daddy Bear, of course. One was holding Little Baby Bear by the scruff of its neck and whacking it on the rump with its free hand. Then he/she threw the baby to its mate, who caught it and continued the punishment. So transparently sincere was the woman, that I almost believed her. Of course, it did not take me long to discover that physically, psychologically, and socially, this would be totally beyond the powers of any koala.

With these notes of caution, less us examine the information on the mystery animal of the north. The first written reference appears to have been in 1871, when a Mr Sclater heard that the son of the Police Magistrate at Cardwell had been attacked by one. In a letter dated 2 August, the Magistrate, Brinsley Sheridan, set him right.

> One evening strolling along a path close to the shore of Rockingham Bay, a small terrier, my son's companion, took a scent up from a piece of scrub near the beach, and followed, barking furiously, towards the coast-range westwards. My boy (thirteen years of age, but an old bushman, who would put half those described in novels to blush) followed and found in the long grass, about half a mile from the spot the scent was first taken up, an animal described by himself as follows:- 'It was lying camped in the long grass and was as big as a Native Dog; its face was round like that of a Cat, it had a long tail, and its body was striped from the ribs under the belly with yellow and black.

My Dog flew at it, but it could not throw him. The animal then ran up a leaning tree, and the Dog barked at it. I got frightened and came home."

It was just dark when the boy came home in a high state of excitement and told me the story From inquiry I found that this is not the first time a similar animal has been see in the neighbourhood. Tracks of a sort of Tiger have been seen in Dalrymple's Gap by people camping there, and Mr. Reginald Uhr, now Police Magistrate at St George, whilst one of the native mounted police officers in this district, saw the same animal my son describes[12].

The next report of a mystery animal was a letter from Walter T. Scott of 4 December that year.

A Mr. Hull, Licenced Surveyor, was lately at work with a party of five men, surveying on the Murray and Mackay rivers, north of Cardwell.They were lying in their tents one night between eight and nine o'clock, when they were all startled by a loud roar close to the tents.They seized their guns and carefully reconnoitred; but the unknown animal had departed[13].

Figure 3.1 Cardwell footprint drawn by Hull in 1871

However, it did leave footprints in the soft soil, and Scott was able to publish a drawing made by Hull (Fig. 3.1). It appears to have measured about 6 cm either way, which would make it somewhat smaller than a cattle dog and, sure enough, it is referable to no known animal. The Aboriginal carving at Carnarvon is just the same, except for an extra toe. Scott interviewed some of the men, and was told that the animal was heard three nights in a row. He also mentioned that a bullock-driver claimed to have seen a tiger in 1864, but as he was a notorious liar nobody believed him.

On 5 June Scott was back with another story[14]. In the Valley of Lagoons Station in the coast range west of Cardwell, Robert Johnstone, with a group of native police, came across a large animal 40 feet [12m] up a tree. It leaped 10 feet [3m] into another tree and climbed down tail first. It was described as being larger than a pointer dog, with a long, thick tail, and a quite round head with no visible ears. The body was fawn-coloured with darker markings, but it was not actually stated that the markings were stripes. Except for the size, it could have been a kind of possum known as a cuscus (*Phalanger* sp.). Johnstone himself described the encounter in his memoirs, after first distinguishing it from the "tiger cat" (*Dasyurus*):

> It was when cutting through the jungle of the Rockingham Range to find a road for the gold escort from Georgetown to Cardwell that I first saw this large animal of the tiger tribe. Unfortunately, I had only a tomahawk, and the brute escaped, but I had sufficient time to note that it was very much larger than any tiger cat I had ever seen, and it did not appear to me to be spotted; but it was in the dark, dense jungle. I examined its lair, which was under an overhanging rock on some dead leaves, but there were no bones of any animals about, so that his jaws must be sufficiently powerful to crush the bones of the paddymelon or rock wallaby, as I saw the knuckle-bones in the droppings near its lair. I stalked the place on two occasions, but was not fortunate enough to find him at home. He is a daring fellow, as on to occasions he came into the camp at night, and took away the salt beef which we had put to soak in the creek, and the trooper, who was left in charge to guard it, saw the brute clearly come into camp at noon and take the beef out of the creek. He fired as it bounded off in the scrub, but missed it. He described it as "all the same pussy, but big fellow all the same dingo." It was a new animal to him, and I have no hesitation in saying that it is a new species, of which a specimen will be got some day. The tracks are more than twice the size of the tiger cat's[15].

The explorer, Dalrymple remembered this story, because the entry of his diary for 3 October 1873, when he was at Mourilyan Harbour and Moresby River, states: "The tracks of many cassowaries and of a wild or tiger cat, similar to that which Mr. Johnstone, Mr Armit, and the troopers of my party saw in the Rockingham Ranges in 1872, were frequent in the wild jungles[16]." It is not clear, of course, how Dalrymple recognized the tracks.

From August 1882 to July 1883 the German zoologist, Carl Lumholtz mounted a series of expeditions from a headquarters in the Herbert River valley. There the natives told him of the *yarri*, an unknown animal which lived on the summit of the Coast Mountains.

From their description I conceived it to be a marsupial tiger. It was said to be about the size of a dingo, though its legs were shorter and its tail long, and it was described by the blacks as being very savage. If pursued it climbed up the trees, where the natives did not dare follow it, and by gestures they explained to me how at such times it would growl and bite their hands. Rocky retreats were its favorite habitat, and its principle food was said to be a little brown variety of wallaby common in Northern Queensland scrubs. Its flesh was not particularly appreciated by the blacks, and if they accidentally killed a *yarri* they gave it to their old women. In Western Queensland I heard much about an animal which seemed to me to be identical with the *yarri* here described, and a specimen of was once nearly shot by an officer of the black police in the regions I was now visiting.

They also believed that a great water would rise if a young man were to pick up a dead yarri, but they agreed to bring him one provided it was carried by their oldest member, Jimmy. In fact, all they brought was a *D. maculatus*. Lumholtz also commented:

No person can spend many days with the Australian natives before finding out that one of their chief traits is their never-ceasing begging. If you give one thing to a black man he finds ten other things to ask for, and he is not ashamed to ask for all that you have, and more too. He is never satisfied. Gratitude does not exist in his breast, and friendship he is unable to appreciate. An Australian native can betray anybody, and confidence can rarely be placed in him. You should never let him walk behind you, but always in front. There is not one among them who will not lie if it is to his advantage. Though it is their nature to be lazy and though they have no inclination whatever for work, yet they can on a hunt develop remarkable energy and endurance[17].

In other words, for whatever reason, Lumholtz had a bad relationship with the Aborigines. So we cannot be sure that they told him the absolute truth about the *yarri*, and there must certainly have been communication problems, as they were required to use gestures. Nor can we tell whether they decided to fob him off with an easily caught tiger cat in place of a *yarri*, or whether *yarri* was merely another name for the tiger cat.

Six years later a Queensland Museum expedition was collecting animals in the Bellenden-Ker area. The report listed *D. maculatus*, which was stated to be:

> an object of dread to the natives of the Herberton district; they even accuse it of carrying off their piccaninies. Exaggerated ideas of it have probably given rise to certain rumours of a great striped carnivore of arboreal habits infesting the Herberton wilds. After prolonged search for the latter in its known haunts nothing but the native cat in question could be found[18].

Now, really! The Aborigines would know quite well that the native cat could never carry off a child. Either they knew of another, unknown species, or they were playing a joke on the white men. One wonders what sort of communication went on between the expedition and the natives, and whether it took place in anything but broken English. Nevertheless, there may well be some significance in the fact that the stories they heard were so similar to those told to Lumholtz.

The next sighting was about 1900, though it was not reported until 1938, when the animal was making news again. It was in the scrub near Kairi, about 4 pm, when Mr. J. McGeehan heard a loud, harsh grating and vibrating sound. He ran over to discover a strange animal expiring from the attacks of dogs. He estimated that it was about 12 inches [30cm] high, with a back, between shoulders and tail 14 inches [36cm] long (remember, this was 38 years before), which would make it the size of a large cat. The fur was finer and shorter than a cat's, the eyes dark, the teeth pointed.

> The most striking part of its appearance was the well defined hoops of colour which encircled its body. These hoops or bands appeared to be about 2½ inches [6¼ cm] in width, and the colours were white and dun alternating in perfectly marked circles. As far as I can remember the alternate colours did not extend to the head, legs or tail. I think that the colour of these parts was dun. The neck was short and stout, and the head was shaped more like a Pomeranian terrier than of a cat, but the pricked ears were not as large[19].

Thick white stripes - there would only have been space for three of them - encircling the body! Previous writers have not commented on how unusual this is. Hardly any species bears such a pattern, nor do individual "freaks" normally bear such well-defined patterns. Equally important, it is not consistent with previous sightings. So what did Mr. McGeehan see? No wonder he claimed few people believed him, but in the previous tear (1937) a person told him he had had similar sightings around Babinda. Almost every witness seems to know another witness.

In late 1921 a sugar planter, P. B. Scougall, along with a Mr. G de Tournouer were riding from Munna Creek to Tiaro. It was about dusk, and they were just about to cross a creek when their horses shied. According to de Tournouer:

> We dismounted ... and were startled to find the cause to be a large animal of the cat tribe, standing about twenty yards away, astride a very dead calf, glaring defiance at us, and emitting what I can only describe as a growling whine. As far as the gathering darkness and torrential rain allowed us to judge he was nearly the size of a mastiff, of a dirty fawn colour, with a whitish belly, and broad blackish stripes. The head was round, with rather prominent lynx like ears, but unlike the feline there was a tail reaching to the ground and large pads. We threw a couple of stones at him, which only made him couch low, with ears laid flat, and emit a raspy snarl, vividly reminiscent of the African leopard's nocturnal 'wood-sawing' cry. Beating an angry tattoo on the grass with his tail he looked so ugly and ready for a spring that we felt a bit 'windy', but on our making a rush and cracking our stockwhips he bounded away to the bend of the creek, when he turned back and growled at us[20].

The next report appears to have been generally overlooked because it does not come from the rainforest of the far north of the state, but from the dry eucalypt scrub in the far south - between Talwood and St George, to be more accurate. In April 1923 a British Museum expedition led by Sir G. H. Wilkins was camped by the chain of water holes known as the Moonie River. It was night, and Wilkins was preparing bird specimens when one of his assistants, the Russian-born Prof. Vladimir Kotoff, shouted: "Come quickly; come quickly with a gun; there is some large animal here at the tent." It disappeared in a blur as the others raced out. The tracks they found the next morning were almost indistinguishable among the dead leaves. The following morning, before dawn, it disturbed the bait they had left, and the scratch marks suggested it was some sort of cat. "Kotoff described it as big as a dog, with a bushy tail and a round, flat head, and striped in colour."[21]

Since Le Souef and Burrell's guide book was published in 1926 and, as mentioned at the start of this chapter, their data was incorporated into Troughton's, now is the time to examine the sightings they reported.

They mentioned, firstly, an experienced naturalist known as George Sharp, who was collecting eggs of the golden bower bird near the head of the Tully River when he heard a rustle in the scrub. It was not yet dark. He turned to see a beast "larger and darker than the Tasmanian tiger, with stripes showing very distinctly" which was gone before he could raise his rifle. Later he met a settler in the Atherton region who had shot a similar creature when it came for his goats. The head and body was eaten by wild pigs, but Sharp did see the skin, which measured 5 feet [1.5 m] from nose to tip of tail. That would have made it as large as a Tasmanian tiger, and solid proof of the animal's existence. It's a pity there was no way of preserving the skin. It is also a pity the authors did not say how they got the story[22]. Did Mr Sharp tell them personally? Did he write them a letter? Did he publish it in some newspaper or magazine? Researchers really ought to be more thorough in their documentation. They didn't even give the date.

Neither did they give a date when Mr Endres of Mundubbera captured alive a very savage animal 'about 18 inches [46cm] high and as long as a large cat; [with a] very short head and neck; striped, but not right round.' This was in the south of the state, and only about 130 km from de Tournouer's escapade.

But let us return to the far north, and a story which the authors attribute to Mr. J. Idriess of Coen:

> Up here in York Peninsula we have a tiger-cat that stands as high as a hefty, medium-sized dog. His body is lithe and sleek and beautifully striped in black and grey. His pads are armed with lance-like claws of great tearing strength. His ears are sharp and pricked, and his head is shaped like that of a tiger. My introduction to this beauty was one day when I heard a series of snarls from the long buffalo-grass skirting a swamp. On peering through the grass I saw a full-grown kangaroo, backed up against a tree, the flesh of one leg torn clean from the bone. A streak of black and grey shot towards the 'roo's' throat, then seemed to twist in the air, and the kangaroo slid to earth with the

entrails literally torn out. In my surprise I incautiously rustled the grass, and the great cat ceased the warm feast that he had promptly started upon, stood perfectly still over his victim, and for ten seconds returned me gaze for gaze. Then the skin wrinkled back from the nostrils, white fangs gleamed, and a low growl issued from his throat. I went backwards and lost no time in getting out of the entangling grass. . . . The next brute was dead, and beside him was my much-prized staghound, also dead. This dog had been trained from puppyhood in tackling wild boars, and his strength and courage were known by all prospectors over the country[23].

The site of this experience was allegedly near the Alice River.

And this is where the absence of documentation is particularly frustrating. J. Idriess was, of course, Ion L. (Jack) Idriess, later to become Australia's most famous chronicler of outback adventures. He once mentioned to Troughton that the piece was "somewhat youthfully over-graphic"[24], but he never explained where and when it was originally published. Nor did he explain why the account also occurs, almost word for word, in D. H. Lawrence's novel, *Kangaroo*[25]. Who plagiarised whom? Lawrence's novel was written in 1922 and researched in 1921. He also had the narrator say: "They published that yarn in the *Bulletin*." I therefore checked the bush yarns section of the *Bulletin* from 1919 to 1921 hoping to find the original story, but to no avail. Until someone finds it, I suggest that the Idriess quote be treated with suspicion. At any rate, Lawrence had obviously heard about the animal.

In 1932 came a brief newspaper report:

Mr. A. W Blackman, of Upper Murray, and a party who made a tour of the Kirrima lands, about 30 miles [49 km] from Tully, claim to have shot what is generally known as a marsupial tiger (called by the Aborigines "*yaddi*"). The animal, when captured, was half as big again as a domestic cat, and was striped like a tiger. It was captured on the fringe of extensive scrub on the Cardwell Range, and it is thought that with a powerful hunt another of the species could be captured[26].

It also mentioned several other species being captured, which makes one wonder what sort of activities the group was engaged in, and what happened to the carcass and skin. Certainly, in 1938 a search was made for the animal by Miss C. Neuhauser, a German scientist collecting for the New York Museum[27], but nothing appears to have come of it.

After that, the scene remained quiet for more than two decades, until another visiting scientist, J. L. Harrison heard of an animal seen in the headlights of a car in the Palmerston National Park. Since Dr. Harrison had recently worked in Malaya, he pulled out some photos of Malayan rainforest mammals. The witness, needless to say, had never seen them before, but commented that the animal he had seen "appeared to resemble a large civet, with the heavy loins and thick base of tail of such an arboreal species as *Paguma larvata*, but with the transverse pattern of *Hemigalus*."[28] Readers will have to take my word that the first species does have very heavy loins, and the last-mentioned bears a series of parallel stripes across its back like a Tasmanian tiger's.

In 1969 came the following story from a Nancy O'Brien:

It was perched on my casement window top, and growling and snarling, and raking the air towards me with its right paw. Its eyes were wide open and a glittering green. So I sat up in bed and shook my walking stick at it and it leaped down. Being bright moonlight I saw the length of its body and that its tail was as long as its body and the stripes on it, from the small of its back to the butt of its tail. I immediately thought of it as a small half grown tiger[29].

Figure 3.2 Animal seen at Cairns by Nancy O'Brien

Her drawing is reproduced as Fig. 3.2. It is unlikely that the lady had a walking stick when she was young, so presumably she was referring to a recent event at her home in Cairns.

It was about this time that Janeice Plunkett decided to make an all-out search for the animal and the people who had seen it. Later she was joined by Peter Makeig. It is hoped that this book will encourage them to publish their 100-odd reports in detail, because so far we have been treated to only the following brief summaries to whet our appetites[30].

Kuranda, 1910: Most of the tiger cats I have killed [how many was that?] were about four feet [1.2m] long and of a fawn colour, with black stripes running across the body, which was fairly long, unlike an ordinary cat.

Kuranda, 1945: He aimed a kick at it, and as the torch shone on its head, to use his words: "I nearly dropped the torch with shock." The creature defying him had a round face and four exposed 'tiger teeth' . . . the other salient point in my opinion was the fact that big savage pig-dogs were terrified of it. He had several at this time, and they usually gave indications that the cat was about by coming upstairs and trying to get under beds or other safe places.

Eungella, 1920: My father had been riding around a portion of a property with his dog, a big blue cattle dog, not afraid of anything, but my father stated that after one small brush with the tiger cat the dog would not approach it.

Bellenden Range, 1925: An animal about as large as a medium-sized dog rushed out and climbed a nearby tree. The animal was very savage. Its coat was beautiful and striped like a tiger.

Sarina, 1950: He said it was as big as a fairly large dog - striped and appeared to have a large head.

Mt Molloy, 1953: The head was a good deal larger than an old tomcat, with teeth, a lot like the extinct sabre toothed tiger (not size but shape).

Mt Bartle Frere, 1968: Head appeared round and broad, its nose shorter and broader than a dog's. Some of its teeth appeared to protrude out and upwards like tusks.

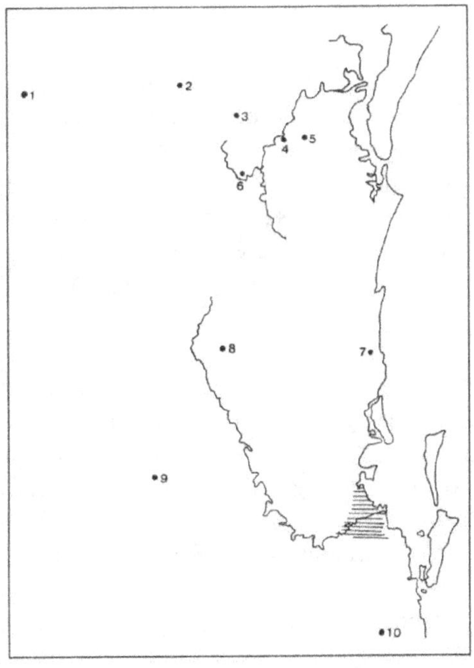

Aramara	3
Bidwell	5
Biggenden	2
Buderim	7
Munduberra	1
Munna Creek	6
Mt Stanley	8
Pechey	9
Tamborine Mt	10
Tiaro	4

Map 3B *Sites of reports from Southeast Queensland shown in relation to the Mary (north) and Brisbane Rivers (south), and the Brisbane metropolitan area (shaded)*

And now for something farther south:

Biggenden, 1904: There were a lot of them about early 1904. My father killed one in our kitchen that year. It was fawny black and yellow stripes. Very large and also savage.

Tamborine Mountain, 1910: My mother lived near Tamborine Mountain ... the tiger cat she said was a horrible big animal like a cat with stripes.

Tiaro, 1915: I can remember shooting one about the year 1915. They would be slightly taller and heavier built than a domestic cat, with large head and strong shoulders. Also striped rings around the body. This specimen had a young one on each teat, approximately ten in all.

This, you might remember, was close to the site of Scougall and de Tournouer's encounter. The reference to young provides a clue to the animal's identity, as we shall see. The next report is only slightly east of that site and suggests that the species was still active there for at least another four decades.

Bidwell, 1954: The cat climbed up a wattle sucker and sat there snarling and spitting. My husband was greatly taken with the markings - some of the stripes he said were nearly a dark orange and the animal was just like a very large cat in shape and size - eventually it leaped out of the tree and faced my husband. He said that he had never seen anything so savage and that he had never seen such big fangs on any animal of that size before and since. He thought for a moment that the animal was going to tear him to pieces.

Aramara, 1948: They were inclined to attack a dog rather than run away and, as far as I can remember, they were a cat with an extra large head mainly in width and extra-long tusks. All were the same colour: two-toned stripes. I think under portion was light fawn. The size varied, the last one I saw, and he would not have been the biggest, but fairly close, would have been 18 inches to 20 inches [46 - 51 cm] high at the shoulder. This one I shot.

Aramara is 40 km west of Maryborough, and so in the same general vicinity.

You might note a certain consistency in the reports, particularly in the background colour being described as fawn. The stripes are nearly always dark. However, Plunkett and Makeig also provide the following story by a bushman/naturalist who examined two animals killed during a raid on a fowl house at Pechey, 30 km north of Toowoomba.

> I saw a pair of such animals a little over 50 years ago [written in 1970]. This pair of animals were of a tawny colour, not unlike the colour of a dark-coloured dingo, and they had off-white bands about an inch [2½ cm] wide running across their bodies, from shoulders to the butt of the tail . . . built after the formation, in practically every way, of the Tasmanian Marsupial Wolf . . . the female was pouched and the male carried his testes between the rear legs as in an O'Possum or like the kangaroo . . . these

animals were at least twice the size of a very large bush or wild tomcat . . . the tail would have been at least eighteen inches [46cm] long and the bodies from tip of nose to butt of tail, at least almost two feet [61cm].

The animals were equipped with long, sharp, and powerful claws, and were said, by old-timers, to be equal in battle to any two dogs . . . the head of the Queensland tiger is after the style of the Tasmanian wolf with extra-long powerful jaws equipped with long, curved, canine teeth as long or longer than those of a full-grown dog fox . . . the pair of animals that I have mentioned above had their habitat in dense wattle forest country.

Here we have something different: long jaws like a Tasmanian wolf's, whereas most of the other reports mention the short, rounded face of a cat. And if there is one thing the average Australian knows is the difference between a dog and a cat. Also, other witnesses describe black stripes, and even when they don't, black is usually implied in the word "stripe". White stripes are a much rarer phenomenon among animals. One is reminded of the much broader, white hoops of McGeehan's creature.

Fig. 3.3. Animal photographed by Rilla Martin in western Victoria, 1964

109

It also brings to mind the Rilla Martin photograph (Fig. 3.3), which was taken in western Victoria in 1964, and has been published in numerous venues since. The more I look at it the more disturbing I find it. It doesn't fit any species, known or unknown. However, the splashes of white sunlight in the foreground and the complete whiteness of the rump suggests that the white shoulder stripes are a light-and-shadow artefact. And although the build and stance of the body is not really what one would expect of a large dog, it cannot be ruled out.

You will remember Nigel Tutt, the chief witness of the Deception Bay monster. After I had finished interviewing him about it in 1989 he casually mentioned that he had seen the "Yedna tiger". At that my ears pricked up, and as he continued my amazement grew. Surely it was too much to believe that one man would have seen both a land and a sea monster, at point blank range under perfect viewing conditions! But he had proof. You see, his daughter, Carol (another Deception Bay witness, remember?) had asked him to write his memoirs for her edification. The result was an unfinished manuscript, entitled *A Vanishing Race*, which describes the days when he and his brother, Charlie were opening up the country under conditions the present generation can scarcely imagine. Mr Tutt graciously allowed me to borrow it, and sandwiched in the middle of vivid descriptions of his pine-felling days was the tale of the creature they had encountered. It has never been published before, so I shall quote it at length.

The year was 1939, the location Mt Stanley, overlooking the little township of Linville in the Upper Brisbane Valley. (It is also not far from a celebrated "*yowie*" sighting, as we shall see in a later chapter.) He and Charlie had seen the occasional spotted marsupial cat (*Dasyurus* spp.) and other animals. They were hiking down the mountain with their packs and making quite a noise when:

> As we rounded a bend in the rough track we both stopped in our tracks; Charlie looked at me; I looked at Charlie: Neither of us believed our eyes; Charlie was first to speak, though his voice sounded rather strange; Do you see what I see he wanted to know? Sure; I saw what he saw all right; - I still didn't believe my eyes.
>
> There sitting in the middle of an old decaying pine-stump was a large Cat-Animal. A few rays of afternoon sun were filtering through the scrub, the large feline

apparition appeared to be relaxing in the warmth of those, sunning itself. We stopped about twenty feet [6m] away from its resting place. It didn't move, just lay and stared at us with a rather aggressive look of territorial possession on its face. We put down the action restricting portion of our load. We didn't put down our axes; Charlie & I were both apprehensive, instinctively we both retained our most effective weapons of defence. This animal was big enough to be dangerous. It was certainly a Cat; it didn't stand up to allow really accurate guess at its height but would be perhaps a bit taller than a large blue cattle-dog, but very much heavier, its legs being abut as thick as the average human leg measured just below the knee. From what we could judge its body would measure forty inches [102m] or more around. Its coat was of rather fine texture fur "Reddish-Ginger" background with very dark brown - almost black - stripes all over its body and also circling its legs. Although we stood and watched for quite a while - We weren't keen to carry our big load too close to its stump; - It made no sign of moving and never took its eyes off us & showed no inclination to vacate its resting place.

They started wondering whether it might not be an escapee from some circus, though it looked too small to be a real tiger.

The day was getting towards its close, our un-Australian King of the pine-stump remained where he was, we had no mind to stand and wait for him to move, we either had to hump our gear back up the hill for half a mile to where an alternate track went down or get past his chosen stump. We weren't keen on getting any closer to him than necessary with our hands full of bulky gear. Eventually we decided to carry our gear past, one of us with a load the other accompanying him with an axe at the ready in case he decided to object to our passing, this ferrying our belongings past took three trips. We kept as far to the other side of the track as possible (About 20 ft). The "Big Cat" didn't move; it just fixed a malevolent stare on us and Sat. It probably trusted our intentions about as much as we trusted its. When we last looked back as the snigging track rounded a bend it was still sitting on its stump. For many years since that strange sighting till well after the end of the second World War there have been periodic reports of cattlemen finding beasts which they believed to have been killed & partly eaten by some creature which they judged to be larger and more powerful than any dingo they could imagine. Also in this area which covers a large and then undeveloped mountainous scrub tract extending over the source areas of the Brisbane, Stanley & Mary Rivers, and also of the "Big" & "Little" Yabba creeks there for years persisted reported sightings of some large Un-Australian animal of the cat family which became known as "The Yedna Tiger"; Yedna [officially, Yednia] is a small one-time Sawmilling settlement in the ranges between Conondale and Jimna.

Perhaps searching through old local newspaper files or interviewing equally old residents would turn up some interesting stories. An animal which had such an effect on two bushmen at such close range is obviously not your ordinary feral cat. I might add that I have not heard any recent reports of the Yednia Tiger.

It is a fact that events as dramatic and strange and of such marked personal significance as this are liable to etch themselves permanently on the brain in what are known as "flash bulb" memories. At the end of the interview Nigel said: "I bet old Charlie remembers it as if it were yesterday." Naturally, I wrote to Charles Tutt in Rockhampton and, sure enough, his description of the animal was if anything, even more vivid than his brother's. Aware of the tricks that memory can play, he stipulated that he purposely avoided contacting Nigel before responding. As you will note, there are significant discrepancies in the brothers' accounts of the circumstances of the sighting. Here, then, are his answers to my questions.

Q 1 & 2. Circumstances of the sighting and what they were doing at the time.

A. The place was in mediumy open scrub (rain forest) near the top of Mt Stanley at the headwaters of the Brisbane River. The weather was cold and cloudy and the leaf litter on the scrub floor was damp.

He gave a long dissertation of his movements to ascertain that the year was 1940. Because of the weather he decided that it must have been May or early June. They walked up the hill later than usual because they wanted to be sure the weather would be fine.

The time when we sighted the "big cat" was between 8 am and 9 am. It was curled up on top of a big old hoop pine stump about two feet [60cm] high and three feet six inches [107cm] across. The stump was situated about seven to ten yards off the snigging track we were walking up hill on, and on our right hand side. (Certainly the distance was less than half a cricket pitch length.) Curled in a semi circle the "big cat' took up nearly all of the top of the stump. A moment or two after I first saw it it moved its head, then sat up with its forepaws straight and its rump on the stump. "Look Nigel, look," I said and I think Nigel had seen the animal at about the same time as I had. It sat almost face on, and turned its head a little extra to look us squarely in the face. It seemed surprised and in a way boldly interested. It coolly looked us over, up and down, then it bounded off the stump, took three or four bounds, paused, looked around at us and stared at us for a couple of seconds, then moved off in a slow trotting, or loping gait. It just seemed to melt into the scrub, without crashing into many bushes or making any other noise.

Nigel and I quickly cut across the track it had left by; in fact we were on to it while it was the last moments in sight. We went to the stump and while looking for any fur or hair a weak ray of sunlight fleetingly broke through the scrub canopy on to the stump. The stump top yielded no fur though it did give an impression of use as a "camp". No doubt a warm spot on a cold morning. Just the sort of thing a cat would like.

Nigel and I then followed down the way the "big cat" had gone a couple of chains [1 chain = 20 metres] and searched. I was carrying a single shot .22 calibre rifle which I usually carried to work. I felt uneasy and I said to Nigel something like "I don't think we'll go any further - the scrub was getting thicker - "I don't think this rifle would be heavy enough to stop that animal quickly if there was need to."

Q 3. How long did the sighting last?   **A.** About 30 seconds, 16 to 20 seconds on the stump and 8 to 10 seconds on the ground.

Q 4. How close was the animal?   **A.** 7 to 10 yards.

Q 5.   How big was it? **A.** Head and body 3'6" (three foot six inches) to 4 feet [107-122cm], tail another 2 feet six inches [152cm]. It was shaped like a light weight tiger.

Q 6. General appearance. **A.** It was lean and strong and sinuous looking. It was not overly well kept looking, nor was it skinny and shaggy. I noticed a few pinched up looking fur or hair: small tufts between its ears and out the back part of its head. It appeared to have a short-haired solid coat all over. No bare or long haired or furred places were seen.

Q 7 & 8. Colour and stripes. **A.** It was slate grey or "middle" grey with very dark grey or black & white stripings and comb like grey and ginger broken stripings, very much like the markings on some strongly marked tabby cats.

The darkest stripes, nearly black that I noticed were a vertical stripe just behind the shoulder, and another on the flank. Other plain though not quite so dark vertical stripes went down its shoulder in front of the darkest stripe and the thigh of its hind leg behind the leading dark stripe. It was dark grey for its body length along the middle of its back and down its tail and had a horizontal pattern of dark and lighter greys along the upper portion of its side (I only saw one side) similar to that which some tabby cats have. The lower part its side was dark grey khaki edged.

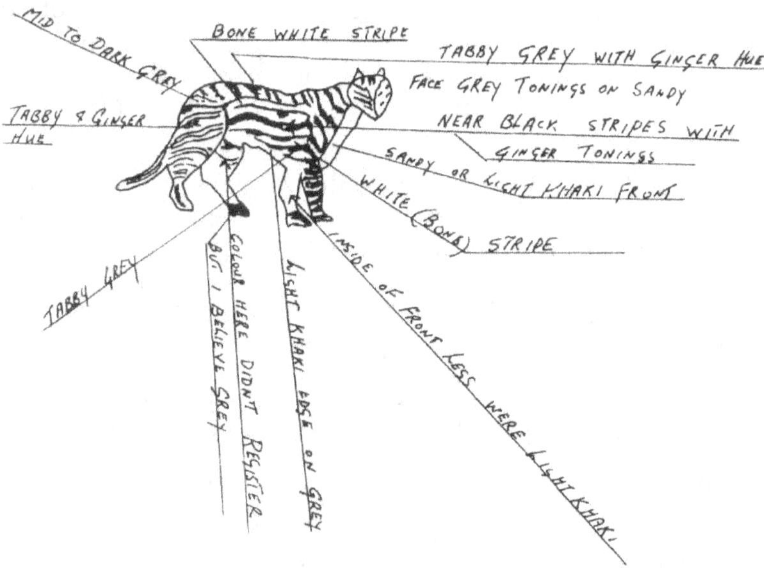

Figure 3.4 Sketch by Charles Tutt of animal seen on Mt Stanley, 1940.

Q 9. Face. **A.** It had a genuine cat's round face but appeared even rounder on its forehead. Its head was large but pretty much in the proportion to its body. It only looked wider than its body from one angle, towards the middle of its run as it ran away. Its ears were short with distinct half circle top edges, and wide apart.

Q 10. Tail. **A.** Only a general view as it ran off. It was dark grey, the same colour as that along the middle of the animal's back. It carried it in a low curve.

Q 11. Behaviour. **A.** When first seen it was lying on its side on the pine stump with the curve of its back towards us. It turned its head unhurriedly around to the right, lifting it, and looked at us for a couple of seconds, then turned away, just as though what it had seen had not registered, but did so afterwards as though it had second thoughts. The second time it turned its head quickly to look, and twisted its body and sat upright almost squarely facing us. It eyed us off with a look, which seemed a cross between interest and curiosity, and uncertainty. (Maybe as prey, or strangers.) Then it stood up on the stump on all fours and bounded off. When it left the stump it was side on to us It could have jumped off the stump and gone directly away from us but it didn't. It left from a side-ways position - down hill. After a few bounds it stopped, looked back then trotted off. I particularly noticed it seemed to swing its front paws well clear of the ground. It left the impression in my mind that its front feet were about the size of a man's clenched fists, and its fore-paws about the thickness of my wrists and forearms.

Q 12. Anything else of significance? **A.** We ran onto the path it left by while it was still in sight and got a view of it from behind. It seemed to disappear suddenly. If it had climbed a tree we should have seen it, and if it left running, we should have seen where it went out of sight, or heard it swishing bushes as the scrub it entered was getting much thicker. I think it must have crouched, but that is only speculation. We followed down onto the edge of the thicker scrub just beyond where we saw it last, but I at least felt uncomfortable and that if an emergency arose my .22 single shot rifle would be neither heavy enough, or quick enough to reload. . . . . Just after we'd finished our searching . . . and we'd returned up the hill a few yards, behind us suddenly there was a loud rustling through the bushes which went in a direction straight down hill and seemed to be being made by a large body charging through them. We remarked to each other, "Did you hear that?"

Charles Tutt also provided a sketch, which is here reproduced as Figure 3.4.

It may be too soon to write off the animal as extinct, even in the crowded southeast of the state, if the news from Buderim is any guide. Buderim is about 80 km east of Mt Stanley, a similar distance north of Brisbane. It is also the oldest town on the Sunshine Coast, very close to the sea, on the main tourist drive, and in the heart of a farming and rural residential area. But down a gravel road to the southwest of the town stands a patch of rainforest, maybe 30 hectares in extent, where 55 year old dentist, Lance Mesh was renting a house in December 1994. As he told it to me 6 months later, he had often heard tales of the "tiger" while living in Atherton, but never expected to find it down south. About 7.30 one evening, he was turning a corner on the way home, when a strange animal froze in his highlights, 50 or 60 metres away. He pulled to a halt, and both man and animal stood mesmerised at each other. Take a good look, he told his 10 year old daughter, Samantha, for she would never see such a thing again.

It was perhaps 75 cm high, and squarish i.e. as high as the body was long. Crouched in alarm, its powerful hind legs formed a sharp acute angle, giving it a superficially kangaroo-like appearance, though the hindquarters did not taper in any way. A powerful tail trailed off into the darkness. Its face was definitely cat-like, with a high forehead, and a strong, heavyset upper jaw. But what amazed him were the stripes. There were 4 or 5 of them, dark and vertical, about 5 cm wide at the spine, and tapering to a point over the ribs. For 20 or 30 seconds it stood facing them, then vanished into the night.

The local newspaper illustrated the story with a picture of a thylacine, or Tasmanian tiger, but never for a moment did he ever identify it as such. However, when he saw Charlie Tutt's sketch, he recognized it right away. Later, he received phone calls from people as far afield as Pomona, Maleny and Mapleton about similar sightings, though he was not convinced about all of them. One man, a geneticist, told a remarkable story. He had returned to his house one afternoon just in time to disturb a striped animal which bolted out a window. Inside, he found his pet cat, disembowelled and partly skinned. According to another resident I have spoken to, this whole area north of Brisbane is a hotbed of such tales.

What are we to make of all these strange stories? A couple of anomalous sightings will be met in later chapters. However, most witnesses describe the animal as cat-like, even mentioning the short, round shape of the face. A couple mention pale or white stripes, but by and large, the descriptions are consistent: an animal as big as a medium-sized dog, cat-like face, long, cat-like tail, dark, vertical stripes, heavy hindquarters, climbs trees, very powerful and savage.

Now, experience shows that feral cats can grow pretty big, and it is easy to overestimate their size. And sometimes, though rarely, their coat colour falls into a pattern of stripes. If there were only one such report, identification would be no problem. But when the same unlikely features turn up again and again over a long period of time, including very early days in remote areas where feral cats are unlikely to have been established, and with an anomalous footprint to boot, the odds are that we are dealing with an unknown species.

A obvious candidate would be *Thylacoleo carnifex*, the marsupial "lion", a leopard-sized brute which hunted the giant fauna in the age before ours.[31] It was another of those peculiar tricks which evolution frequently plays. While all the other carnivorous marsupials belong to the more primitive classes, along comes one of the higher forms, the Diprotodonta, a relative of the possums and the kangaroos, to occupy the niche occupied on other continents by the big cats, even to the extent of being semi-arboreal.

It is easy to imagine that, faced with the country drying up and its natural prey dying out, *Thylacoleo* shrunk to a more manageable size and retreated to the isolated patches of dense scrub which were probably the cradle of the species. The most persistent reports come from far north Queensland, especially the rainforest belt. However, there have been a number of good sightings from scattered southern parts of the state, particularly the area around Tiaro. In how many of these areas does it still exist? Over the decades many species have become locally extinct.

Nevertheless, despite the attractiveness of *Thylacoleo* as an explanation, there are a number of obstacles. The first is the tooth structure, which was derived from that of a possum. Other predators possess a row of small front teeth (incisors) between a pair of elongated canines. In *Thylacoleo*, however, the canines had disappeared, and its killing teeth were a pair of long incisors right in the front of both jaws. Its snarling face would thus have presented quite a different aspect to that of a cat, and it is surprising nobody commented on it, not even those who claim to have killed one.

The second is the few references to reproductive anatomy. The Pechey female was said to have had a pouch. Admittedly, the witness did not say how close he got to be able to describe it, and we don't know whether it was even seen during the breeding season. Also, the animal was said to be dog-like, and thus may not have been the same species as the others. The one shot at Tiaro in 1915 was said to have had ten young, one attached to each teat. This would suggest (though it is not certain) that it possessed a rudimentary pouch consisting of just a flap of skin at either side. Such a feature is typical only of the primitive marsupial predators, the Dasyuridae, whose mothers frequently have to drag large number of young around, clinging to their teats or fur, even when they are so big as to be a hindrance. *Thylacoleo's* pouch would have been fully developed, like that of its kin. However, it is unlikely that even a dasyurid of that size would been able to carry so many young. Of course, we have to rely on the memory, and truthfulness, of only a single witness.

Finally, *Thylacoleo's* hind paw was very similar to that of a ringtailed possum. However, it walked on the toes of its forepaws, which possessed four clawed toes of more or less equal length, and a thumb which could be turned at right angles to the others[32]. This does not sound much like the known footprints. True, the Cardwell footprint might be incomplete; there might have been a thumb mark to the side which was indistinct and/or overlooked. Conversely, the Aboriginal carving at Carnarvon Gorge may have depicted the forepaw with all toes aligned. The trouble is, they are of equal size, whereas *Thylacoleo*'s thumb was shorter and stouter than the others. But if the Queensland tiger is not *Thylacoleo*, then it has no counterpart in the fossil record.

If the legendary animal does exist, how can it be located? A group of American biologists had an idea. One of them, William Lawrence of the University of California, even interviewed a witness from Millaa Millaa who claimed to have captured a litter of "tiger" kittens some years before. After an unsuccessful attempt to rear them, they were buried in the forest.[33] (I have not been able to contact Dr Lawrence about this, and would appreciate it if he would contact me.)

The upshot was a proposal to send three biologists and thirty volunteers from the London-based Operation Raleigh on an expedition from Cooktown. One team would spend two weeks travelling from Cooktown to Koombooloomba Dam, where they would join a second team. From there groups of five to ten would radiate out into the forest for a week before rafting down the Tully or Herbert River. In the process, they would interview local inhabitants, check for tracks, scats, and hair, conduct spotlight searches at night, and possibly set up simple traps to catch the whole animal, or even simpler traps to pick up hair samples for later analysis. What a pity the authorities refused to grant permits!

Personally, I can't say I was disappointed. Although some of the expedition leaders and advisers had visited the north Queensland rainforest before, I suspect they are still psychologically in the Northern Hemisphere, unprepared for the sheer ruggedness of the terrain in question. Groups of five to ten outsiders roaming the jungle would be just asking to get lost, not to mention falling foul of the country's inimitable attractions, such as unseen precipices, poisonous snakes and the giant stinging tree. It would be questionable whether even known species, such as the cassowary, could be found in such a manner, and there is absolutely no evidence that the North Queensland tiger actually inhabits that particular patch of scrub.

In short, if it were as simple as that to solve the mystery, somebody here would have done it years ago. When a species is unknown to science, it is for a good reason, and this one is certainly one of the rarest and most elusive of all.

ADDENDUM

When I wrote about the Carnarvon footprint engraving at the beginning of the chapter, I assumed it was well known officially. To my surprise, however, in the quarter century since then I have discovered that I appear to be the only person aware of it. Those who mention it always cite my book. The current staff of the Carnarvon National Park don't know about it. They used to, and they should, but they don't. With this in mind, it is time I set the record straight.

Carnarvon Gorge is situated at approximately 25° S, 148° 10' E, and consists of a spectacular complex of gorges, now served by a large number of walking trails. More to the point, the cliff faces and rock shelters also feature spectacular examples of Aboriginal art, the most spectacular being on the hard-to-access Art Gallery.

Carnarvon Gorge is not easily accessible to a person like myself acting alone. However, in 1978 and 1986 I booked excursions with companies providing camping tours of the canyon. Because I had taken a large number of photos on my first visit, I left my camera home on the second one. I could have kicked myself! Here is an extract of my diary for Saturday 29 March 1986. At the time, we had done a complete circuit, and were heading back to camp.

If I had had my camera with me, I would have taken photos of both the engraving and the sign. As it was, I made a rough sketch of it on a scrap of paper, and later transferred it to my diary. I shan't copy it here because it was very crude but, like Mr Hull's sketch, it displayed the same oval pad, not present in any known native animal, and with five toes - not four - in a line above the pad, but I think somewhat thinner than on Hull's footprint.

For various reasons, I haven't been back since - at least not to the Art Gallery. You can find plenty of photos online of the art at that site, but none of them, as far as I am aware, covers the specific small nook which bears that engraving. Don Hitchcock, who has published a large number of such photos[34] tells me that he knows nothing about it. In 2016 a correspondent, Chris McLean decided to make written enquiries to the authorities at Carnarvon Gorge about it. It turns out no-one now knows anything about it. The sign directing attention to it no longer exists. Some time in the last third of a century, when facilities were being up-dated, somebody decided to remove the sign.

But I know the engraved footprint is there. I saw it. And the only reason I did so was that a sign directed me to it.

As for the actual footprint drawn by Mr. Hull, the original publication stated that it had been "reduced by half". However, I always felt that made it too small. As it turns out, Alfred Hull's diary was being published in Queensland newspapers within a few months of being recorded, but under the pseudonym of "Taff of Tolosa", Tolosa being the name of his property. Here, therefore, are the relevant entries for August of 1871.

> 24th. - Left camp this morning in the boat, and rowed up the Murray to the Bellenden Plains landing place, about twenty-five miles up the river . . .
>
> 26th. - Shifted camp lower down the river, and were disturbed in the night by the alligators [crocodiles] bellowing and a native tiger roaring close to our camp; the tiger came within one hundred yards of our tent, but we could not get a shot at him, owing to the darkness and the scrub. I believe it is not generally known that there is such a thing as a native tiger in Queensland, but it is nevertheless a fact.
>
> 27th and 28th. - Working down the river; scrubs very dense and swamps deep, and lined with cutting rushes from nine to ten feet high. Where the country is dry, which is rarely the case, on this (the south) bank the soil is poor and sandy; on the north side, from the Bluff upwards, the country is far better, being dry and open, lightly timbered, and well grassed. Saw the tracks of the tiger and measured them - four inches long by four and a-half inches wide [10 x 11½ cm] - so that there is no doubt about the existence of a very large animal of the cat tribe in these scrubs[35].

You will note, first, that the size of the print is now more reasonable: consistent with something the size of a large dog or small leopard, as the animal is normally described. It would appear that the drawing had been "reduced by half" when originally submitted in a letter, and then halved again for publication.

Secondly, the site was on the south bank of the relatively small Murray River, less than 25 miles [40 km] from its mouth. That would be about 30 km northwest of Cardwell, at about 18° S, 145° 50' E.

Thirdly, the tracks were discovered on 27 or 28 August 1871, an unstated distance from the site of the roaring. The roaring and the tracks were assumed, but not proved, to be connected. There was no reference to roaring three nights running, but it is possible that, on previous nights, it was not close enough to be considered worth recording. The roaring itself is a mystery, because I know of no other account of such being heard in the bush.

As far as the "Tantanoola Tiger" is concerned, I can do no better than to refer you to a recent book, *Snarls from the Tea-tree* by David Waldron and Simon Townsend[36]. The latter is a keen investigator of mystery cats in Victoria, and his half of the book details the evidence and methods of investigation. The first author, however, is a professional folklorist (among other things) who has provided a detailed and fully documented history, not only of the Tantanoola Tiger, but also several later predator crazes, all of which ended with the killing of an aberrant dog.

The Rilla Martin of 1964 photograph was almost certainly a hoax. Shortly after the death of prominent cartoonist, Bill Leak (1956-2017), a journalist related how, at the time, Bill and family were living in Goroke in the Wimmera, where his father, Reg was a postmaster. Since the local newspapers were reporting stories of strange, striped animals, Bill's father, along with a mate, decided to have a bit of fun by cutting out a piece of cardboard in the rough shape of a thylacine, painting it appropriately, and taking a photograph with a Box Brownie camera. They handed it around a group of friends for a laugh, when suddenly it all got out of hand. The photo was published in the *Wimmera Times*, and next thing they knew, it had gone viral. The cardboard cutout was disposed of, and

> Bill's dad pulled his young son aside and told him gravely,
> "You must never speak of this to anyone. Never tell a soul.
> Not while I'm alive[37].

Now, we shouldn't automatically take such revelations at face value. There is such a thing as a false hoax. To put it simply, whereas an ordinary hoaxer runs the risk of becoming a laughing stock, or else he gloats in private with a handful of friends, other people discover that they can gain their 15 minutes of fame, and be more likely to believed, if they falsely claim to have faked a famous photograph, footprint, or other artefact. This being said, such a claim carries a high evidentiary value. Also, the original photograph was always difficult to refer to any known, or even unknown, animal. Since it appeared, the putative photographer, Miss Martin, "went to ground" and never spoke about it again. Also, there does not appear to have been any ulterior reason for revealing the alleged hoax. Therefore, I consider the case closed.

On the other hand, the quotation by Ion Idriess was genuine. He was writing to *The Bulletin* under the pseudonym of "Gouger", and his article was published in the issue of 8 June 1922, on page 20. D. H. Lawrence had researched his book the same year, and had it published in 1923. So it was Lawrence who was the plagiarist.

In March 1923 an expedition under a Mr. Reg Kendall set out from Sydney for Cooktown intent on heading for the Palmerville Ranges to look for the animal. Once a base camp had been established, they were expected to be joined by Mr. le Souef, the Curator of Taronga Zoo. The expedition began with much fanfare, and apparently fizzled out, because nothing was later heard of it. More important, from our point of view, is that a number of background stories were published in the newspapers[38].

Since the expedition started from Sydney, I have every reason to believe that the ultimate source of the stories was le Souef himself. Remember, this was three years before he and Burrell repeated them in *The Wild Animals of Australasia*. He mentioned, not only the Sheridan and Idriess' experiences,and the Cardwell footprint, but also the encounter by George Sharpe, but in slightly different words to the later version. This suggests that it relates back to some much earlier document. Tellingly, it included new information.

> Even Mr. Robert Grant, late of the Australian Museum, is positive that the marsupial tiger is no myth. He fossicked about for years in Queensland after fauna, and although he did not actually see the beast, he secured very convincing evidence that it haunted the mountains, and was extraordinarily rare.
>
> First emphasising the proved reliability of the blacks, Mr. Grant related a most interesting and strange narrative of his experiences, as far as the tiger was concerned, in the wilds of the north.
>
> Sergeant Whalon, of the native police, introduced Mr. Grant to the subject of the marsupial tiger on the banks of the Mulgrave River. He said that it was carnivorous, and well known to the natives. Many of their dogs hunting among the scrub and boulders of the mountain tops never returned.
>
> The natives were on the verge of hysteria. All their dogs were being slain and devoured, and superstitiously the natives regarded the tiger with frantic terror. Not even the most extravagant inducements could persuade them to accompany Mr. Grant to the vicinity of the animal's lair. They refused to venture within miles of the mountain peaks.

Sometimes, the jabbering natives said, one or two of these tigers would slink down from the mountains. The men would say no more than this. So Mr. Grant had to assume that these alarming visits flung the blacks' camps into pandemonium.

Once when Mr. Grant was in the scrub with a companion he came across the tracks of an animal that he knew nobody in the world - except blacks and a few white men - had ever seen before. The imprints were fresh and as big as Mr. Grant's hand.

When did this take place? At the date the above account was written, Robert Grant had been dead for several weeks. In 1907 he had been promoted to Chief Taxidermist at the Australian Museum, but he had been employed in similar capacities long before. An internet search reveals that he is more famous today by virtue of his adopted son, the Aboriginal soldier, Douglas Grant. A toddler orphaned in a massacre, he had been found by Robert Grant and his wife in 1897, when they had spent several months collecting in the Bellenden Kerr Range area. I conclude, therefore, that the incident with the "tiger" took place in that time frame, about thirty years before the 1923 expedition.

Let us now return to what I prefer to call the "Plunkett Papers": the reports collected in the early 1970s by Janeice Plunkett, now known by her married name, Kay Makeig. The papers, or at least copies of them, are in the possession of Paul Cropper, who graciously allowed me access to a large section of them. It became apparent that most of the important information has already been published - see pp 106 - 109 - and this rather scant, but there is a bit more which can be culled from them. For example, the 1904 Biggenden incident probably occurred in the northwest of New South Wales, Biggenden merely being the current (1970) address of the witness. We also have the following testimonies, all written in 1970.

Tiaro, 1910 - 1912. This brings us to a familiar district and time period. A Mr. David Stratford related an event in the area eight kilometres south of Tiaro, between the Mary River and Tinana Creek. His two older brothers went out possum hunting one moonlit night, and instead ended up treeing a "tiger cat". That itself indicates that it was not any sort of dog. When the cat jumped down, it fought with their foxhound, seizing its nose in its teeth an refusing to release it until its masters bludgeoned it to death. They also treed another a hundred yards away. After a lapse of more than fifty years, the author did not provide any description, except to say that "They stepped the first and said it was about eight feet [1.5 metres] from tip of tail to end of nose" which, even the dimension was reduced by a quarter for exaggeration, is still pretty big. They estimated its weight at 30 pounds [13½ kg], which sounds like an underestimation for something that size.

Ingham, c 1950. A Mrs Daisy Kelly wrote two letters to Janeice, and the first one is very telling.

> I hereby assure you that 20 years ago [written in 1970] when I lived near the rainforests situated about 30 miles [50 km] from Ingham, my 3 children and I have seen animals of the same description you mention in the newspapers; that is heavy muscular bodies, striped hindquarters, very strong claws, the hind part to me looked like a dog, but the head has every appearance of an overgrown tom cat. My dogs (heavy cattle breed types) would tackle them, but always ended up with their heads and shoulder blades torn to the bone. Really, they are very fast moving and VERY shy.

She added that they were nocturnal, and would kill poultry. The local name as "scrub native cat", and there were two other types of native cats (I presume the spotted ones, *Dasyurus*) in the rainforest, and that her son claimed the animals were still there. A few months later she wrote again, telling how she she had since spoken to her son, and to other timber cutters, who also confirmed the existence of the animals, although they moved so fast they were unable to say whether they were striped or spotted. Then she related the following anecdote;

> One very interesting incident came out of one interview. (I actually saw this animal - dead - but had forgotten the details). He found one up a 70 feet straight trunked tree eating a freshly killed fully grown wallaby. Fresh blood on the ground led him to look up and locate the animal, which was shot dead.

Anything which can kill a fully grown wallaby and carry it up a tree is obviously not a feral cat, or any known marsupial. And the lapse of twenty years is not excessive for a reliable memory.

Outer Brisbane, 1914. This is a really interesting case, if accurate. A Mr. J. Ardell claimed that, when he was living in the Seventeen Mile

Rocks area of outer Brisbane, he saw a cat-like animal the size of an Alsatian dog, with stripes on its side.

Mossman, 1930. I don't know what to make of this story, because the coat pattern is unusual. It is best just to quote the letter verbatim and let it stand on its own merits. The author was called Andrew Mason. It may be relevant that, although was still living in the same area in 1970, he appears to have had only two encounter in 40 years.

> Back in 1930 my wife and I were hunting wild pigs in the Baileys Creek area, situated north of the Daintree River, 30 miles [50 km] from the sugar town of Mossman, North Queensland. Our dogs treed a tiger cat which I shot. It weighed about 25 lbs. [11.3 kg], was about 4'6" [137 cm] from nose to tip of tail. The body was marked with sooty black & dirty yellow stripes not very contrasting running lengthwise, the marks on the tail were round the tail in rings. The hair on the body was coarse & on the tail was stiff and wirey. This one was a male & had a strong musty smell. The teeth were carnivorous & the jaws long. The face had a flat appearance from the front.
>
> Again in 1944 I shot another male cat at Myall Creek 2 miles [3 km] south of Cape Tribulation; it was stealing my fowls in the night. This one was smaller but with the same markings. I do not think that it was fully grown.

So there you have it. With reference to the individuals being male, I have seen this in other reports, and I suspect they mean to imply: it didn't have a pouch, so I don't know whether or not it was a marsupial. In case any reader is in the same position: there is something you ought to know: although in marsupials the penis is normally retracted when not aroused, its site can usually be discerned, and it is *behind* the testicles, not in front. Furthermore, in dealing with a thylacine (see next chapter), you ought to know that a thylacine possessed a small pouch for the testicles. Also, anyone familiar with a dog should know the solid sheath which holds the penis.

With access to the Plunkett Papers, Tony Healy and Paul Cropper included a number of other previously unpublished encounters in the relevant chapter of *Out of the Shadows*, which I mentioned in the second introduction as a companion book to this one[39].

They also dated the encounter by Nancy O'Brien at 1968, and included her testimony is words identical to the ones quoted previously, but from a different source. However, her sketch which they included was different (Fig. 3.5).

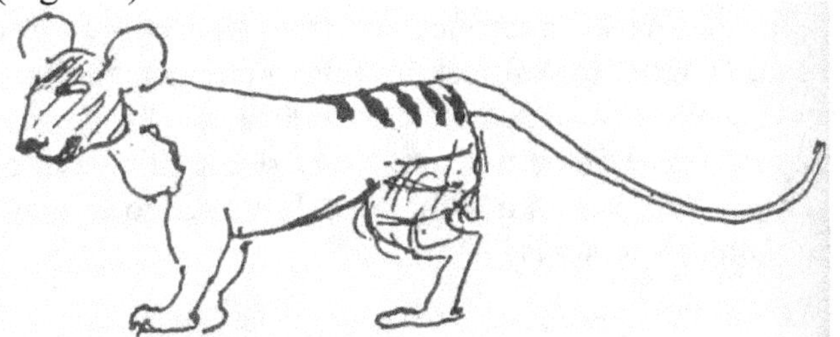

Fig. 3.5. *Second sketch by Nancy O'Brien.*

Why is this important? As will be seen in the addendum to Chapter 5, there is good evidence that some extremely outsized feral cats have evolved in the last several decades. Most are monochrome - black, grey, or tawny - but it cannot be ruled out that some possess the more common striped tabby coat pattern. That throws a shadow over any report of striped, cat-like animals in the last (say) fifty years - such as the one seen by Lance Mesh.

However, you will notice from Fig. 3.2 that Mrs. O'Brien has depicted her cat with rounded ears. That this was no accident is shown by Fig. 3.5, where that characteristic is not only repeated, but exaggerated. This cannot be a feral cat, because their ears are pointed. (Yes, I realise that some descriptions of the "tiger" suggest pointed ears, but one cannot be certain.)

Personally, I consider that the alleged marsupial tiger is in the unhappy position of tending towards extinction before it has even been officially recognized. Its last holdouts, however, are likely to be far north Queensland.

Why, you may ask, have no skeletons been found? The reason is clear: apart from the obvious fact that it is rare, and the country it frequents is hardly suitable for the preservation of bones, it is a predator. The bodies of prey species lie where they are killed, but predators typically choose their own place to die; they crawl away into some obscure nook when they are wounded or sick. Dr. Grover S. Krantz made a similar observation concerning the North American scene: bear footprints are a hundred times more common than those purported to be from the bigfoot or sasquatch, but one practically never finds the skeletons of bears in the wild[40].

What about road kill? Again, if you examine road kill (which you probably don't), three things will become apparent. Firstly, it is the common, rather than the rare, species which mostly fall victim. Secondly, unlike small animals, large ones are more likely to get away, or at least survive long enough to get back into the undergrowth. Finally, crows and other scavengers - the vacuum cleaners of the bush - ensure that they don't stay recognizable for long. No, I don't think patrolling the back roads of the country looking for road kill is a good way to discover a large, rare, unknown species.

REFERENCES

[1] A. S. LeSouef and H. Burrell (1926), *The Wild Animals of Australasia, embracing the mammalogy of New Guinea and nearer Pacific islands, With a chapter on the bats of Australia and New Guinea by Ellis LeG. Troughton,* George G. Harrap, London

[2] Ellis LeG. Troughton (1941), *Furred Animals of Australia.* Angus and Robertson, Sydney

[3] 'Mystery "beast" terrorised farming town for 15 years.' *Daily Mirror* (Sydney), Wed. 15 March 1989. Also, Neville Bonney (1976), *The Tantanoola Tiger*, Luthan Publishing House, Adelaide. (I have not read this book, and am relying on secondary references.)

[4] Samela Harris (1968) Hold That Tiger! *Walkabout* 34(6): 28-31 (June)

[5] Untitled, *Sunday Sun* (Brisbane), 10 Sept. 1972

[6] "Lion' on the loose - report to police.' *Courier-Mail* (Brisbane) Wed. 2 Feb.72. 'Mystery on the Beenleigh trail'. *ibid.* Thurs. 3 Feb.72

[7] 'Craignish Creature.' *Sunday Mail* (Brisbane) 11 Feb.1973
'"Craignish creature" a fox, says museum.' *Courier-Mail* (Brisbane) (probably) 25 July 1973

[8] Although I didn't keep the original reference, a secondary source, with photo, is the *Gold Coast Bulletin* 10 Aug.1973, quoting an article by Joan Starr in *Hoofs and Horn*, 1967.

[9] R.W. Mckay '"Monsters" of mystery. Seen but never caught. Queer tales' *Sydney Morning Herald* 9 Dec. 1939

[10] 'A Springbrook "Tiger"' *Courier Mail* (Brisbane) 22 May 1923

[11] Matthew Prior (1664 - 1721) *Alma*, Canto III, lines 13 - 14

[12] Brindsley G. Sheridan (1871) letter   *Proc. Zool. Soc. Lond.* pp 629-3

[13] Walter T. Scott (1872) letter   *Proc. Zool. Soc. Lond.* p355

[14] Walter T. Scott (1872) letter   *Proc. Zool. Soc. Lond.* p796

[15] Robert A Johnstone (1903) *Spinifex and Wattle, Reminiscences of Pioneering in North Queensland* (This was published in *The Queenslander* between 1903 and 1905. The specific paragraph occurs on pp 9 and 10 of the issue of 27 June 1903.)

[16] 'North-East Coast Expedition', *Rockhampton Bulletin* Mon 20 April 1874, page 2

[17] Carl Lumholtz (1890) *Among Cannibals: an account of four years' travel and of camp life with the Aborigines of Queensland*, John Murray, London, pp 100, 101, 174, 175

[18] Biology of Bellenden-Ker, as ascertained by the late expedition under Mr. A. Meston.   *Report of the Department of Agriculture for the Year 1889-90* (Brisbane)

[19] J. McGeehan (1938), Description of wild animal seen on Atherton Tableland.   *N. Qld. Nat.* 6(54): 3-4

[20] G. de Tournouer (1923) 'Incident near Tiaro'. *Brisbane Courier* 7 April 1923

[21] Capt. Sir G. H. Wilkins, M C (1928) *Undiscovered Australia. Being an account of an expedition to tropical Australia to collect specimens of the rarer native fauna for the British Museum, 1923-1925* Ernest Benn Ltd, London, p 29

[22] Le Souef and Burrell (ref. 1) p 330

[23] *ibid.* pp 330-331

[24] Troughton (ref. 2), 6th edition, 1957, p 49

[25] D. H. Lawrence (1923), *Kangaroo*, Martin Secker, chapter 6

[26] 'Shot near Tully. Marsupial tiger'. *Courier-Mail* (Brisbane) 12 Dec. 1932

[27] 'Bush Tiger' *The World's News* 11 May 1938

[28] J. L. Harrison, (1962) Mammals of Innisfail I. Species and distribution. *Aust. J. Zool.* 10: 45-83

[29] letter quoted in 'Tigers, devils, monsters and things that walk in the night'. *Wildlife in Australia* 62(2), p54 (1969)

[30] Peter Makeig (1970) Is there a Queensland marsupial tiger? *N. Qd. Nat.* 37 (152): 6-8. 'Hold that tiger.' *The Sydney Morning Herald* Sat. 30 May1970, p 23 (Duplicates the reports in the first reference, and contains several more.)

[31] R. T. Wells, D. R. Horton and .P Rogers (1982) *Thylacoleo carnifex* Owen (Thylacoleonidae, Marsupialia): marsupial carnivore? **in** *Carnivorous Marsupials*, vol. 2, pp 573-86 (Michael Archer, editor, published by Roy. Zool. Soc. N.S.W.)

[32] R. T. Wells and B. Nichols (1977) On the manus and pes of *Thylacoleo carnifex* Owen (Marsupialia). *Trans. Roy. Soc. S. Aust.* 101: 139-146

[33] 'Proposal-in-Brief for a 1989 Operation Raleigh Queensland Cryptozoological Expedition' (provided to the author by the organiser, Victor A. Albert).

[34] https://donsmaps.com/carnarvon.html (accessed 17.10.2020)

[35] Taff of Tolosa, 'A surveyor's diary', *The Brisbane Courier*, Tues, 17 Oct. 1871, p 3.

Taff of Tolosa, 'The northern rivers', *The Queenslander*, Sat. 21 Oct. 1871, p 11

Malcolm Smith (2012), The Queensland tiger: further evidence on the 1871 footprint, *J. Cryptozoology* 1:19-24

[36] David Waldron and Simon Townsend (2012) *Snarls from the Tea-tree. Big cat folklore*, Arcadia, Melbourne. See also my review at https://malcolmscryptids.blogspot.com/2013/01/snarls-from-tea-tree-review.html

[37] 'Jack the Insider: the prank that took 53 years to debunk' *The Australian*, Sat. 24 March 2017

[38] 'Marsupial Tiger. Australia's wild animal. Mountain hunt. Savage terror of Palmerville Ranges', *The Sun* (Sydney), Tues. 27 March 1923, page 14 - and many later newspapers.

[39] Tony Healy and Paul Cropper (1994) *Out of the Shadows, mystery animals of Australia*, Ironbark Press, pp 106-110

[40] Grover S. Krantz (1999) *Bigfoot Sasquatch Evidence*, Hancock House, pp 9-10

CHAPTER 4

THE THYLACINE MOVES TO THE MAINLAND

It was 6.27 am, Thursday 18 August. John Chevalier and sister Sharon, part of a larger bushwalking group searching for caves, were suddenly woken by a low coughing outside their tent. A large animal was eating a half loaf of bread they had left out the night before.

It stood like a monument, side on to us for 30 seconds [said John]. It was as large as a great dane dog. Its head was like a wolf's and its hindquarters larger than its front quarters. It was a dark ginger color and had vertical stripes across its back which became lighter towards its neck. There were three stripes under its chest and it had foot claws like a dog[1].

Figure 4.1 *Harts Creek animal, based on a sketch by John Chevalier*

Surprisingly, they didn't know what it was. Any zoologist reading that description or examining the sketch (Figure 4. 1) would immediately recognize it. If it had been seen in Tasmania in 1934 it would have aroused little comment. But it was 1984. If the place were still Tasmania it would have been hailed by many as proof that the long-lost Tasmanian tiger or thylacine (*Thylacinus cynocephalus*) was not extinct after all. But it was not Tasmania. The site was Harts Creek, 3 km south of Lake Pambula, in the extreme southeast of New South Wales. Interestingly, Linda Gibson, of the Australian Museum, said that a dozen or so similar reports were received every year.

Probably most of you know the bare bones of the thylacine history.

It officially passed into the realm of extinction in 1936, when the last captive specimen died. Since then innumerable expeditions have set out to search for it - all without success- and innumerable sightings have been made - mostly by people who were not looking for it. However, I shan't entertain you with the story of this search. Firstly, it has already been done - and in much greater depth than this book allows[2]. Secondly, although pessimism runs deep, nobody would be really astounded if the species were confirmed to be still alive. In Tasmania, that is. On the mainland it's a different matter.

Now, before we all get too excited, let's get a few things clear. Everything said in the previous chapter about mangy dogs applies double to the thylacine. The thylacine has the same build and face as a dog. It is its stripes and hindquarters which give it away. A row of 15 to 20 vertical stripes - not many animals have that sort of pattern - extends from the shoulders to the root of the tail, which is long and whiplike. Over the hip they are so long they almost reach the knee, but get progressively shorter towards the front. The hindquarters taper into the tail in a manner reminiscent of a kangaroo's. A thylacine cannot curl its tail over its back like a dog, nor even wag it very much from side to side.

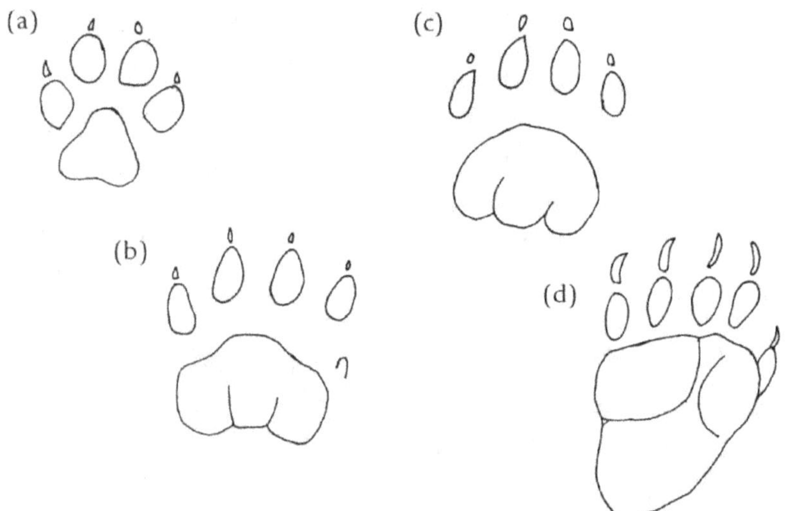

Figure 4.2 Footprints of (a) *Dog* (b) *Thylacine front* (c) *Thylacine rear* (d) *Wombat*

As for the footprints, have a look at Figure 4.2(a). If you see anything like that: a subtriangular pad with the side toes back from the middle ones, then it doesn't matter what you saw, the animal is a canid: a dog, fox, dingo, or dingo-dog cross. Surprisingly, as Figure 4.2 demonstrates, a thylacine's spoor is more likely to be confused with that of a wombat. However, unlike a thylacine's, a wombat's trail tends to shuffle from side to side. Should anybody wish to go into this is a serious way, my best suggestion is to pick up Guiler's comprehensive guide book[3] and study it in detail.

One is not heartened by the fact that few of those who report a thylacine get a good look at it. Most of the sightings in Tasmania itself lasted less than 30 seconds[4], and most of these (made from a vehicle) less than 5 seconds. 69% took place at night. Furthermore, when thylacine fever hits an area, its residents tend to lose their critical faculties. Take, for instance, this story from Benalla, northeast Victoria[5]. A postman was on his run 25 km from town when something crossed the road 80 metres away. It was bigger than a fox with a greyhound's long, skinny tail. If it had anything resembling stripes, he didn't mention them. "It wasn't a normal sort of a dog, and it wasn't a fox," he said, "so what could it be?" How about an abnormal sort of dog? There are a lot going round.

It seems to me that if a mystery animal doesn't have stripes, you need to have some pretty good reasons to call it a thylacine.

Nevertheless, the species was present over much of the mainland in prehistoric times until displaced by the dingo, introduced by early visitors from Asia. The thylacine humerus found at Tunnel Creek, Western Australia may not be as young as the other bones found in the deposit, but it is fair to mention that some of these have been dated by the radiocarbon method at no more, and probably much less, than 180 years old[6]. The most recent specimens of known age are 3,000 years old[7,8].

The sinkholes of the Nullarbor Plain deserve much greater exploration by fossil hunters, because of the habit of local wildlife of falling down the shafts and perishing inside. In 1966 a sensation was created by the discovery of a mummified thylacine in a cave 110 km west of Eucla, W.A., subsequently christened Thylacine Hole[9]. Decomposition had converted most of the soft tissues into a tarry substance, but the tongue and left eyeball were still recognizable, and the skin and hair so well preserved that the stripes were still visible. It looked

so fresh that for a while it seemed the species might still be alive on the
Nullarbor. Alas! Three separate radiocarbon tests established its age at
between 4,600 and 4,700 years[10].

The Wolmadjeri people of the southern Kimberleys know of a
dog-like predator, the *waldagi*, which is neither dingo, dog or ghost, and
which an anthropologist[11] thought might be a thylacine. In 1964 Mrs M.
Sack made a tape of tribal songs near Marble Bar, including one by an
old man about a dingo pack with a striped leader[12]. These people were
probably aware of the prehistoric thylacine paintings in the Hamersley
Range. However, apart from these two dubious references, there is no
evidence that mainland Aborigines knew anything about the thylacine,
and even less that the white settlers did.

So why do so many people keep seeing the beast on the mainland?

The zoologist most involved in the search in Tasmania, Dr Eric
Guiler, recognized the obvious: if clear, detailed reports of sightings
made by sensible people can be considered reliable when they come
from Tasmania, one cannot scoff at similar reports from the mainland. In
his book[13] he listed a number of such reports. Unfortunately, the sources
are usually unreferenced newspaper clippings or personal letters
addressed to him. This is not terribly appealing to those of us who like to
make our own judgments, and it is hoped that he will publish them in full
somewhere else.

He refers, for instance, to a clear multiple sighting near Buckingham,
Western Australia in 1980 at a distance of 25 yards. The grey-brown,
dog-like animal was about 20 inches [50 cm] tall and had a thin tail and a
series of very dark, vertical stripes on its rump.

In 1970 a sighting at Nannup led to a full-scale search by residents
and Forestry Department officials[14]. But one can hardly put much
confidence in the report from Harvey, 140 km south of Perth the
following year. The animal was the size of a fox and "reddish-brown
around the head, pure white on the side, and had a black tail[15]." In other
words, anything less like a thylacine would be hard to imagine.

Sid Slee is so convinced that they are lurking around his property
near Busselton, W.A., which adjoins the Yoongarillup State Forest, that
he has the words, "The Haunt of the Marsupial Wolf" suspended below
the property name,"Hillside" and has written a book with the same title[16].

I would be happier if he had explained how the thylacines he has
seen over five decades were identified. One was a light biscuit colour,

one was black, and one was dark biscuit on the back. A few stripes would have helped. The exception was the one that popped out not 20 feet [6m] in front of him, and took off in a characteristic thylacine manner: by kicking its hind legs together like a kangaroo or rabbit, so hard that it leapt off the ground, and kicked gravel over Sid's feet. It was light yellow in colour, with a thin strip of dark chocolate around its eyes and lips. A strip of dark chocolate ran down its back from ears to tail, with six or seven dark stripes over its back leg.

I am not completely happy with this account. A thylacine is supposed to have light, not dark, marks around its eyes, it does not have a line down its spine, and it has more stripes than that. On the other hand, a dog is not supposed to have any stripes at all. An optimist would suggest it was a different race. I prefer to suspend judgment. This fellow was estimated to be seven feet [213 cm] long. In 1980 he measured footprints that were 4 foot 8 inches [142 cm] from the first to fourth foot. Pretty darn big thylacine! The largest specimen ever measured (and incidentally, the first) was only 79 cm from shoulder to root of tail, and 190 cm in total length. An ordinary male would be at least 20% shorter[17].

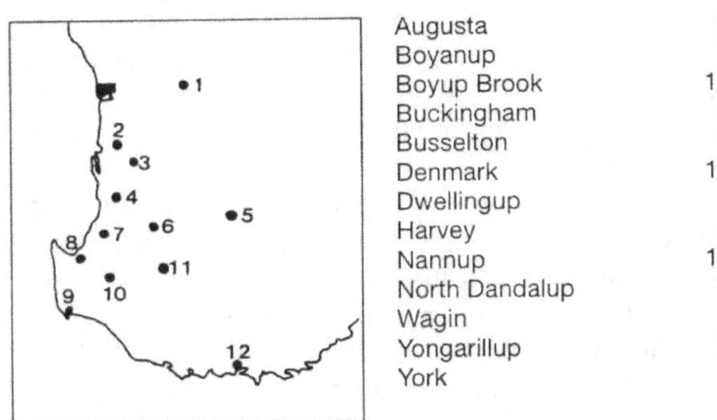

Augusta		9
Boyanup		7
Boyup Brook		11
Buckingham		6
Busselton		8
Denmark		12
Dwellingup		3
Harvey		4
Nannup		10
North Dandalup		2
Wagin		5
Yongarillup		8
York		1

Map 4A Sightings in Western Australia

There are some other items which tend to back up Mr. Slee's contention. He has, for instance, recorded kangaroos killed and eaten in clean, methodical manner foreign to a dog, but typical of a thylacine or big cat (see next chapter). He even published a photo of one such kill next to the print of what looks like a thylacine's hind foot. The accounts he gives of other people's sightings suffer from the same ambiguity. One was a brindled animal, one a stripeless animal, one had a few dark bands on its body, but the brush on its tail identifies it as a dog. Another witness saw something with a rigid tail and an un-thylacine fan of three stripes. Significantly, she stated it was mangy looking. Even the sighting made by Joe and Freda Carmody in 1972 at a range of 30 feet [9 m] is so-so. It was the right shape, but the position of the sun behind it prevented them from seeing stripes. Incidentally, according to Guiler, the Carmodies have collected reports of more than 20 sightings, and repeated that enough reports have been emanating from the Nannup region to be investigated by the Department of Fisheries and Wildlife[18].

Meanwhile, back at the Slee property, Kevin Cameron had entered the picture. An expert, part-Aboriginal tracker in the employ of the Agricultural Protection Board of Western Australia, he gave a day by day account of a year long hunt for an animal which left an unusual smell, and prints with five toes on the front paw. Both cats and dogs have five front toes, but the fifth, or dew, claw is so high it seldom appears on prints. Staff at the Western Australian Museum identified them as abnormal dog prints, and from the photos published by Mr. Slee I have to agree. However, the other set of prints on the same photo are far more promising.

Moreover, Mr. Cameron, his sons and his dogs met the animal(s) on a number of occasions. The closest was sitting on a log 30 feet [9 m] away in broad daylight on 13 January 1984. The detailed account he gave was virtually a classic description, from the tip of its dog-like head to the bristles on the tip of its rigid tail. They did not pursue it because they believed it was a mother. A pouch hung low between its hind legs.

From the details of this hunt, I am convinced that Kevin Cameron was a genuine hunter who honestly believed he was tracking a thylacine. In fact, if he was telling the truth about the animal on the log, that is what he did see. This is important in view of what came next.

On 24 April 1986 the *New Scientist* made world news with a series of photographs taken by Cameron of an alleged thylacine[19]. In vivid colour, they showed a grey animal with fawn stripes digging furiously behind a rock and log, its back arched and very long tail stuck out like a ramrod. Its head, forequarters, and most of its hind limbs were hidden from view. Needless to say, this provoked not a little comment in subsequent issues of the magazine[20]. The most obvious criticism was that the posture and position of the animal was exactly the same for in all photos, something that would have been impossible even during the stated time lapse of 20 to 30 seconds, let alone the much longer period indicated by the shadows on the grass.

Athol Douglas, who originally brought the photos to the attention of the world, has backtracked a bit[21]. He acknowledges that the film had been cut, frames were missing, and the photos taken from different angles. He also had colour separation tests done on the photos, which revealed a gap of several hours between the first and subsequent photos. He now believes that the animal was shot after the first photo, and its carcass repositioned for the remainder.

I find this idea preposterous. It would be quite impossible to kill an animal and then reposition it, without any wounds showing, in precisely the same place and posture as before. It could also be wondered what could be the motivation. Cameron is known to have regard for the commercial value of the photos. (He also asked $53,000 to disclose where they were taken.) However, obviously a close-up shot of an unmistakable thylacine carcass, complete with head, would be the most valuable of all.

Besides, as I pointed out afterwards, the animal isn't very convincing[22]. Admittedly, it would be hard to find a dog with that sort of tail. But the hindquarters do not really taper. That is largely an illusion created by the angle between tail and rump. Furthermore, both the background and the stripes are much lighter than on authentic thylacines, and the latter could have been produced by bleach, dye or paint.

All in all, the evidence is against the Cameron photos being authentic - which is not to say that he never saw a thylacine.

Douglas then decided that the Thylacine Hole carcass deserved a reassessment, and with his 40 years' experience in the Western Australian Museum, he was well equipped to do so[23,24]. He produced pretty cogent reasons for believing the animal did not die where it was found, and considers it was moved there, for motives unknown, by earlier visitors to the case. This I find a little unlikely, but concede that it could have been moved by flood waters. He also gave good reasons why it could not be so well preserved if it were really 4,600 years old. He believes that contamination by carbon dissolved in water has given a false carbon 14 date to a recent carcass.

Maybe - I am in no position to question his qualifications in the carcass preservation department. However, radiocarbon dating is based on the fact that old carbon has less of the radioactive C_{14} isotope than fresh carbon. It is thus possible for an old specimen to be contaminated with fresh, dissolved carbon to produce a false recent date. It is harder to see how C_{14} could be washed out of a recent specimen to produce a false old date. Until that is explained, I will stick with the old date. Pity. Douglas also stated:

I have interviewed witnesses from the areas of Augusta, Boyanup, Dwellingup, Boyup Brook, Wagin, Bannister, Denmark, Nannup and Busselton, all of whom, without prompting, have described known facts and characteristics of the thylacine.[25]

Reports are still coming in from Western Australia, mostly of dog-like animals with stripes of some sort and tails that stick out. None of them fits the thylacine description exactly. One was seen by a ranger at North Dandalup in 1989, but because the sun was behind it he could not tell whether it was striped. But at only 20 metres, he could tell it was neither dog, fox, nor cat. The animal observed near York in July 1993 was brown coloured with beige stripes. The precise pattern is not stated[26].

To give an idea of what we are facing, take the animal seen three times in May and June 1994 near Mt Helena[27]. According to four real estate agents and a journalist, it was long and skinny, with a tapered tail like a kangaroo's. Its colour was fawny grey, with creamy stripes across its rump and tail. A thylacine should have black stripes, but no dog, not even a mangy one, could look like that. From the photo, I cannot decide whether the prints belong to a thylacine or a dog. Despite the poor quality of the reproduction, the prints are clear enough, but they seem to have features of both species. Being a Queenslander, I am tempted to christen it *Thylacinus claytoni*. This is a Clayton's thylacine: the thylacine you see when you're not seeing a thylacine[28].

Let's move a bit further east, and see what Guiler[29] has to say about South Australia. Huon Johnston of Sydney phoned him and described an experience when he, his wife and three others were crossing the Nullarbor Plain on horseback. At Nullarbor Station he went out to look after the horses and saw a thylacine close enough to see the stripes and the bull-terrier-shaped head (the sign of a male).

Near Moonta, on the Yorke Peninsula, Mrs. D. J. Kaye saw a ginger-coloured animal with black stripes on its back. That was at 8.30 am on 14 March 1981. She was certain it was not a dingo, but said it was mangy looking - a warning sign.

It is the far southeast, from Lake Coorong to Nelson just across the border, that has been the centre of persistent sightings. On the night of 1

November 1962, nineteen year old Ian MacRae saw one outside Port Macdonnell. It was light brown with black stripes running across its back, and as big as an Alsatian. It was reported to has been seen three times in the previous year[30]. A rabbit hunter claimed to have seen one near a waterhole several times. Once he saw two. He shot one with a .22 rifle and followed it for 5 miles [8 km].

Mr. A. Cockington of the South Australian Field Naturalists Society interviewed various witnesses, and sent Guiler plaster casts and photos of the spoor. As far as the latter was concerned, they did not belong to any known species, let alone the thylacine, and were probably deformed. The claws were huge, and pointed straight down in what must have been a very uncomfortable position.

In 1968 a Government stock inspector, R. F. Lighton watched a thylacine through field glasses for a quarter of an hour[31]. Regrettably, he did not say where.

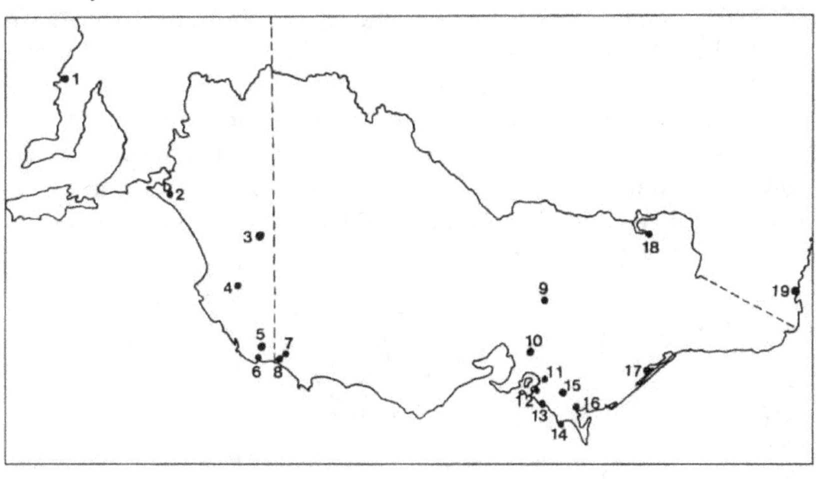

Borderotwn	3	Moonta	1
Cape Liptrap	14	Mt. Gambier	5
Drik Drik	7	Nelson	8
Foster	16	Olinda	10
Grantville	12	Port Macdonnell	6
Harts Creek	19	Tallangatta	18
Lang Lang	11	L. Victoria	17
Leongatha	15	Wonthaggi	13
Lucindale	4	Yea-Healesville Rd.	9
Meningie	2		

Map 4B Sightings in Southeast Australia

Samela Harris visited the southeast for two days that year and found that 100 people claimed to have been witnesses. Only a few were published, but they sounded interesting[32].

- Jack Victory, Park Commission Park Keeper: head like a dog, rump with tapering tail, brown, striped with grey towards rear, viewed through telescope at 400 yards.
- Millicent business man: "a heavy-looking dog with stripes on its back and a thick tapering tail which looked like a mangy rat's tail, only much larger."
- Don Gilette: sketch shows tapering hindquarters and broad, hooplike stripes on rear half of its body, reaching around the abdomen in an un-thylacine manner.
- Penny Gneil: sketch shows tapering hindquarters and hooplike stripes over front part of body, but not rear. (Thylacines are never like that.) Sighted by seven persons near Coorong.
- Rosalie Anderson, aged 12: fast-moving and doglike, with tapering tail like a kangaroo and striped body. Ran alongside the Lucindale school bus for about a mile [1.6 km].

The last happened in July 1967, and was widely publicised in the press. Rosalie's mother, Dawn Anderson of Spence, interviewed her daughter, the other children, and the driver, Bob Jackson. Eventually, she produced a sketch of The Animal, which anyone could see was an unmistakable thylacine (Fig. 4.3).

Figure 4.3 Dawn Anderson's sketch of the animal seen from the school bus.

Thus began The Animal Project. With the help of another housewife, Kath Alcock she compiled two large dossiers of newspaper clippings, correspondence, and signed testimony of witnesses from as far afield as Mt Gambier, Meningie and Bordertown[33].

Mrs Anderson eventually sighted The Animal close up on three occasions - once for a quarter of an hour. Unfortunately, no description is available. However, the two women were able to make some generalisations about the testimony of the witnesses they interviewed.

Few of the witnesses had heard of the thylacine before, but most recognized it when shown a photo. All of them agreed The Animal was unknown to them. It was dog-like, with an unusual loping gait, and a placid temperament. It did not appear afraid of cars. They all said the tail was like a kangaroo's: thick at the base, tapering to a point, and carried stiffly behind it - just like a thylacine, and quite unlike a dog. Where they disagreed was in describing the head as either pointed or thickset, the body either brown, grey or golden, and the stripes as either black or white. It was pointed out, of course, that under the right lighting conditions a light animal with dark stripes can appear to be dark with light stripes. And the differences in head shape is typical of male and female thylacines[34].

Mrs Anderson found some hair at the site where some children watched The Animal grooming itself for several minutes. Hair samples are not as easy to identify as you might think. Peter Aitken, the Curator of Mammals at the South Australian Museum, thought it might be fox fur, but he could not be certain. But he admitted to having a file "three feet thick" on The Animal as well.

Let us look at some reports from the Anderson-Alcock files. In January a Mr Buzzacott watched an animal cross the road 30 or 40 yards away. The time was 4.30 to 5 pm. In the few seconds available he noted that it was much larger than a fox, and had a long face. It was a kind of grey-blue with light off-white stripes down the back and tail. The tail was long and thin and hung rigid, the back was high and thin, and in front the animal was thickset. White stripes on a grey-blue background is hardly typical of the thylacine. Unfortunately, it is hardly typical of anything else.

The two women managed to take photos of many footprints, and the one published in their article[35] is impressive but, not being an expert, I am not prepared to be more definite. They once followed the tracks of an adult and a youngster. When the smaller tracks disappeared for no reason at all, they assumed the maker had returned to the pouch. Another track was found in July 1968 after a sighting by a wool auctioneer, Trevor

Taylor. They compared them to those of the family sheepdog, and found many differences. Mr Taylor had been able to watch the animal for a long time, for it was not too concerned about him, though it halted every time he gave a whistle. It was 18 to 20 inches [45 - 50 cm] high, with a broad head, pointed ears, and a snout longer than a fox's. It had a "[m]ost distinctive tail, longish, thick at the butt and running with a downward curve to a point, did not appear furred. Looked like a kangaroo's, except that it thinned off closer to the butt." The colour was brownish, with a blackish saddle-shaped marking over the shoulder and black markings over the back and flanks. In other words, whatever it was, it was not a thylacine.

Mrs Anderson discussed the sightings with Adye ["Adair"] Jordan, who captured the last (official) thylacine in 1930. He agreed that the South Australian animals could be nothing else.

What more can I say? These sightings have occurred over a very large area, and there is a broad consistency about the descriptions which, although they do not always fit the classic description of a thylacine, fit it better than even a whole tribe of mangy dogs. Obviously, too, many more sightings are made than recorded. I have no way of knowing whether they are continuing.

It is Victoria which appears to be the heart of the mainland thylacine range. Back in February 1987, Peter J. Chapple of Rare Fauna Research Society (of which more next chapter) told me they had more than 900 reports of thylacine-like animals, of which the majority were from Victoria, but had found no conclusive evidence themselves.

In 1990 a number of people contacted journalist, Graeme O'Neill about their sightings[36]. One man twice saw animals without stripes, but with tapering hindquarters about 30 km from Cape Liptrap in 1989. Ten years previously a mother and daughter had seen lope across the road near Foster "a canine-like animal with gold-beige colouring, a long tail and a dark-brown striped back".

Even more impressive stories came from the Grampians. In October 1986 a farmer spent five minutes one morning watching two males prance skittishly around a female. We are not told how he was able to distinguish their sex, a factor which would be important in telling a marsupial from a placental. However, they were fawn in colour, with chocolate stripes across the rump and tail, and again the rump tapered into the tail.

The farmer contacted a primary school headmaster, who had another story to tell. He, his wife and three children had been driving near Drik Drik when they came abreast of an animal only 10 metres away. It was as big as a labrador, with a pointed snout, a fawny-brown colour, and dark stripes on its sloping hindquarters. Its kangaroo-like tail was held horizontally.

Not all the reports collected by O'Neill were so specific, but they still indicated some animal quite different from the run-of-the-mill dog. He also quoted Dr Robert Warneke, who said that, although he did not believe in the existence of a mainland thylacine, he had kept records of similar sightings for three decades, particularly from the Wonthaggi-Tarwin-Foster region of south Gippsland. So Dr Aitken is not the only zoologist who keeps dossiers! Again, a lot more sightings than are actually made public.

In the same area a skinny animal with huge jaws and a striped back was seen by Mrs Pam Haigh, her sister-in-law, niece and three children[37]. They were on a busy road near Grantville, when it ran across with "a strange sort of trot", a feature mentioned in many of O'Neill's reports. A couple of days later she overhead two men in a shopping centre taking about seeing a similar animal.

Another thylacine is said to have crossed the road near the Leongatha Golf Club, when it was spotted by retired school principle, Gordon West only 20 metres away. One of his townsmen, Neil Wray-McCann, has been searching for the thylacine ever since he saw one in the Walkerville area in 1975. He chased it on his motorbike to within 30 metres, and could see that it was mangy[38]. In neither of the above reports were any details given to confirm the identity.

What sort of reports has Dr Guiler got?[39]

- 1967: very detailed description from Lake Victoria.
- January 1970 and February 1973: near Kallista in Dandenongs, three witnesses, night, not certain of identity.
- 1970: two sightings near Kalorama.
- 1971: Tallangatta.
- 1978: group driving from Yea to Healesville in the afternoon.
- 1978: Range Rd, Olinda.
- 27 Nov.1976 and 26 Nov. 1979: 3 witnesses, two sightings, 3km from Lang Lang.
- 1981: Cape Liptrap-Point Smythe area, family had clear view at 250 yards.

- 1981: near Lake Buchan.

Thylacines are not the only Tasmanians to cross the strait. In 1912 a Tasmanian devil was killed at Tooborac, about 100 km from Melbourne, but it was generally considered to have been introduced[40]. Keeping them was not illegal in 1912, and they do make affectionate pets. However, it was a bit unexpected to hear stories of a devil at the Newport Lakes[41]. That's a Melbourne suburb, and the month was July 1988. As far as I know the rumour was never run to ground.

The thylacine plague has not spread far into New South Wales yet. It is only fair to mention, however, that Rex Gilroy claims to have seen one at Blackheath in December 1972, and to have taken plaster casts of prints at Wallangabba[42]. I gain the impression that a lot more are seen than are actually reported.

When the Thylacine Hole carcass was first reported, it inspired Mr Paramonov to publish the notes he had made in 1949 of an animal he had seen in broad daylight at a range of 15 to 20 metres. It was dog-like, grey-brown in colour, but with hindquarters tapering into the tail, and a set of almost horizontal stripes on the hindleg. In other words, this was another case where un-thylacine markings were joined to hindquarters which no other animal should have.

He continued:

> The most remarkable feature was the strange manner of running; although the animal was swaying regularly sideways, the hind part of the body made a kind of bobbing, up and down movement; the impression was as if the animal was drunk[43].

So, if there is one thing our research should have taught us: "out there" are a lot of animals with funny walks. This one was literally "Back o' Bourke" : to be precise, on the Bourke-Wanaaring Road - just where you would not expect to find a thylacine.

In 1976 and '77 there came news - with photos - of a group of eight thylacines being kept under observation by two farmer families, using conservationist, Bruce Jacobs as their spokesman. One was seen to be carrying young in her pouch. When I first saw the 1977 photo I was impressed, but not any more. The ears are too pointed for a thylacine, and the snout too short and pointed, almost foxy. From the viewing angle it is not clear if the hindquarters are tapered, but - and it might be just the bad reproduction - the stripes look like they were painted on the negative. Also, thylacines were not known to be pack animals.

The site was kept secret to prevent disturbance by outsiders, but was said to be close to the N.S.W.-Victoria border[44]. In all fairness, it must be pointed out that the Chevalier sighting, mentioned at the beginning of this chapter, also occurred near the border.

The only report Guiler heard from the Northern Territory was of a pack of scavengers seen by a bull-catcher. One member was a dingo-like animal with rings around its body[45].

Queensland? Well, there is the Cootharaba Devil, reported around Pomona, Cootharaba and Warpungah. About 1972 Neil Dowsett was living on a cattle property 18 km east of Pomona, near Lake Cootharaba. One evening their spotlight caught a predator "over a metre from head to tip of the tail; greyish in colour with dark vertical stripes on its back" which let out a growl like nothing they had ever heard[46]. Next morning the tracks led to a sick cow which had been attacked by something with long claws and sharp teeth. An old timber cutter told them about the Cootharaba Devil, which he believed was a mutant cat. All eight witnesses likened it to a Tasmanian tiger.

Of course, it might have been a south-east representative of the North Queensland striped cat. For that matter, some of the sightings reported by Janeice Plunkett in the last chapter might have been of thylacines. Many of the accounts are not too specific. However, the next one is pretty clear cut.

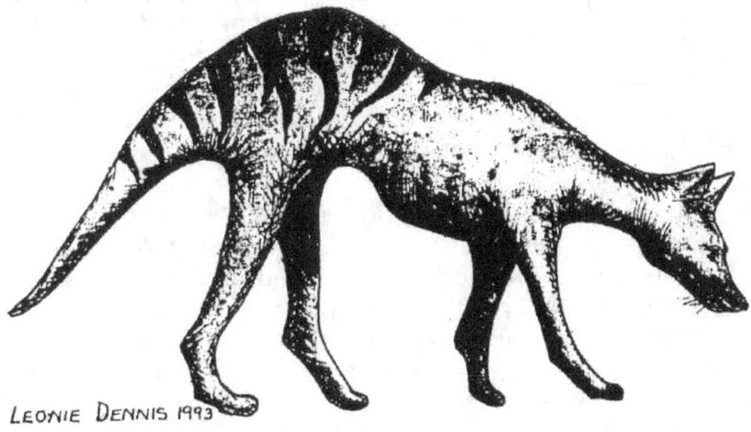

Fig. 4.4. *Leonie Dennis' original drawing of the Sunshine Coast beast.*

One afternoon in July 1993 Greg and Leonie Dennis were driving on the Coolum-Yandina Road when a striped, brindle-coloured animal raced across the road and disappeared into a ditch[47]. An experienced artist, Leonie drew its portrait as soon as they got home. Thus, from Fig. 4.4 one can see that it has the definite doggy face of a thylacine, even if its hindquarters are unnaturally high-set. It is therefore quite different from the cat-faced beast seen by Lance Mesh not 20 km to the south, as the crow flies.

Then, on 8 August 1995, a remarkable experience was had by 58-year-old Roy Swaby[48]. A retired marine engineer, Mr Swaby lives on a bend of the Gregory River, south of Woodgate, Qld. In fact, it is not far upstream from where the Burrum sea serpent appeared the following month (chapter 2). On the night in question, he had gone out in his truck to buy a few cigars, and was on the way home. The road threads a stretch of national park and crown land which together add up to a hundred square kilometres of extremely dense wallum scrub. Roy and his wife are authorised wildlife carers, and he is always on the lookout for sick birds. Besides, the road was very dark, so he drove with both spotlights and headlights switched on.

A couple of kilometres from his home, he turned a corner, and was changing gears when a grey kangaroo flashed panic-stricken across the road.

"Then I saw it. ... This incredible sandy-coloured striped animal leapt out from the side of the road a full 15 feet [4½ m] and into the glare of my 100-watt halogen spots and four headlights.

It stopped on the road, turned to look at me and fell back on to its huge hindquarters, its large green-yellow eyes glowing in the light, and then it opened its jaws and snarled at me.

I have never seen anything like it. The white teeth were large and the jaws like a crocodile, like a mantrap. It took two steps and then suddenly crouched and sprang again, 15 - 20 feet [4½ - 6 m], this time into the scrub.

I was 20 metres away from it and my lights lit up the road and the creature like it was daylight. I could even see whiskers. . . .

The animal was 4 - 5 feet [1.2 - 1.5 m] long and its huge tail was another 2 - 3 feet [60 - 90 cm]. The stripes started halfway down its back.

I thought it was like someone had cut a dingo in half and a 'roo in half and joined them together. Except from those massive teeth and jaws. And it was sleek and healthy-looking."

Mr Swaby came home white-faced and shaking. A quarter of an hour later, in front of witnesses, he sketch what he saw (Figure 4.5). He confirmed to me that the limbs were long, and the hindquarters raised - rather like Leonie Dennis' animal. The next morning he found footprints 120 mm long and 100 mm wide - much larger, in fact, than those of his German shepherds. However, the photograph was not clear enough to allow a proper identification.

Figure 4.5 Roy Swaby's sketch of the Woodgate tiger, made immediately after the incident

When I phoned Mr Swaby the following month, he was still obviously overwhelmed by the experience. He said that he put the gears into neutral when he saw it, and the truck just coasted along. The distance narrowed from 50 - 60 metres to only about 20, and the beast was in sight for 15 - 20 seconds. He counted 15 to 20 dark stripes, patterned just as depicted on the sketch. He was amazed by its tremendous strength and grace. It sprang like a cat and its body rippled like a cheetah's.

But it was the way it opened its jaws that left him lost for words. It was "like a man-trap - like a snake - like a crocodile". They spread a full 160 degrees. Its face disappeared behind the huge gape of the jaws. Only after I had elicited this information - without leading questions - did I tell him that this was a classic thylacine yawn-threat. Indeed, there exists a famous photograph of the last captive thylacine displaying such a threat, but the photographer hadn't realised its significance until it was too late. The late David Fleay told me how, immediately after he had taken the snap, the thylacine turned and sank its teeth into his thigh.

Two days after the event, Mr Swaby went to the Bundaberg library, found a lithograph of a thylacine, and immediately recognized the animal he had seen. I must say, I can't fault him there. The creature was much bigger than any known thylacine, but if it had been seen in Tasmania, no-one would have had any doubts about its identify.

In 1973 came a newspaper report that a zoologist, John Winter was investigating sightings on the Atherton Tableland[49]. Since I had known Mr (now Dr) Winter at university, I immediately wrote to him, and was rewarded with a six paged typed report[50].

There were four sightings, of which two reached the press, in the Longland Gap area, centring on the Herberton turn-off of the Ravenshoe-Atherton Road. No more than 6 weeks and 1½ km separated the most distant encounters. Winter talked to one of the witnesses, Rhonda Gadaloff on the phone, and met three others: Janet Crump, Ed Morton and Bill Weare. He interviewed them separately, taking pains to avoid asking leading questions, though he did attempt some misleading ones, like "Did the stripes run along the body parallel to the backbone?" Only at the end of the interviews did he show them drawings of the thylacine, in two books, Troughton's *Furred Animals of Australia* and *A Guide to the Native Mammals of Australia* by W.D.L. Ride[51]. Here, then, are the results.

1. Witnesses Janet Crump and mother, about 8 pm, sometime in December 1972. Very lean and hungry looking animal (not mangy) with vertical stripes from shoulder to rump, which started at the spine, but did not encircle the belly, and a long thin tail held diagonally down. It was not nervous of the car, but stood watching as the vehicle disappeared.

2. Ed Morton, Honorary Protector of Flora and Fauna and his boss, Bill Weare, beekeeper and former crocodile hunter saw an animal about 9 or 10 am on a fine, sunny day, probably 23 December 1972. It had a dog-like head with ears very erect, a short, thick neck, and was in very poor condition, but not mangy. (It might be noted that the Tableland had been particularly dry that year.) The tail was dog-like but not bushy, according to Morton, and straight and held diagonally down, according to Weare. He also thought the animal was 18 inches [46cm] at the shoulder and 2 feet [61cm] long, and that it was dark brown with several vertical stripes coming well down towards the belly. Morton said the vertical stripes ran from shoulder to rump, possibly at a slight angle. It moved off in no great hurry at the approach of the car.

3. About 11 pm on the fine night of 23 December 1972, Mrs Rhonda Gadaloff saw an animal she estimated to be 12 inches [30cm] high with stripes 3 to 4 inches [7½ to 10 cm] broad, which also walked to the side of the road and watched the car go by[52].

4. At 10.15 pm on 13 January 1973 Len Watson, a 35 year old miner, Ron Tucker, 52 and his son Harry, 17 saw an animal with a small, triangular, pointed mouth and small, round ears, a very short neck and a body 2 feet long and 18 inches high. The underside was parallel to the top, the legs straight, and a tail 18 inches long and the same thickness throughout held straight out behind and ending in a rounded tip. It was a light tawny brown with dark, vertical stripes 1½ inches [4cm] wide. It walked like a cat in front of the car and stopped for a moment before disappearing[53].

To Winter this sounded a lot like a thylacine. In fact, Ed Morton actually thought that the thylacine drawing in Ride's book was closer to his mystery animal than the one in Troughton's. It should be mentioned, though, that no-one had actually described the tapering hindquarters of the thylacine. In fact, Weare later stated that "it tapered off more hound-like to the rear."[54]

The upshot was that Winter camped in the Longland Gap area for five days and four nights, laying ten wallaby traps baited with freshly killed chickens and a fresh road kill of a pademelon. He also laid scent trails between the traps, and patrolled the main road in a vehicle at night. Results: one white tailed rat caught, and three dingoes sighted. He added that a forester in Atherton claimed to have seen a large ginger cat with distinct stripes climbing a tree in the rain forest.

At the same time there came stories of the "Cape Tribulation Tiger" on the Cape Tribulation side of the Daintree River[55,56]. The ferryman, John Allen was collecting reports. It was said to bigger than an Alsatian, with a tail half as long again as a dog's and to be dirty grey in colour, with hair visible only on its back, a tiny head, short neck and nose, short, rounded ears, two pig-like tusks protruding from the upper jaw, and a blood-curling, yodelling dry. Sounds like some sort of big, feral dog.

When he returned, Winter received a letter from a Mr. F. A. Arnold:

> As a young man (born 1900) a brother and I, while opening up a new cane farm at Waugh's Pocket near Innisfail in 1923/4 lived in a small house surrounded by

scrub (Rain Forest). Late one night we heard our fowls disturbed and proceeded to investigate. My brother grabbed the kerosene table lamp & I grabbed a new axehandle. I was in the fowl house with the animal when the lamp blew out. The door was of course closed. When it was relit the snarling animal was low down in one corner & I was high up in the other. However we killed it and next morning seeing it as a novelty we studied it closely. Being extremely busy & broke we threw it away in the scrub & have thought little of it since but as I was the one locked in with it & who dragged it outside, the tension & excitement of those few minutes left me with very clear recollections of the animal & the incident.

He marked the paragraphs on the original newspaper article to show that Watson & Tucker's description applied to his animal, and commented:

My added description would be - coarse sparse hair similar to a pig's; - slight upward curve at end of the straight tail, - Dog type feet - A mouth of strong dog like teeth - It was a male, purely dog type animal with no hope of climbing a tree - The black stripes carried down along the tail I.E. across the tail as on the body - For want of a better name we called it a native cat, but it was not a cat - It Being a male and at that time not having heard of a marsupial tiger I do not recall any indication of a marsupial nature -

Actually, it is not hard to tell whether a male animal is a marsupial. In marsupials the penis, which is usually forked, is normally only visible when erect, and it inserts behind rather than in front of the testicles.

F. Arnold is now deceased. His brother, L. O. Arnold remembered the episode, but was unable to provide any details when I contacted him.

The latest report comes from Cape York Peninsula[57]. Former Ansett captain, Percy Trezise had been living at Jowalbinna property, near Laura for 18 years. On the night of 20 July 1993 he had placed out scraps for the dingoes when his sister and brother-in-law arrived. The animal which stood in their headlights just 15 metres away looked like a dingo head on. But when it turned to pass through the fence, they saw its light belly and the long stripes on its back. It was in view for 3 to 4 seconds.

Mr Trezise was able to take plaster casts of the big paw prints. He found another set later on and followed them for miles. He states they are unlike dingo spoor, with which he is well familiar, and considers them similar to drawings of thylacine tracks. At present he is keeping watch with tripod, camera and flash.

In a letter to me (8 Feb. 1994) he gave further details. He is familiar with dingoes. One big male, in fact, has been around long enough to be given the name, Brownie, and is not adverse to being photographed. But it is a different matter with the thylacines, of which he calls the male Thylus and the female, Thylene. The latter turned up with a pup in September.

He believes they have a lair in a nearby rocky escarpment. Unlike dingoes, they do not hunt together, and they approach his homestead only during the dark of the moon, leaving footprints much heavier than a dingo's. Then, as he put it: "The female comes at the bait like a lioness, she bounds in, you hear the jaws crunch, then bounds away, gone in a split second."

He constructed a huge trap with a garden gate at both ends, but on the one occasion both gates sprung, Thylene still got the better of it. "About midnight she had a go, went in like a full forward on the burst, hit the bait and sprung the trap - and made it out the east gate before it fell 3 feet [90cm] and she had to move about 8 feet [2.4m]. By the way she clawed gravel it hit her on the rump."

There must be numerous stories around like this if you look for them. Shortly after Mr Trezise's story was published, a farmer from Lakeland Downs rang him and reported that he had a similar pair on his property. He saw them run like cats after his cattle, and they killed his dog on a chain.

Mr Trezise was also in the Windsor Tableland in 1977 when he photographed a footprint of some marsupial, bigger than a dingo, which was capable of climbing. Not unnaturally, he related it to the animal seen by Robert Johnstone in 1873 (chapter 3). Unfortunately, I've been advised that the slide is too faint to be of any use. But what an interesting place north Queensland must be, with a danger of confusing two distinct unknown marsupials!

What about further north? Don't laugh. Thylacine remains have been found in Papua New Guinea[58] where, presumably, they were driven to extinction by the introduction of the New Guinea dog, a close relative of the dingo which outpaced them on the Australian mainland.

But recently, a remarkable story has come out of Irian Jaya, the

Indonesian half of the island. It involves Ned Terry, a retired grazier who had spend much of the previous fifteen years searching the Tasmanian bush for thylacines. One October - I think it was 1990 - there came a telephone call from a stranger who had settled nearby. He had been a missionary in Irian Jaya for seventeen years. One day a colleague had screened a film of unusual Australian animals to the natives in a remote, highland village when the natives suddenly went wild at the picture of a thylacine. They called it *dobsegna*, and said it lived in the nearby mountains.

Immediately, Ned contacted a missionary in the area and obtained a description of the *dobsegna*:

> "Head and shoulders like white man's dogs, but with strong mouths," came the reply.
> "Tail is long and thin, almost the same length as the body. From ribs to hips they have no intestines, meaning they are very thin in that area, and that part has stripes[59]."

Ned immediately recruited his cousin, Robin, and together they visited the site, the last lap of the journey by helicopter. When he showed the natives a photo of a Tasmanian tiger, they instantly identified it as a *dobsegna*. The beast evoked a superstitious terror among them.   It had a reputation for ferocity, and for killing people with a blow from its tail, and they used its droppings for black magic. But it was established that they knew a lot about its biology.

Ned and Robin, with a couple of guides, were taken by helicopter to a mountain reputed to be *dobsegna* territory. Unfortunately, there was no game. The hunters' snares were empty and, needless to say, they saw no *dobsegna*. Considering the density of the forest, I doubt if they would have had a chance, even in a good area.

Well, that's Ned Terry's story. He did not reveal the name of the site, and the photos he produced could just as easily have been taken in the independent side of the island. I would be a lot happier if he had explained how he managed to get a permit to visit the interior of Irian Jaya. The Indonesians don't like outsiders seeing how they treat the natives, and have put most of the interior out of bounds. However, I suppose the missionaries could have arranged permission.

Although the existence of the *dobsegna* relies of just one man's word, but it is not itself improbable. Indeed, a thylacine report from New Guinea would be more credible than from the Australian mainland, simply because it is so little explored.

But how do we explain the repeated mainland reports of dog-like animals with tapered hindquarters and stripes at least on the rear half of the body? Has the legendary Tasmanian tiger been living there all along, and never before been observed by settlers, or entered the lore of the original inhabitants? Unlikely. So what's the alternative? In the early days of the century showmen used to drag captive thylacines around on display. Did a pregnant or pouch-gravid female get away in both Victoria and Western Australia?

You don't like that idea? Then how about hypothesis number 3? All the mainland witnesses are either mistaken or lying. Every last one. Because if just one of those stories is true . . .

ADDENDUM

I have to admit that it this mystery - not big cats or yowies, as described in the following chapters, but the idea of thylacines on the mainland - which give me the most trouble. I also have to admit that most of this chapter should be considered folklore rather than cryptozoology. There are just too many "thylacines" which don't really fit the pattern of a real thylacine. For example, how many references to "stripes" involve the genuine thylacine pattern of 15 to 20 unbroken black vertical bands rather than (say) the broken pattern of brindled dingo hybrids, which amount to three percent of the dingo population. Dr. Corbett, a dingo specialist, made the comment that:

> **In Victoria, sightings of similarly coloured animals sometimes give rise to the forlorn hope that thylacines still exist in the bush[60].**

As an example of what I call "thylacine fever", we might consider the case of the "monster" of Wonthaggi in Gippsland, Victoria. Out of the blue, Paul Cropper sent me 106 - yes, 106!- photocopies from two now defunct Wonthaggi newspapers covering 34 years' of reporting on the animal. It must have taken him hours of research.

The initial "monster" made headlines from December 1955 to July 1957, and it is clear from the reports that they were dealing with, initially, an oversized feral cat, and later by several large feral dogs[61]. In 1958 the return of the "monster" was announced, and so began a series of reports, all of which were consistent with large dogs, all different from the original "monster" and usually from each other. However, in 1962 someone reported seeing a thylacine, after which the only things worth seeing were thylacines - and the reports continued all the way up to 1986.

I analysed these accounts[62] and, by and large, I was not impressed. Just the same, there were a few, albeit with low levels of detail, which would have been taken seriously if they had occurred in Tasmania. And that is the problem: there are just enough plausible cases to make one wonder what is going on.

The animal seen by Mr. Swaby near Woodgate is the best. Not only was the description spot on, but its behaviour was totally un-doglike ie it gave the typical thylacine gape-threat, of which few non-zoologists are aware, least of all Mr. Swaby.

This event had a sequel. About half past six in the morning of Sunday 11 May 1997, a Jim Wieland saw a strange animal by the side of the road in Woodgate National Park, only about four or five miles from Mr. Swaby's adventure. He phoned the ranger, who phoned Mr. Swaby, who phoned me, and I was able to telephone the witness just nine hours after the event. It had lasted only four or five seconds, at a distance of 20 or 40 metres. The animal was darker than a fox, as big as a good-sized cattle dog, with definite, although not prominent stripes on the rear. The tail was almost as long as its body, and tapered like a kangaroo's. I was not convinced it was a thylacine, but the location was significant[63].

The Atherton beast investigated by John Winter sounds very good. You will remember that one of the witnesses was shown two drawings of a thylacine, and considered his animal was closer to one than the other. The sighting at Harts Creek was very good, if Fig. 4.1 is accurate. Likewise, the one near Lucindale (Fig. 4.3).

Some of the Plunkett Papers, mentioned in the last chapter, are relevant. In other words, although Miss Plunkett advertised for reports on the striped marsupial cat, several of the accounts sound more like a thylacine. Thus, Grace Baldwin, writing in 1970, specially stated that what she and her husband saw one clear, fine morning in 1964 near Goodiwindi, Qld was a thylacine. They saw stripes, but were vague about them because -

> The hindquarters were sloped, the rear legs having a long elbow, the tail was long by comparison and, at the butt, kangaroo like. In fact, the extraordinary hindquarters took my eye to such an extent that I probably missed other details.

A policeman, W. A. Leith, also writing in 1970, reported that, in September 1967, when he was stationed at Babinda, he saw one about two miles [3 km] from The Boulders. In other words, this was closer to the coast, but not that far from the Atherton Tableland sightings identified by Dr. Winter in 1973. It was about 7 a.m. on a popular walking track, when his Doberman Pinscher dog suddenly turned back with its tail between its legs. He then came across an animal as big as a medium sized dog about ten yards away, which remained in view for about ten seconds.

It had large vertical stripes on its body and its body appeared to slope downwards towards the rump. It had a long stiff tail. It had a peculiar gait, something like that of a dingo as it slinks away. I only had a rear view of the animals' head as it looked rearwards towards me.

It is noteworthy that, unlike the "marsupial tiger" encounters, where the delay in reporting was commonly several decades, these two sightings are based on memories only six and three years old respectively.

East Gippsland, Victoria has long been a hotspot for alleged thylacine sightings, and on 1st June 1997 journalist Andrew Rule wrote an article about it in which he did something unusual for journalists in this field: instead of simply reporting the information volunteered by the witnesses, he questioned them with a meticulous attention to detail. Among the large number of cases, I found two particularly interesting[64].

The first sighting took place just four months before, on 1st February, with an excellent witness, a former assistant police commissioner, Fred Silvester, and his wife. Their garden in Seagull Drive, Loch Sport abutted onto the bush. Mr. Silvester had heard of "tiger" sightings by other residents, but knowing how inaccurate so many witnesses can be, he was sceptical.

Then, at 9 o'clock that morning, he say a strange animal standing at his fishpond, and despite his experience as a shooter, he could not identify it. Having alerted his wife, they moved to the verandah, only ten metres from the animal, and watched it for about 30 seconds, when it looked at them and loped off with a peculiar gait. It was about as big as a medium sized dog, with a long head like an Alsatian's, and ears which were vertical rather than floppy. It was brownish in colour, with dark stripes which his wife described as "reddy tan". They ran from the shoulders down to the butt of its tail, which Mrs. Silveston estimated was

10 centimetres wide at that point. They both agreed that the tail tapered to a point like a wallaby's.

The second account was based on a sighting in the late 1970s ie twenty years before. Normally, I was be chary about such a story, but I have included it because of the separate witnesses, and because of the behaviour of the animal. Rule interviewed both 74-year-old John Anderson, former soil scientist and farmer, and his daughter, Anne. The location was his property in a coastal grazing area between Sale and Seaspray - which is not all that far from Loch Sport.

On the day in question, Mr. Anderson went out with his kelpie to check his property, and when an animal loped away about 20 metres from his position, he initially mistook it for a wallaby. Then he saw that it was something different: as big as a kelpie, rusty brown in colour with dark brown stripes from the loins backwards, and the tail thick at the butt. Its gait was unusual. He could have shot it then and there, but held fire because he had no idea what it was.

When he arrived back at the house, he found 16-year-old Anne had preceded him. She had set off in the opposite direction to her father's, chasing rabbits with her border collie, Devil. Suddenly, what was apparently the same animal shot out from the tea trees. It was a bit bigger than her dog, brown tan in colour, with darker markings around it from mid-loin to the tail, and again, with an unusual gait. Devil chased it to within 15 feet [4½ metres] of her. As it turned to face him, she noticed its short, thick, triangular ears, which did not appear dog-like. What it did next was crucial.

> 'The dog ran towards him. The animal's muzzle stayed straight. That is, the top didn't move, but he dropped his bottom jaw right down . . . like a medieval drawbridge over a moat.' She mimes this, holding one hand flat, dropping the other down through more than 90 degrees to form a gaping 'mouth.' 'Then,' she continues, leaning forward in her chair, reliving the moment, 'he made this really bizarre sound. It was a weird 'yip, yip!' from the bottom of the throat. The hairs went up on the back of my neck. I was terrified. So was my dog. He turned around and bolted. I was left standing with nothing but a stick. I ran all the way home to tell Mum, but the dog beat me.'

Back home, they consulted a book on Australian mammals, and she recognised it as a thylacine.

So there you have it: memories twenty years old, admittedly, but two independent witnesses, in broad daylight, at close range, a reasonable description, plus the yawn threat, and a most un-canine vocalisation. (The thylacine's vocalisations have been variously described, and many were quite distinct from those of a dog[65].) If this had happened in Tasmania, it would have been taken very seriously by zoologists.

Gary Opit is a professional freelance zoologist with a detailed knowledge of Australian wildlife and an even greater penchant for cryptozoology than I. Like me, he was asked to contribute a chapter to Rebecca Lang's book, *The Tasmanian Tiger: Extinct or Extant?*[66]. Thus, when people contact him and enquire about a strange striped animal they have seen, he keeps an open mind. He points out most people know little about the thylacine, but they are familiar with common wildlife in their area, and when they see something quite unusual, they do not jump to the conclusion that it is an allegedly extinct animal somehow transposed from the Apple Isle. Rather, they assume it is a known, but uncommon member of the local fauna, and want to know what it is.

As a result, he believes that it survives in small numbers on the mainland in the rugged mountain ranges such as "the Grampians, Great Divide, Nightcap, Macpherson and the Border Rangers." As wildlife consultant for ABC North Coast Radio, he had collected 65 sightings from northeastern New South Wales alone, and quite a few from elsewhere.

For a start, he himself claims a couple of sightings. First of all, he quotes Carl Lentz (whom we have met in chapter 1) about a male animal he shot and skinned in 1894 behind Mudgeeraba in the Gold Coast hinterland of Queensland. Although he reported it in 1967, he obviously kept notes, or else he had kept the skin, because his description was detailed. He said it was six feet [1.8 metres] long from nose to tail, which would have been exceptional for a thylacine. However, the stripes which ran downwards on the flank, and around the tail, were not black, but "light pale blue-grey", with marble sized orange or yellow spots on the flanks as well. This does not sound like a thylacine. Also, it had five bright orange rings around its eyes, compared to white markings in a thylacine.

One unusual feature was " 2 extra long sharp fang teeth, one and five eight inches [35 mm] long besides the 4 ordinary incisor teeth." A dog has six incisors in each jaw, while a thylacine has (? had) eight in the upper jaw and six in the lower[67]. My feeling, therefore, is that this was an aberrant dog which not only possessed an unusual coat pattern, but the incisors next to the canine teeth were abnormally long, making it appear that it had a double set of canines and fewer incisors.

The point is, Dr. Opit believes that he saw the same thing in the spring of 1969 on a lonely stretch of the Gold Coast Highway. It casually walked across the road in front of his car about 11 o'clock at night: an animal of general canine shape, but with a waddling marsupial-like gait reminiscent of a brush tailed possum. It had "thickly brindled fur" and a thickly furred tail with seven bands across it.

He also told how, just after dark on 3 February 2007, he watched an animal of the appropriate size for about five minutes in the headlights of his car at a distance of about 20 metres. He saw what he believes was the same animal three more times over the next two years. Significantly, however, he described the animal as dark brown in colour, but he did not describe any stripes.

Personally, I don't think any of these was a thylacine. Nevertheless, while it pains me to disagree with a fellow zoologist - and a more successful one at that - on this occasion, I have to admit that some of his reports are a lot more cogent. It would be impossible to condense the whole of his chapter, but three accounts in particular caught my eye.

The first was from a schoolteacher called Mark. We must, however, bear in mind that, although the incident occurred in 1970, it was not reported until at least 1997. Anyway, Mark was working during the school holidays on a banana farm at Crabbes Creek, in northeastern New South Wales, when the owner's German shepherd rushed to attack an animal sheltering in an old, partly collapsed banana packing shed. Suddenly, it backed out, and then there emerged an animal almost as large with brown stripes on its back and a thick, stiff, kangaroo-like tail. The amazing thing was that it opened its huge jaws to an extent greater than the dog, and produced "a bizarre coughing bark-like sound unlike anything that they had heard before."

The second report was, in fact, the first one he had received. In January 1982 he met Laurie and Judy Arnott, and they told him of what they had seen on Friday 5 March 1965 in the Mooralla District of the Grampians in Victoria. In the early evening they slowed to open a gate, when a strange animal leapt into the middle of the track just five metres in front of their car. Displaying no fear of the now stationary vehicle and its headlights, it sat in a crouched position with its forelegs off the ground, its butt resting on the ground and its tail held stiff and horizontally about 15 cm [6 inches] off the ground. That tail was as long as its body, about 6 cm wide, and did not taper, but ended abruptly. It was covered with short, sleek, grey-brown fur. The important point was a series of dark brown stripes which began at the shoulders and continued to the haunches, as well as the first quarter of the tail. As with a genuine thylacine, the stripes were shorter behind the shoulder and increased in length towards the rear. They were all the same width, and continued more than half way down the side, where they narrowed to a point.

This is a perfect description of a thylacine. It was the size of a large red-necked wallaby, and at first they thought it was some unknown species of wallaby, until it dropped onto all fours, and they saw that the forelegs were of a similar size to the hindlegs. Suddenly, it leapt like a coiled spring had powered its hindlegs, and disappeared into the darkness. They never saw it again, although a local beekeeper admitted that he had been seeing such animals about a fortnight. Dr. Opit questioned them separately over the next few days, and finally he showed them Dr. Ride's book, *A Guide to the Native Mammals of Australia*, which had two drawings of the thylacine: one on all fours, and one of it rearing up as the keeper rattled its bars. They told him that the second drawing was very similar to what they had seen.

Finally, Opit moved to the south east area of South Australia, in areas covered by Figure 4B, and started picking up various accounts, of which the most interesting was by Lindsey Laurence, a farmer at Western Flat. On a hot summer night in 1972 he came within 10 metres of one. No description was provided, but it was stated that "it rose up onto its hind legs, opened its jaws remarkably wide and hissed loudly at him." With that behaviour, there is no way this could have been a dog or fox. Nevertheless, the thylacine was known to not only use a gape threat, but also a hiss.

What does this all mean? In the first edition, I mentioned the possible recent date of the Tunnel Creek humerus. However, in 1997, when *The Australian Magazine* was running an article on mainland thylacines, they sent it to the Institute of Geological and Nuclear Sciences Ltd. in New Zealand for testing, and they came up with a date of 4,000 years[68]. How disappointing! We must accept that there is no physical evidence of thylacines on the mainland later than 3,000 years ago. Also, based on the ease at which normal animals can be confused with thylacines, a high standard of proof rests on any claim for their existence. Just the same, a number of sightings do meet the standard. The frequent combination of stripes and a long, stiff tail, along with, on occasions, specifically thylacine behaviour, would be music to the ears of any zoologist or naturalist it they came from Tasmania.

It is not only the presence of such sightings which is disturbing - why weren't they reported before? - but the fact that they are not localised. They are dotted all over the place. No documentation exists for any deliberate introduction to the mainland, and even if there were, it would not explain the wide distribution.

For his book, *The Last Tasmanian Tiger* (2000), Robert Paddle did a remarkable job of combing through early nineteenth century documents, and thereby uncovered evidence of thylacines on the mainland[69]. In 1855, a Victorian naturalist called "Cambrian" wrote that, although he had personally never seen a live one, he claimed to have examined the head, feet, and skin of a thylacine killed in the Blue Mountains, west of Sydney. This is not the sort of thing a naturalist could mistake. Paddle also referenced an 1839 lecture by a prominent South Australian scientist, Dr John Litchfield, who mentioned rewards being offered for them in that state, although their ravages were by then limited to the thinly settled areas. Not only that, but there were Aboriginal references to thylacines in the Flinders Ranges area in the first part of the nineteenth century. To be sure, he did not suggest that they are still extant, but in Opit's opinion[70], a relict population always existed at low levels, and with the removal of their competitors ie Aboriginal hunters, dingoes, and wild dogs, their numbers have increased such that they are now being observed in coastal nature reserves.

Maybe. But you will now see why mainland thylacines give me more headaches than any of the other mystery animals.

Personally, I consider a more likely location for thylacine survival would be the island of New Guinea, especially the western half controlled by Indonesia. The mountain chain backbone of the land has turned it into a patchwork of "ecological islands": peaks and valleys separate from each other, where species are able, indeed forced, to develop in isolation.

Dr Tim Flannery, one of Australia's leading mammalogists and palaeontologists, who has spent decades on mammal surveys on the island, indicated that he does not rule out the presence of thylacines in some of these isolated patches, but with a couple of caveats[71]. Firstly, it takes time and effort to gain the trust and acceptance of the native people, who can easily be led to tell you what you want to hear. Secondly, in the areas of the sightings, the wildlife has been devastated by overhunting, meaning that resident thylacines would face a scarcity of prey.

Be that as it may, in March 1997 a local Indonesian Governor, Jose Buce Wenas announced the presence of an animal resembling the Tasmanian tiger in the Jawawijaya Regency, in particular, in the districts close to the PNG border around the Kurima Tableland, Oksibil, and Okbibab. He had been informed by local missionaries that the predators lived in caves and came out in the evenings to hunt in packs and attack the locals' livestock[72]. Oksibil is located at 5°06'S, 140°40'E, and contains an airport and a mission station.

Wenas' story was second hand, and a bit jumbled. For a start, thylacines were not known to hunt in packs. Also, he claimed they were a metre high, which would make them the size of a real feline tiger. On the other hand, there is no "thylacine fever" in New Guinea. It is not an interpretation people tend to put on unknown animals. Indeed, the newspaper initially did not know what to make of it. They assumed it was some sort of feline tiger, and had to consult a local zoologist to set the record straight (and even his answer was inaccurate).

In April the same year came an announcement from Kayat Sutaryo, the head of forestry in Irian Jaya, as the Indonesian half of the island was then called, that villagers in the Baliem Valley had reported thylacines attacking their chickens, dogs, and pigs, and that the animal was too fierce to capture[73]. Indonesia's Nature Conservation Agency was said to be planning to undertake a study.

All this makes sense. The Baliem Valley, with its chief town of Wamena (4° 06' S, 139° E) is a major tourist centre, and one place which foreigners can easily reach. Meanwhile, Oksibil is located at 5°06' S, 140° 40' E, and contains an airport and a mission station, and you will remember that Ned Terry arrived at his destination by helicopter.

However, it was clear that foreign journals were receiving confused signals, for the same report added:

World Wide Fund for Nature naturalist, Richard Kalelego, says an expedition he headed in 1993 found Thylocine *[sic]* **footprints in forests in the Carstenz Mountains.**

Mount Carstenz is called Puncak Jaya ("glorious peak") in Indonesian, and being located at 4° 05' S, 137° 10½' E, is quite a distance from both the Baliem Valley and the border areas mentioned by Wenas. To make matters more confusing, on the same day, the Jakarta correspondent of the *Sydney Morning Herald* reported:

> The official newsagency, Antara, said a team from the Government's Natural Conservation Agency would conduct a field study on the slopes of Mount Cartenz, where locals say they saw several Tasmanian tigers, or thylacines, foraging for food at night[74].

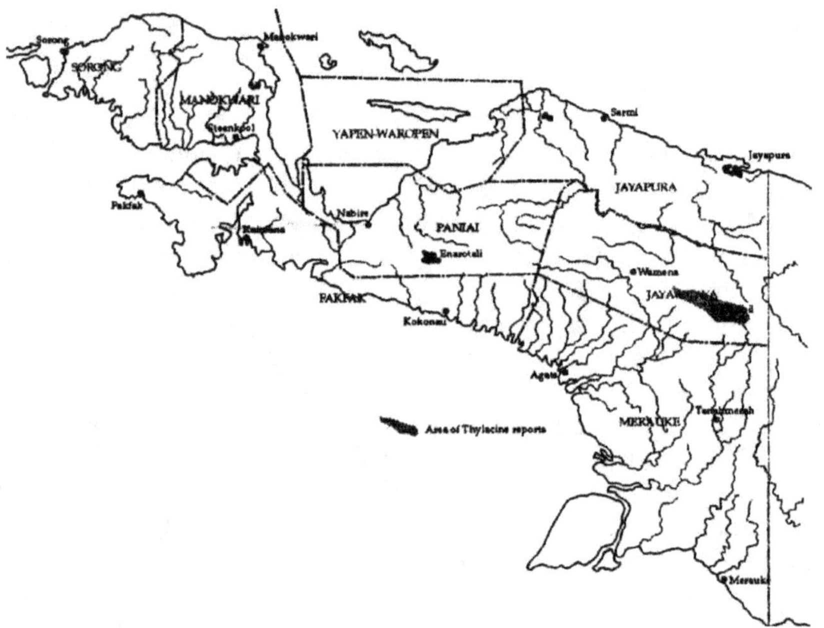

Map 4C: *Franz's map showing the area of thylacine reports in Irian Jaya.*

Then, in 2000, I received a letter from an Austrian called Franz (he has asked me not to publish his last name), who told me that, nearly every year since 1976 he had been visiting Indonesian New Guinea with a friend in order to study the culture, but also the fauna and flora[75]. (And, yes, I did do a websearch of his full name to obtain independent confirmation of the fact.) He had been to a particular area three times, and on the last occasion - I believe it was in 1992 - the natives saw a letter bearing a picture of a thylacine on an Australian stamp, and recognized it.

Map 4C is the map he included with his letter, with shading showing the area of thylacine reports. As you can see, it is wholly within the Jayawijaya Regency, starting in the eastern section of the Baliem Valley and extending westward to Oksibil. This was written before he had heard of Wenas' reference to Oksibil. He said that the people in the area involved live in small settlements in the dense rainforest around 1,5000 to 2,000 metres, and the alleged thylacines are in the mountainous country higher up. The natives keep the skulls and teeth of animals hunted on the walls of their huts, and it might be possible for a zoologist to check them for possible thylacine remains. They do not keep the skins.

On his journeys Franz takes photos of both local animals and those of Africa and South America, and when I contacted him again in 2013 he told me he now includes a painting of the thylacine. He pointed out that the natives normally failed to identify the non-native animals, which means that they don't just say they recognize them in order to please him. After 2000 he concentrated on the southern part of the province of Papua ie eastern Indonesian New Guinea, and only one person recognized the thylacine. He was an immigrant from a village located at 1,900 metres in the highlands. According to him, the species lived higher still, in a region of marsh grasslands with tree ferns and shrubs. Then, as soon as Franz reached one of the villages in a certain untouched highland valley, he found people who recognized it, although it was obviously very rare..

Interestingly, Franz said that, despite coming and going since 1976, he had never seen an echidna!

When I published Franz's and Wenas' information on my blog, I received some feedback. For example, an anonymous commenter in 2013 said he saw one in Jawawijaya when he was posted there for three years, but he gave no further details except that the pelt was grey. In 2011 Chad Arment, an American author on cryptozoology, said that, in the 1990s, an American animal importer told him he had collected reports on the subject.

Dr. Karl Shuker, who may be the only person to actually make a living from cryptozoology, also had something to add[76]. In 2003 an explorer of Irian Jaya named Ralf Kiesel had told him that, since 1995 there had been rumours of thylacines from the Yali region in the northeast part of the Baliem Valley, and from the Carstenz National Park - which you will remember was mentioned in the 1997 press releases. Kiesel also told him of the experience of a Papuan friend of his called Jan Sarakang. In the 1970s he and a colleague were camped at an altitude of about 2,400 metres near Mt. Carstenz one night when two dog-like animals, an adult and a cub, paid a visit. They failed to see any stripes, but they were amazed at their stiff, inflexible tails and enormous gape when they yawned.

Finally, In 2019 a Sydney based documentary film maker e-mailed me to say that he had made enquiries at Turnobil village, on the PNG side of the border, and found two hunters who were able to identify the animal.

Does all this sound fanciful? Remember, the big island up north has no tradition of "thylacine fever" such as exists in some parts of Australia. Also, by using methods typical of cryptozoology, Dr Tim Flannery himself managed to discover two new species of tree kangaroo: the dingiso (*Dendrolagus mbaio*) in the Indonesian half of the island, and the tenkile (*D. scottae*) in Papua New Guinea[77]. The latter was particularly significant. His quest began when, while being medivacced, he noticed an unusual claw worn by a native attendant and purchased it, realising it must have come from a new species of tree kangaroo. But it took seven years to locate this extremely rare and endangered animal in very restricted areas of the Torricelli Mountains.

So don't be surprised if some other unknown species turn up in that labyrinth of mountain peaks and valleys that constitute our northern neighbour. Let's hope that we find them before they become extinct.

REFERENCES

[1] 'Tiger' outside their tent. *Courier-Mail* (Brisbane) 17 Aug. 1984

[2] Eric R Guiler (1985) *Thylacine : the tragedy of the Tasmanian tiger* Oxford University Press, pp 9-33, 139-169

[3] Guiler (ref. 2), pp 45-47

[4] D. E. Rounsevell and S. J. Smith (1982)   Recent alleged sightings of the Thylacine (Marsupialia, Thylacinidae) in Tasmania. **in** *Carnivorous Marsupials*. vol. 1, pp 223 - 6, Michael Archer, editor, published by the Royal Zoological Society of N. S. W.

[5] 'Postie gives mail on 'tiger'.' *The Sun* (Melbourne) 21 Aug. 1990

[6] Michael Archer (1974)   New information about the Quarternary distribution of the Thylacine (Marsupialia, Thylacinidae) in Australia.   *J. Roy. Soc. W. Aust.* 57 : 43 - 50

[7] Jeanette Partridge (1967) A 3,300 year old thylacine (Marsupialia, *Thylacinus*) from the Nullarbor Plain. *J. Roy. Soc. West. Aust.* 50 : 57 – 59

[8] John H. Calaby and C. White (1967) The Tasmanian Devil (*Sarcophilus harissii*) in northern Australia in Recent times. *Aust. J. Sci.* 29 : 473 - 5

[9] David C. Lowry and Jacoba W. J. Lowry (1967) Discovery of a Thylacine (Tasmanian tiger) carcass in a cave near Eucla, Western Australia. *Helictite* 5: 25

[10] Jacoba W. J. Lowry and Duncan Merrilees (1969) Age of the desiccated carcass of a Thylacine (Marsupialia, Dasyuroidea) from Thylacine Hole, Nullarbor Region, Western Australia. *Helictite* 7: 15-16.

Duncan Merrilees (1970) A check on the radiocarbon dating of desiccated Thylacine (Marsupial "wolf") and dog tissue from Thylacine Hole, Nullarbor Region, Western Australia. *Helictite* 8: 39 - 42

[11] E. Kolig (1973) Aboriginal man's best foe? *Mankind* 9 : 122 - 4

[12] Guiler (ref. 2) pp 11-12

[13] Guiler (ref. 2), pp 170 - 5

[14] 'A tiger, by jingo!' *Telegraph* (Brisbane) 3 Nov. 1971

[15] *ibid.*

[16] Sid Slee (1987) *The Haunt of the Marsupial Wolf*, 41 pages. Privately published.

[17] Malcolm Smith (1982) Review of the Thylacine (Marsupialia, Thylacinidae). **in** *Carnivorous Marsupials*. vol. 1, pp 237 - 253, Michael Archer, editor, published by the Royal Zoological Society of N. S. W.

[18] Guiler (ref. 2) , pp 173 - 4

[19] Athol M. Douglas (1986) Tigers in Western Australia? *New Scientist* 110 (1505): 44 -7   (24 April 1986)

[20] Letters were published in the issues of 14 May, 29 May, 12 June and 24 Sept. 1986

[21] Athol M. Douglas (1990) The thylacine: a case for current existence on mainland Australia. *Cryptozoology* 9 : 13 - 25

[22] Malcolm Smith (1992) Mainland thylacines. *Cryptozoology* 11: 136 - 138

[23] Douglas (1986) (ref. 19)

[24] Douglas (1990) (ref. 21)

[25] Douglas (1990) (ref. 21) p 22

[26] Sharon West (1993) Mystery Animal Association of Western Australia, *Newsletter* No. 4, pp 6-7

[27] Sharon West (1994) Mystery Animal Association of Western Australia, *Newsletter* No. 10, pp 5,7

[28] My overseas readers, and many younger Australians, will be unfamiliar with this snippet of Australian slang. Clayton's is a non-alcoholic beverage, billed as "the drink you have when you're not having a drink." See https://en.wikipedia.org/wiki/Claytons

[29] Guiler (ref. 2), pp 171 - 2

[30] 'S-E animal "mystery"' *Adelaide Advertiser* 2 Nov. 1962

[31] 'Tasmanian tiger believed sighted.' *Science News* 93 (24): p 569 (15 June 1968)

[32] Samela Harris (1968) 'Hold that tiger!' *Walkabout* 34 (6): 28 - 31 (June)   (The photo is Rilla Martin's snap of the Oozenkadnook tiger.)

[33] Heather Parker (1970) 'Is it the Tasmanian tiger?' *Australian Women's Weekly* 37 (39) pp 35, 56, 61 (25 Feb. 1970)

[34] Guiler (ref. 2), p 35

[35] Parker (ref. 33)

[36] Graeme O'Neill (1990) 'Strange sights in the bush.' *Melbourne Age* 16 June 1990

[37] 'Tassie Tiger spotted by shocked family.' *Daily Mirror* (Sydney) 13 June 1989

[38] Paul Bird (1991) 'Tassie tiger hunt on the mainland!' *Australasian Post* 11 May 1991

[39] Guiler (ref. 2) pp 171-2

[40] Troughton, Ellis LeG. (1941) *Furred Animals of Australia.* Angus & Robertson, Sydney, p 47

[41] 'Is it a devil? Is it a dog? Or maybe the ... Lakes-ness Monster!' *The Western Times* (Footscray) 17 Aug. 1988

[42] Guiler (ref. 2) p 175

[43] S. J. Paramonov (1968) Is the Tasmanian Tiger extinct on the Australian mainland? *W. Aust. Nat.* 10 : 171 -2

[44] ''Tiger' now in baby mystery' *Sunday Telegraph* (Sydney) 27 March 1977 (Also refers to an article the previous year, which I have not seen.)

[45] Guiler (ref. 2), p 174

[46] Neil C. W. Dowsett (1982) 'Tasmanian Tiger alive and well.' *People* 16 Feb.1982

[47] Toni McRae (1995) 'Beast of Buderim' *The Sunday Mail* (Brisbane) 18 June 1995

[48] Toni McRae (1995) ''Buderim Beast' made man shake.' *The Sunday Mail* (Brisbane) 27 Aug. 1995. I also interviewed him by telephone on 2 Sept. 1995.

[49] 'A "tiger" hunt in Queensland bush'. *Sunday-Mail* (Brisbane) 28 Jan. 1973   (John Winter's name is incorrectly spelled Wintour.)

[50] I have since copied his entire report, along with the relevant newspaper articles online at https://malcolmscryptids.blogspot.com/2014/09/a-thylacine-in-north-que ensland.html

[51] Troughton, Ellis LeG. (1941, 1967) *Furred Animals of Australia.* Angus & Robertson, Sydney, facing p 48.
Ride, W. D. L. (1970), *A Guide to the Native Mammals of Australia,* Oxford University Press, Melbourne, p 93

[52] 'Aloomba woman reports seeing Tableland beast.' *Cairns Post* 18 Jan. 1973

[53] 'Another strange beast sighted on Tableland.' *Cairns Post* 17 Jan. 1973

[54] Keith Willey (1973) 'Nth Qld sightings: Mystery monster of the rain forest.' *Pix/People* 5 Aug. 1973, pp 6-7

[55] Willey (ref. 54)

[56] See ref. 53

[57] Desmond Zwar (1993) 'Tiger Hunt' *Sunday Mail Magazine* (Brisbane) 3 Oct. 1993

[58] Hobart Van Deusen (1963) First New Guinea record of *Thylacinus. J Mamma*l. 44: 279- 280

[59] Simon de Salis, 'The Tassie tiger is alive & well and living in New Guinea!' *People* (exact date not recorded - probably 1991)

[60] Laurie Corbett (1995) *The Dingo in Australia and Asia*, UNSW Press, Plate 8

[61] I copied the relevant articles online at https://malcolmscryptids.blogspot.com/2014/10/the-wonthaggi-monster.html .

[62]
https://malcolmscryptids.blogspot.com/2014/11/thylacine-fever-in-wonthaggi-district.html

[63] Malcolm Smith (2014) 'Thylacine sightings outside Tasmania' **in** Rebecca Lang (ed) *The Tasmanian Tiger: Extinct or Extant?*, Strange Nation Publishing, pp 89-99, at 94

[64] Andrew Rule, 'Australia: Agenda - Tiger Tales - It's out there somewhere … or is it?' *Sunday Age* (Melbourne) 1st June 1997 (I discussed these in slightly more detail in ref. 63.)

[65] Robert Paddle (2000), *The Last Tasmanian Tiger, the history and extinction of the thylacine*, Cambridge University Press, at pp 63-69

66   Gary Opit (2014) 'Evidence for the continuing survival of the thylacine' **in** Rebecca Lang (ed) *The Tasmanian Tiger: Extinct or Extant?*, Strange Nation Publishing, pp 111-127

67   Thomas, O. (1888), *Catalogue of the Marsupialia and Monotremata in the collection of the British Museum (Natural History)*, British Museum (Natural History), London

68   Mark Whittaker, "Look! There's one!', *The Australian Magazine*, 15-16 Nov. 1997, pp 12 - 18

69   Robert Paddle (ref. 65)   pp 22 - 23.

70   Opit (ref. 66) at 115

71   Whittaker (ref. 68)

72   *Suara Pembaruan* ("Voice of Renewal", a Protestant newspaper) 25 March 1997. See my translation of the report on https://malcolmscryptids.blogspot.com/2011/10/thylacines-in-indonesian-new-guinea.html

73   'Indonesia checking sightings of extinct Tasmanian tiger', Radio Australia (ABC), Tues. 15 April 1997. http://www.abc.net.au/ra/newsrael/25828.htm (dead link)

74   Louise Williams, 'Tribes report tiger sighting' *Sydney Morning Herald*, Tues. 15 April 1997 - online.

75   See my blog at https://malcolmscryptids.blogspot.com/2013/10/thylacines-in-indonesian-new-guinea.html

76   http://karlshuker.blogspot.com/2013/05/the-new-guinea-thylacine-crying-wolf-in.html   (accessed 2020)

77   Tim Flannery (1998) *Throwim Way Leg, tree-kangaroos, possums, and penis gourds - on the track of unknown mammals in wildest New Guinea.* Text Publishing

CHAPTER 5

THE   ABC   OF   ABCs

One of the more persistent cryptozoological mysteries is that of the ABCs: Alien Big Cats. All over the British Isles, Europe and North America, cougars, black panthers, and lions have been spotted, some of them so frequently they have become local legends[1]. Such stories are not as ridiculous as you might suppose. Until recently the countries in question had few laws against the keeping of dangerous exotic wildlife. In fact, a couple of ex-patriate Australians once kept a lion in a furniture shop in London[2].

But, of course, the one place they could never turn up would be good old isolated, quarantine happy Australia. So when I saw a book entitled, *Savage Shadow,* and subtitled, *The search for the Australian cougar*[3], my immediate reaction was: "This guy's got to be a crackpot." The only reason I bought it was that it was cheap, second hand, and obviously out of print, and I thought (incorrectly) that if I didn't take it I'd never get the chance again.

Now the cougar, puma, mountain lion, or catamount - *Felis concolor* to us zoologists - is a highly adaptable predator which ranges, or used to range, over most of North and South America from desert to dense forest. Secretive, solitary and elusive, it rarely falls prey to hunters unless they are assisted by specially trained dogs. It could easily live in Australia, and remain undetected for a long time, if anyone were crazy enough to introduce them. But before we jump to that conclusion, let's ask ourselves what sort of thing could possible give ordinary, if uncritical people the impression they were seeing cougars. Even the biggest feral cat is far too small. The native marsupial "cat", *Dasyurus geoffroyi* is smaller, much rarer, and covered with white spots. As always, the prime suspects are feral dogs.

Feral dogs come in all sorts of sizes, shapes and colours, but tend to go in for long muzzles and medium length, bushy tails. Individual deviations from the mean are very common, but if we hear consistent reports of short faces and long, tubular tails over a wide area, where they obviously refer to different individuals, the chances are we are not dealing with dogs. Dogs tend to hunt in packs. They are rippers and tearers, worrying their prey to death by repeated assaults. A dog kill will have wool and blood and bits of flesh scattered all around. Neither can feral pigs ever be mistaken for cats. However, they do tend to scavenge carrion, and they leave the carcass just as messy as dogs do.

A thylacine has (had) long jaws, vertical stripes, and hindquarters tapering into a long, not very flexible tail. No formal research has ever been done into thylacine hunting technique, but anecdotal evidence suggests they were solitary hunters who killed and fed a lot more cleanly than dogs[4].

Cats have short faces, long, tubular tails, heavy hindquarters and fluid motions. They tend to be solitary hunters, and kill by piercing the neck bones of their prey with their long, pointed canines. They kill cleanly and feed tidily. Their paw prints differ from those of dogs, and they need not be in proportion to the body. Those of a cougar are seldom more than 9 cm across, those of a black panther more like 7cm, but a big dog's can often top 10cm.

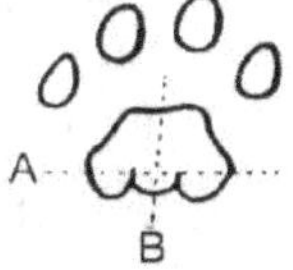
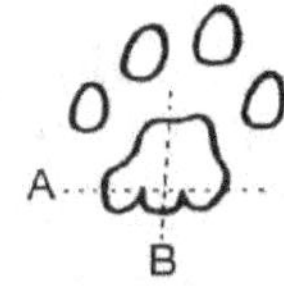

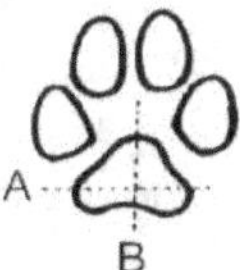

Front track of cougar. Note how heel pad differs in shape from rear track. Front foot is also larger and will be ahead of or partially overlapped by rear.	Rear track of cougar. Note small, tear-drop shaped, widely spaced toes. Note little toe and non-symmetrical shape of foot. Note squared-off front of heel-pad and 3 lobes at rear.	**small head** **rounded ears** **long tail**
Typical dog track. Note large toes, rounded front of heel, smooth (not lobed) rear of heel, and near-perfect symmetry. Front and rear tracks same size and shape.	Cross section (A) of heel pads of dog (——) and cougar (- - - -). Note that dog is higher in centre while centre lobe of cougar is same or lower than side lobes.	Longitudinal section (B) of heel pads of dog and cougar. Note that dog is highest in rear while cougar is same height or slightly higher in front. Dog slopes gradually in front — cougar is squared off.

Figure 5.1 Comparison of dog and cougar footprints (from Downing and Fifield, used with permission.)

Figure 5.1 will give you some idea of shape. The overall shape of a dog's print is rounded, the toes more or less the same size, and large - each more than 44% of the width of the heel pad. A cougar's print is tear shaped, the toes thinner and asymmetrical, the outer toe smallest, and the second from the inside longest. Claw prints are less likely to be present, and tend to be thin. The heel pad of cat prints have three lobes in the rear and tend to be truncated in front. In cross section they tend to be deepest towards the front, while a dog's is deepest at the centre rear. Cats tend to hunt alone; dogs rarely do so. A dog will seldom deviate from the path of least resistance (say a road) except to urinate. A cat's trail, on the other hand, weaves as it seeks the cover on the edges, and they have a predilection for walking along logs, wooden guardrails and rocks.

If all this seems straightforward, you're wrong. A lot depends on the surface of the ground, and whether or not the animal is running or turning. Downing and Fifield, who have been following cougar reports in the eastern U.S. for years, and who provided me with this information[5], warn that any dog track can be made to look like a cougar's, and vice versa. Anybody who wants to be able to distinguish the tracks, they said, should examine several thousand dog tracks of different breeds, and compare them with those of a cougar. Not many people in this country would fit that bill.

For these reasons, as well as the poor quality of the reproductions, I have not been overly impressed by the photos of alleged cougar prints which have turned up over the years in the popular press.

Now, back to the *Savage Shadow*. I soon discovered that the author, David O'Reilly did not fit the usual crackpot profile. In fact, as bureau chief of *The Australian* in Perth, he had more than his share of investigative journalist skills. But one day in 1978, when there was little in the way of news available, he got involved in the saga of the Cordering cougar. In the stolid farming district of Cordering, near Collie, something was lurking, slinking like shadows, letting out blood-curdling screams in the night, and killing sheep. In one season alone, grazier Dennis Earnshaw had lost $3,000 worth of lambs. They were killed cleanly, their throats torn out, their internal organs delicately eaten, without any of the mess associated with dogs, dingoes and foxes. In broad daylight he and his brother, Ross had spied a large yellow animal with a long tail, and a similar, gingery animal following behind. At 6.15 pm another day, in drizzling rain and evening twilight, he and his wife had watched something like a lioness, light brown, with powerful back legs and a long tail, lope across the road 25 metres in front of their car.

Not only that, there were footprints - large ones, some with the marks of a fifth toe. And Earnshaw was able to show O'Reilly scratch marks on the sides of gum trees - invariably trees angled at 45 degrees, easily climbable, with horizontal boughs where a cat could lie. The only animals that can claw trees like that are cats. And scratches 15 cm long and 2.5 cm apart obviously did not belong to your average back yard kitty.

The hunt for the Cordering cougar(s) was on. They hunted it with spotlights, while the press and the TV cameras tagged along. A man called Bert Pinker wounded it with a .243 bullet at 200 metres. They hunted it with a starscope, an expensive Vietnam War device which intensifies the illumination of starlight. Between two eye blinks O'Reilly himself saw "a robust cat-like figure moving at startling speed, in huge bounds, into the scope's view." Another hunter later saw a big cat place its paws on a tree and make the scratches they'd all be puzzled by. They called out an ex-cougar hunter. Don Neuman by name, he had migrated from Montana in the 1960s. "Man, you sure got cougars," was his response to the dead stock the farmers showed him. They hunted it with dogs. Unfortunately, costs and quarantine ruled out any hope of importing trained cougar dogs. A German shepherd breeder, Rick Richardson, trained one of his dogs to follow the scent of a bundle of rags placed in the cougar cage of the Perth Zoo. They then turned it loose in the haunts of the Savage Shadow and watched it chase an invisible trail and go wild over trees which might have been marked by its quarry. They found scratch marks, and a footprint bigger than the dog's.

O'Reilly soon discovered that Cordering was not unique. Unknown to the rest of the country, the Western Australian press had been carrying stories about cougars and "panthers" for years. (And still is, as far as I'm aware.) Take, for instance, this account by journalist, Brian Pash. George Moir, a farmer from Kulja, 250 km north east of Perth, told him that about September 1972 two black panthers appeared and started rounding up his sheep. He gave chase in his utility truck.

> They were black all over, at least 2 ft [60 cm] high with a long slender body and a tail the same length as the body and curling at the end. My fastest speed was 45 mph [73 kph] and I couldn't catch them up. When we came to a fence one of them took it in his stride and the other, which was lagging, crashed into the wire. It recovered quickly and climbed over like a cat. At the next fence they went over

with no trouble[6].

He lost them when he had to stop to open a gate. A fauna warden
followed their tracks for 5 miles [8 km]. One evening he (Moir) shot at
one which was raiding his pig sties. Pash was able to name other people
who had seen them. Tracks were also found, including the prints of cubs.
They were breeding.

Pash continued with a follow-up story[7]. The panthers had struck
again in the Moir property. On another property, Ron Johnson had baited
a trap with a dead sheep and set it 8 feet [2.4 m] up, which would have
discouraged most dogs. Unfortunately, he could not cover the top, and
whatever sprung the trap got out. There were tracks bigger than the
bottom of a large cool drink bottle. He chased the animals twice at
speeds up to 50 mph [80 kph], but they could go where he couldn't. By
now eleven people were said to have seen them. Not only that, but Mr W.
Adams of Cunderdin stated that he had seen something similar in the
district ten years before, but was afraid to say anything. Three years later
one of them turned up elsewhere[8]: in the Harvey-Brunswick-Australind
area and sometimes the Darling Range. Four occupants of a car saw
something walk across their headlights. Said Mrs Freda Shalders: 'It was
solidly built, pitch black, and cat-like in the way it moved. It had an
almost stumpy tail. The face was like a cat's but large and thick. After a
minute it loped away into the bush.' A Bunbury vet, formerly of East
Africa, and three farmers had also seen something similar.

Now, that puts a new complexion on things. A cougar can be grey or
tawny, but practically never black. Black is a colour phase of the big
spotted cats. Are there two species of foreign cats loose in Western
Australia? Coincidentally, there are persistent reports that the cougar is
making a comeback in eastern North America, where it has been
officially extinct since the turn of the century. In some areas a third of the
animals sighted have been black[9].

O'Reilly was also shown a photo - not a very clear one - of a big
black cat taken by a certain Barry Morris. However, it did not originate
from the Cordering area, but more than 1000 km away, on a station
northeast of Carnarvon. Interestingly enough, the Carnarvon area was
also the site of an unusual road kill in September 1993. This one was
better authenticated, because the two fisherman who found it took it to
the authorities. According to the description and photograph, it was
reddish brown with black spots, as tall as a kelpie, thickly built, with
long legs, long, pointed ears, and a tail as long as its body. Its canine

teeth were curled back almost like a boomerang, and one of the toes on both front feet appeared to have two nails growing together[10]. I can only assume it was some sort of badly deformed dog, the victim of some unusual mutation syndrome. However, one of the men who found it (Ron), believes there are more in the area. Truckies he has spoken to claim to have seen strange animals crossing the road.

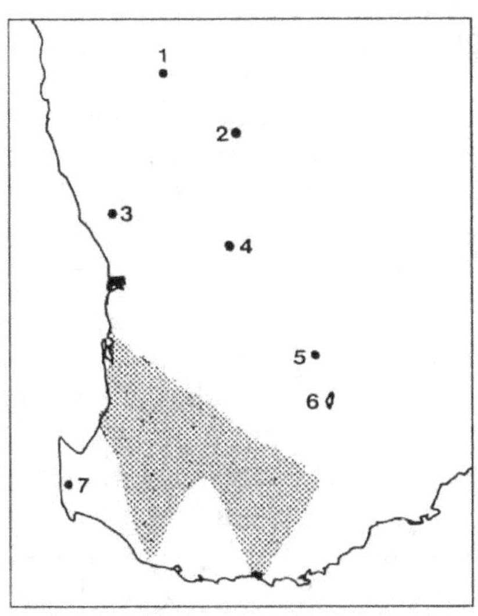

Stipled: centre of infestation
Dots: outlying appearances

Cunderdin	4
Gingin	3
Kulin	5
Kulja	2
Lake Gace	6
Latham	1
Witchecliffe	7

Carnarvon and Exmouth are well to the north of the limits of the map.

Map 5A Big Cat reports from Western Australia

Meanwhile, back in 1978, stock losses were mounting. Two brothers, 160 km south of Perth, together lost 600 lambs, reducing their lambing rate for 1978 from 95% to 50%. People had even sighted female cougars with cubs at foot (Arthur River and Rosa Glen.) Something had to be done. At a public meeting on 27 March 1978 the Cougar Committee was established. Questions were asked in Parliament. By this time the government had already sent a veterinary surgeon, Peter MacKenzie, and their top dogger, Alan MacKenzie into the district. Unfortunately, for various reasons, the two officials and the farmers quickly fell out. The official report - you can read extracts of it in O'Reilly's book - ultimately attributed all killings to dogs, foxes and pigs, while insisting that none of the other evidence was conclusive of cougars.

The farmers then hired a private vet, Peter Brighton, who had previously worked for the Department of Agriculture. Brighton was reported as being amazed at the consistent pattern of the killings. Victims were repeatedly killed instantly by a savage bite at the back of the neck.

The separation between puncture marks varied from 3 to 10 cm, and the wounds were up to 10 cm deep. In one case the teeth punctured two vertebrae lengthways and came out the other side. Now, this sort of pattern spells C-A-T with a capital C. I immediately wrote to Brighton and asked him in effect: was this true, did he still have his original autopsy notes, and could I borrow them for a few weeks? Back came the brief reply:

> Thank you for your enquiry. The pages you have photocopied do give an accurate summary of autopsies. However, my own personal photos and autopsy reports were removed from my house in my absence in '84 by two men driving Commonwealth plates. I am unable to give you detailed data off those reports. I am still interested in my ongoing public occurrences in local media including the thylacine sightings!

Readers can draw their own conclusions from that.

Why would two qualified vets come to such radically different conclusions, and which is right? I prefer not to make accusations of incompetency, or develop any sinister conspiracy theory. The Cordering area would have to be unusual if there were no predation by feral dogs, or secondary scavenging of carcasses by dogs, foxes, pigs, eagles etc. MacKenzie's initial impressions were probably based on fact. When it became clear to the graziers that he didn't support their pet theory, it is likely they ceased bringing him the most promising carcasses. That privilege fell to the vet of their choice who, from all accounts, was allowed a significant number to work with: sixty sheep and kangaroo carcasses over a period of two years. I have to admit that the photos included in O'Reilly's book tend to support the cat hypothesis. Brighton was also said to have identified cat hairs in large scats presented to him - as if a big cat had ingested its own fur while grooming.

Then there was the Ian Milroy questionnaire, which the farmer of that name drafted, and which the Cougar Committee forwarded to anyone thought to have had a sighting. To quote the Member for Warren, David Evans in Parliament on 22 August 1979:

> It is interesting to note the areas involved which can be gleaned from these reports. They include areas such as Northcliffe, going back as far as 1963; Pemberton in 1966; Wellington Dam; South East Latham; North Borden; Capercup; Harris River; Collie; Donnybrook; Grimwade;

Palgarup; Duranillin; North Dinninup; Cordering - three reports; Donnybrook; Witchcliffe; Bokal; Denmark; Arthur River; and South Collie. That will give an indication of the extent of the area over which such animals have been seen[11].

Over the whole of the southwest, in fact. (See Map 5A.)

Mr Evans was quoting from 30 reports. Exactly how many questionnaires were eventually returned I do not know. Some came from as far north as Exmouth and Carnarvon, giving credence to the Morris photo. I invite the Committee, or whoever holds the information now, to publish it in a reputable journal, such as *Cryptozoology* (see the final chapter). Information is not very valuable unless it is capable of analysis. It would be useful to know, for instance, what was the average length of the sightings, the distance, time of day, and whether any pattern emerged.

For instance, we are told that two colour types were described, jet black and some shade of brown or tawny, but the respective proportions were not mentioned. It would obviously be valuable to separate daylight and darkness sightings when dealing with colour. Equally, one might ask whether both colour types were seen in the same district, or whether some other geographic pattern can be discerned.

Practically everybody emphasized that the animal was definitely cat-like. Many simply compared its height to that of a collie, labrador or alsatian, but 30% stipulated one height: 2 foot 6 inches [75 cm]. There were tales of long legs, heavy builds, round heads, bright eyes, screams in the night and growls close up. Thirty percent nominated the tail - long, tubular and curly - as the most outstanding feature. But the vast majority were impressed by its movements: slinky, soft, silent, and fast. Just like a cat.

The A.P.B. (Agriculture Protection Board) officer at Kojonup, Graham Blacklock was initially skeptical at the story told by Steve Bellotti. The farmer had gone out one night in his truck to investigate a sound like a very loud cat fight, only to meet the glowing eyes of a cat the size of a farm dog.

He summoned two of his neighbours, and their wives. They saw it too: sitting on a ridge of rock not 30 metres away, as big as a dog, with short legs, thick body, short neck, small rounded ears, and a very feline face. One of the men blasted it with a shotgun. It rolled end over end, long tail swirling, then shot off at a tremendous speed. Becoming curious, Blacklock started following up other reports from the Kojonup area, and himself saw the thing on the Bellotti property one night, though the sighting was inconclusive. He also examined the dead stock. Now Blacklock, already familiar with big cats in his homeland of South Africa, is a believer.

O'Reilly ended with two reports. Trevor Rowe, aged 14, visiting his uncle's property near Latham, saw an undoubted cougar just 60 metres away at 6.30 am. That was in January 1950. Then there was Cliff Munyard, who drove up to within two or three yards of a sandy brown animal identical to a cougar at dusk not far from Broomehill. People in Tambellup and Mt Barker told similar stories. On a stormy night later in the year he was in the Lake Grace - Kulin area when he heard a scream from the bushes and a large cat-like animal ran out. That was in 1949.

This, then, is the story told by the journalist I initially assumed to be a crackpot. If he is reading this, I hope he accepts my apology. The savage shadow has not disappeared, and it is currently being hunted by a motley crew of enthusiastic amateurs.

In September 1988 a TV cameraman called Mike Voss went to investigate "black panther" reports from the Denmark and Mt Barker areas. Twenty kilometres west of Denmark he happened to stop his vehicle when, just 150 metres away, he saw the rear end of the said panther disappearing into the scrub. It was as big as a lion, he claimed[12]. It was the morning of Thursday 16 January 1991 that Ernie Palm was diving back to Albany from Nyabing when he saw what he first thought was a fox standing in the middle of the road. But on coming closer he realized it was a cougar, light sandy in colour, and between 75 and 90 cm [2ft 6 to 3ft] tall[13].

In 1990 the *Australasian Post* published a story of the goings-on around Bridgetown[14]. The article was illustrated with photographs of lambs decapitated as cleanly as with a butcher's knife, and a lamb slain with a single puncture in the skull. (It also sported "a rare shot of a puma taken near Albany in 1966", but which I recognized as originating from Surrey, England the same year[15].) There were the familiar tale of blood-curdling screams in the night, of carcasses with their entrails so thoroughly consumed that not even a teaspoonful of residue was left, and of a black panther crossing the road in front of a grader in the early morning. But the most dramatic were the stories of Evelyn Thorpe and Gerry Bowles.

With regard to Mr Bowles, I think the best idea is to quote in full the letter he graciously sent me five months after the event.

On Sunday the 17th of June 1990 I had been working in my shed on my wife's car, and about nine thirty pm I decided I had done enough for the day, as my wife at that time was in Perth with her family. I left my shed turned off the lights & locked the door. At that moment I heard something move to my left & shone my torch in that direction, & I saw a large cat like animal about nine feet [2.7 m] from me. I was so afraid I leapt over a washing machine which was behind me, & into my van which was fifteen feet [4.6 m] or so from the shed, where I knew I would be safe only to discover that the battery was in the shed as I had used it to start my wife's car, so I was stuck in the van several metres from the house. The weather was very stormy, pouring rain & thunder & lightning. When I leapt over the washing machine I dropped the torch & lost my glasses. A few seconds after getting into the van I felt it rock gently, & when there was a flash of lightning on the passenger side I could see the wet hairy chest of an animal. Its front legs were on the roof of the van which is six feet four inches [193 cm] from the ground high, & every now and then it would rock the van not hard, but in a sort of playful manner. There was no aggression, but I was afraid, as it was between me & the house & I didn't know what to do. Then I remembered there was a can of D15 which is an Amway product flyspray, so I then wound the driver's side door window down, & started to tap on the door, & the roof & for a while to no avail, & after a while I felt something touch my hand & I froze. I gently pulled my hand inside & I grabbed the spray & sprayed out of the open window & dropped the can, leapt out of the passenger door & ran for the house, & I checked the time & it was ten thirty pm. I went & had a shower & got myself some supper & all the time I was doing this my hair was on end & a cold chill down my spine. It was outside watching me as other than our bedroom we only have net curtain up at our windows as we are in the country. This went on until I went to bed at about 2.30 am.

At this stage I didn't know what to do because I knew no one would believe me so I said nothing to no one. At this time I was looking after a big sheep farm as the farmer &

his wife were away, & I was finding the odd lamb dead & its rib cage opened up & all its innards eaten. Then two days on we had a sheep warning over the radio so I took my wife who was back home with me. We went into the farthest back paddock where all the new lambs were first to check them & I had the farmer's sheep dog with me. We went into the paddock & up to the far boundary fence where there were three lambs on the outside. Anyway, I got out of the ute & the dog went with me & I checked the fence to see where they had got out. Then I raised the lower part of the fence so I could drive them back. At this stage the lambs leapt past me to the far corner of the paddock & the dog took off yelping to the ute, & I called her but she took no notice. I went up to her & she was shaking, & she just wanted to get into the ute, so I let her in with my wife & she cuddled up to my wife still shaking. Anyway I tried in vain to get the three lambs back but they wouldn't go towards the hole I had made. By this time it was getting dark so I left them & sealed the fence, I continued on round the paddock & at that stage I noticed all the sheep had gone. Anyway on the way out we noticed one ewe carrying on so I stopped & as soon as I opened the door the dog was out & went to round the ewe up & then noticed a lamb a few metres away so I went over & it was dead. Its tail had been ripped out, its head was crushed & it was bleeding & warm. My wife noticed it had two holes in its head & on its side, claw marks in blood about an inch [2½ cm] apart & about 3/16 [½ cm] thick. We left the lamb there & the next morning it had been eaten the same as the others. It was like it had been done by a surgeon & every one was the same. Now it wasn't killing in numbers. It would be one every two or three days so it was only killing for food. I was concerned not so much the volume but the way it killed. At this time I didn't know anything about these cats roaming in our country. I called the local ranger who said he didn't know & said it was not dogs & he didn't think it was a fox & I pointed out that a fox couldn't crush a skull like these were & he agreed but couldn't give me an answer.

I was talking to a guy that night & he said we had wild cats roaming around & I said feral cats & he said no, big jungle cats & I said is that so, remembering my ordeal a few days past but said nothing about it. The following day I phoned the local vet & I put it straight on the line & asked him the killing pattern of a mountain lion. He was quiet for a moment then asked me what I meant so I mentioned the sheep so he said you tell me about the killings & eating pattern so I did. Anyway we talked for about half an hour about tests he had done & the proof he had about these cats but the government departments wouldn't listen & didn't want to know, & the next thing I knew I had the TV people at my door, newspaper & so on.

I was afraid to go out at night so I started to make enquiries about this cat as it was hanging around my property, & I had found out a lot about it & I'm not afraid of it any more so I spend a lot of time in my shed & at night if it's not raining the door is open & it sits outside watching me. It can see me but it doesn't know that I can't see it. Then one night I went out at the shed & I saw it run down my drive about fifty metres from the shed & two weeks later at 7 30 pm I was going out to my shed after tea, & when I got to the end of the house I had the feeling it was very close so I stopped & shone my torch to my left & there it was no more than ten feet [3 m] from me. I blinded [it] temporarily with the torch as it's a good one, so I had a chance to have a good look at it. It was gold in colour. Its face had white markings each side of its nose with black thickish lines above & around the white. Under its nose is white & the white goes up round its eyes. It's light coloured under its chin & down under its belly. Its head is sort of round & small with smallish ears & not pointed but sort [of] rounded at the top. Its hind quarter is higher than its shoulders & its tail is about half of its body length & thick. My van was parked just in front of where it stood & it's about five foot [1.5 m] wide & its body length was longer than the van width. Overall length from nose to tail tip would have been close to ten feet [3 m] & at the shoulders it would have been over a metre high. I didn't shine the torch into its eyes on purpose but it gave me a chance to see the rest of it & as soon as it became accustomed to the dark it leapt clean over my van & into the night & the Wed night of the same week my wife saw it sitting on our fire wood pile about eight metres from the back door.

Yes it's true it is a regular visitor to my property. It's very inquisitive, & I hope one day I will be able to hand feed it. It's a beautiful looking animal & I believe it's a female. I could be wrong but as we all know opposites attract. One thing I've noticed is when we get the moon from about half to full & past it's never around but other than that it's here most nights. Also I've noticed if there has been a strange car on my property it wouldn't come too close but of late it doesn't seem to worry, so given time I know I will befriend it. My wife has a pet lamb & he knows when the cat is around, as it's the only time he goes to his pen of his own accord. I also run 13 ewes & a ram & there's been no problems with them & on Monday night this week it walked down our back path from one end of the house to the other. We were in bed at the time & it was too dark to see it but it stopped at our bedroom window which is always open, as we listened to it sniffing at the fly screen & I spoke to it as I quite often do when it's close, & we know it's by our water tank & watches at night when we play cards.

So who said life is boring down at the farm? I might add that Mr Bowles opened the letter by stating he had misplaced the *Post* article. If he hadn't I would have thought he was taking the description directly from the photograph of a cougar on the second page. It must be an exceptionally large one.

At the same time (1989) the Thorpes were building their home on the outskirts of the town while living in a shed. John Thorpe went out one night to investigate a movement near the construction site. Wife Evelyn and daughter Elizabeth stood by the shed shining a spotlight into the long grass. Suddenly, to their horror, they saw a large, sandy-coloured cat crouching and circling behind John as if preparing to attack. As they screamed warnings, and trained the light on it, the beast took off, but it has been seen regularly since, and was reported to have eaten the cat's food left out the back[16].

He is not the only one to have such an experience. It is reported (it is not certain in what year) that a timber cutter who knew nothing about the cats was casually following a trail in the Yarloop/Waroona area when he had a feeling he was being watched. Turning, he was horrified to see a big black cat stalking him. Fortunately, he was able to drive it away by turning on his chain saw. A better documented experience was that of a member of the Mystery Animal Association of Western Australia, called Paul. In January or February 1980, while camping far to the northeast of Perth, he decided to go for a walk in the heat of the day with his dog, a big border collie. The dog suddenly startled a huge black cat, which raced up a nearby sapling. It was hard to tell who was the most terrified, the man or the cat. Both stood rooted to their respective spots for several minutes, then the cat came down, coughing and snarling, while the dog cowered behind its master until its adversary had fled. There had been only about 20 feet [6 m] separating them. Paul described it as taller than the dog, and at least 5 - 6 feet [1.5 - 1.8 m] long, including tail, with a broad face and large blue eyes. Its teeth were huge, and its paws as big as hands. And it was black[17].

The Association consists mostly of people who have had experiences with the mystery animals. When Sharon West decided to form it in late 1992 she wrote to several country newspapers. Within three months she had 70 reports, and they are still coming in[18].

It is hard to know where to start. Black cats heavily outnumber those of light colours. High pitched nocturnal screams are almost *de rigueur*. Then there are the footprints. Those found near Northcliffe in 1993 were as big as a man's hand[19]. Ditto those at West Gingin the same year, where there had been a lot of screaming[20]. Mrs West herself measured prints at the edge of Waroona Dam, near Dwellingup. They were 13 cm [5 in] wide and long[21]. In the hills near Harvey (same year) the prints were 13 cm wide and 20 long[22]. All of these were probably made by dogs, for they are far too big for either a cougar or a black panther. However, there are also reports of dead kangaroos, many of them probably road kills, with their heads removed. A remarkable, not to mention horrible, predation technique was reported from Tambellup a few years before. Pregnant ewes had been had their genitals bitten and up to two kilos of flesh eaten from their vulvas while they were still alive. One ewe had actually worn a bare patch in the stubble trying to get away from her attacker. The fleeces of all these ewes were 3 or 4 cm thick. None of it had been torn out, but when the hapless animals were put down and shorn, the skin underneath was found to bear scratches a centimetre or so in depth[23].

Meanwhile, at Kendenup reports have been coming in, not only of a black cat, but of another the size of a German shepherd, with a long tail, and the face of a lynx. Its colour is said to vary from dark brown to bluish black, but with light brown spots the size of oranges[24]. I rather hope that is a lighting effect. I also rather hope that the residents of the Lake Clifton-Mandurah area are mistaken. The silvery grey cat of Lake Clifton sounds almost normal compared to the striped cat of Melros, while on 7 June 1993 a bear turned up in a back yard. It stood on its hind legs, and left scratch marks on the asbestos fence over which it escaped[25].

But it is in Victoria that the hunt is really on. Here, as In Western Australia, a Parliamentarian has got involved. Tom Austin, the Member for Ripon has been pressuring the government to take action, and has become the patron of the Central Victorian Predator Research Foundation[26].

It is also the home of Rare Fauna Research (RFR)[27], which we met briefly in the last chapter. This dedicated band of amateurs contains between thirty and forty associates from all over the state, and beyond, plus three main investigators, Bernie Mace, Peter Chapple and Nick Costello. Both Bernie and Peter took a year off their respective careers to do fieldwork full time. As secretary of the group, Peter's home is full of newspaper cuttings, eye witness reports, and casts of footprints.

The activities of this group beggar description. Set up in late 1984, by February 1987 they had amassed files on 4,000 sightings of anomalous creatures, mostly cougar-like, but 900 thylacine-like[28]. By October 1988 they had completed 708 night drives and 243 extended field trips. Peter Chapple comes from Silvan, in the Dandenongs, and had heard rumours of the big cat, but he had spent many hours in the bush, and tended to scoff at anyone who claimed to have seen one. He will never forget the precise moment he became a believer. It was 10.45 pm on 9 August 1981, and he was negotiating a bush trail near his home town.

> The moon was out and my torch nearly so. I switched it off to preserve what was left of the battery, but as I neared a bend in the track, the moon most unreasonably went behind a dark cloud. I switched the torch on again to see around the turn, and shone the beam straight into the eyes of a huge grey cat less than three metres away. If I had fainted and fallen forward, I would have headbutted it! As best I can say, it stood about 60 cm at the shoulder, was uniform silver-grey in colour, with very fierce bright eyes and upright, but fluffy-looking ears, rather like those of a koala. At no stage have I ever intimated this was a puma, but I believe that most, if not all, the other big cats I have seen were pumas[29].

Earlier, he had given the distance as five feet [1.5 m], which sounds more reasonable[30], but at the time that was the last thing on his mind. The animal let out a strange growl. He switched off the torch and stood, terror-struck, waiting for the attack. A few seconds later he switched it on again. The beast was gone, as if it had never existed. He cannot remember how he got back to the main road, except that he hurt his back in the process.

The second time he was more composed. It was 12 February 1983, about 7.45 pm daylight saving time, and still fairly light. His girlfriend was using a public phone at Yarra Junction. He glanced across the nearby paddock and watched a black animal sniffing around in a nearby paddock about 100 to 150 metres away. Four or five minutes later, it looked up, and suddenly he realised it was a cat, heavy in the body, and small in the head, with pronounced ears and a long, thick, heavy tail. Casually, and arrogantly, it leaped over a small log, completely obscuring a larger log parallel to its body. Only when Peter was able to measure the larger log did he have any idea of the cat's size. It was two metres long and almost a metre high. That would make it as big as a lion or tiger.

Nick Costello had his conversion earlier. In early 1974 he was a passenger in a car which turned a bend near Erica. A black cat with a long tail, and a very muscular body four feet [1.2 m] long slinked across the road 20 yards ahead. Something similar was seen at Licola in 1979 at a greater range, only this one had the build of a tiger, and an estimated length of six or seven feet [1.8 - 2.1 m]. Both sightings occurred in daylight.

Peter then gave me a list of twelve sightings made by members of the group between July 1984 and July 1988. All took place at night. Half of the animals were black[31].

The following year they obtained photographic evidence. There were six witnesses to the photos from South Australia, but the one published[32] shows a black cat out of focus, and it would not be hard to fake it, if that were their intent. Another associate got two clear shots of a black cat the size of a doberman on a bush track in front of his car. To my knowledge, they have not yet been published.

It would be impossible to detail the hundreds of articles appearing in the Victorian regional newspapers, particularly the *Maryborough Advertiser*. John Higgins, the editor of said newspaper, even produced a detailed profile of the predator, based on the reports of several hundred people, including police and journalists[33]. While I am loathe to quote generalisations without information on the data on which they are based, it provides an excellent overview by one who has been following the situation for many years. Besides, as a professional journalist, his reports of individual incidents carry weight.

For instance, I don't know how much reliance can be put on the statements that small numbers of the predator were reported by the early settlers. But he did mention an animal with a 3½ foot [106cm] head and body length, and a tail more than two feet [61 cm] long caught in a trap at Kyneton in 1942. Later, a Maryborough man told how he had been playing beside the road between Halls Gap and Dunkfeld in 1944 or 1945 when he heard the sound of a chain dragging. Then he saw a black animal the size of a dog with a chain around its neck just 10 metres away[34]. Of course, it might have been a dog.

According to Higgins, the animal is invariably described as feline, and the size estimated as from six to nine feet [1.8 - 2.7 m]. It is similar to a lioness, but much more slender, and with a relatively small head. Ears, if observed, are reported to be small. The tail is nearly always mentioned, for it is nearly as long as the body, as thick as a man's forearm, and sweeps downwards with a definite upward hook at the end. There are two colour phases. One is sandy, ginger or brown, and the other slate blue to black. Pencil-like markings can be observed on the face, particularly of the lighter phase, with a darker line down the spine. Higgins gives examples of different coloured animals being seen together, and even of a brown female with a black cub. Any suggestion that feral dogs might be involved can be put to rest by three observations of the animal climbing trees. In one case, near Dunolly, a predator moved from tree to tree to effectively escape from a local councillor with a gun. Again, there are the familiar stories of blood-curdling screams in the dead of night, but a correspondent pointed out that they could quite easily have been made by the barking owl *(Ninox connivens)*, also known as the "screaming woman bird"[35]. This owl, incidentally, can also be heard in southwest Western Australia.

Stock killings are another matter. Time and again we read of farmers protesting that they know the work of dogs, and are convinced their lambs are being slaughtered by something quite different. According to Higgins[36], 20 to 30 lambs per property per season is quite normal, and he knew of losses as high as 80. He also lists adult sheep, goats, calves, a horse, kangaroos, rabbits, hares, koalas, young red deer and foxes. How he could be quite sure of all these, I don't know, but he did investigate one kangaroo kill which was still warm i.e. the predator had probably been disturbed by the man who found it. Marks on the ground recorded how the kangaroo had been chased 50 metres, and then dragged 200 metres into a high reed bed next to a creek. The neck was broken, without any puncture marks, but a circular wound was found on the groin, so clean there was not a trace of blood. There was also a set of punctures on the shoulder, and four deep gashes on the chest, with the same spread as a man's extended fingers. Interestingly enough, when they searched the reed bed they found a whole collection of dead sheep, lambs and kangaroos of various ages. That description alone should be sufficient to prove that something foreign is in the area. This was the work of a cat, and nothing but a cat. Higgins also claimed that livestock tend to be killed by biting the neck or choking or, in the case of larger animals, by dislocation of the neck. Sometimes the heads are bitten clean off as at Bridgetown, W.A.

He then went on to describe the predator's typical eating habits. Students of the Western Australian (not to mention North American) scene will find nothing out of place. The kill is dragged onto the tops of rocks, into creek beds, or otherwise sheltered areas. In one area there is a small depression behind a couple of thistles which is littered with lamb feet. A couple of miles up the road the prey are eaten in an empty dam. Invariably, a small opening is made in the groin, and the intestines and internal organs consumed. Often grass is then scratched over the half-eaten carcass, but on the second night the rest of the animal goes. Typically, it is extracted completely through the hole in the groin, leaving only the ribs and spine in a covering of skin. As an alternative, the whole skin is peeled away back to the neck and turned inside out. Nothing more unlike the usual doggy blood-and-guts approach could be imagined. Those, then, are Higgins' generalisations, and all the newspaper reports I've seen of killings tend to bear him out[37]. Together they spell one word: CAT.

The Bung Bong killings, for instance, were widely publicised, as well as being investigated by my friend, Paul Cropper[38]. Bob Crook, owner of 1000 ewes, had lived in the area for 40 years, and didn't believe the predator stories. That was until 24 April 1990, when he started losing two or three lambs a night, until the score came to 60. The remains (some good photos were provided) fitted Higgins' stereotype exactly except (Paul said) that they were eaten in the open, while a creek bed would have provided good shelter a few hundred yards away. Whatever ate them was not small; some of the ribs and leg bones were bitten clean through. Then, on 7 June several people watched a big cat moving around a rocky outcrop just a few kilometres away. The outcrop, Paul discovered, overlooked a creek which fed into the creek near to Mr Crook's property.

Then there was Geoff Woess, who was driving along minding his own business when a black cat leisurely crossed the road 100 metres in front[39]. It was bigger than an Alsatian, with a tail a metre long, and on the wet ground where it entered the bush it left four good prints. Not only was Mr Woess a former sceptic, but he owns a private zoo near Maryborough with a lion, a lioness, a puma and a black panther. In fact, he was on record as saying that he would have thought it was his own cat if he didn't know it was locked up. Rob Wallis, of Moyston, does not own a zoo, but he had been a zoo warden in England, and knows big cats. So when he made a cast of a footprint 13 cm long and 10 cm wide, he took it to the curator of mammals at Melbourne Zoo, Ernst Weiher. According to the latter, it could have been from a jaguar or a leopard, but was more likely a puma[40]. In fact, the only reason he did not treat it as proof of pumas in Australia was that Mr Wallis could not prove he got it in the Grampians. I myself am not completely convinced by the photo, and it must be considered outsized.

Nevertheless, Mr Wallis told Paul Cropper that he had seen the Grampians beasts three times[41]. About 6 am one day in January 1971 he was photographing birds at Lady Sumner's Bridge, on the road from Ararat to Halls Gap, when his sons called out to him. Out of the scrub walked two pumas, smoky grey and speckled with fawn. Some nearby kangaroos froze in terror, but the cats ignored them all as they passed just six metres in front of him, then casually crossed the bridge. But they had chosen their moment well. He had just finished shooting a roll of film. Then, around 12.30 pm in July 1989, he stepped outside his door for a smoke when a piercing scream, which he immediately recognized as a puma's, came from 100 metres in front of him, and went on for three or four minutes. The day before, his neighbour had found a dead sheep on his property - no need to tell you how it had been killed. A week later, he had just driven past Moyston en route to Ararat when he passed a cat sitting, staring up at tree. Seated, it was about a metre tall, totally fawn except for some white and black markings near the ears. That was at 6.35 am.

Just ten days later, he was returning from Moyston and approaching the edge of a nature reserve when an animal ran across the road in front of him. He had it in view for 10 seconds. It looked like a puma, but its fur shone jet black. Even its long tail was shiny. Its head was round, and held lower that its powerful shoulder blades. Wallis went white and cold at the sight of its rippling muscles. From nose to tail tip it would have been 8 feet [2.4 m], and he estimated its weight at 200 pounds [90 kg]. When Paul visited the place, along with Bernie Mace of Rare Fauna Research, they heard of another sighting 14 km away.

These are not the only sightings by zoo keepers. I have at least one other recorded in my files, plus individual sightings by three different policemen and a policewoman. A black animal with "large, luminous green eyes" was sighted just outside of Kyneton at 12.30 am 14 March, 1993. Too big to crawl under a gate standing half a metre off the ground, it left massive footprints to be examined by the police as soon as it was light. They were said to be 7 feet [2.1 m] apart[42]. In the Euroa district a man called Neville has been hunting the cats for years. One day in 1993, his hunting mate, Peter flushed a black cat at a distance of 20 yards, but its weaving flight among the trees made it impossible to shoot. Neville then managed to flush it again by releasing the dogs, but again the prey escaped[43].

Cats can be curious and, apart from that last one, these have been given few reasons to fear man. Higgins has heard stories of people being followed by them, invariably at a distance of 50 metres, halting every time the human does[44]. They themselves don't like people following them, but will sometimes allow a person to walk parallel to them for up to two kilometres. Curiosity got the better of one female. Having watched a person enter an outhouse, she and her two cubs went down to inspect it. (Best cure for constipation ever devised.) Another time, the same trio copied the work of their Bridgetown, W.A. compatriots, and rocked a caravan. Another frightening encounter recorded by Higgins was that of a husband and wife gold prospecting team. Having just descended a very deep hole, they heard the sound of an animal bounding, then looked up to see the puzzled expression of a huge cat staring down at them. Thirty seconds later, its curiosity satisfied, it wandered away. (We are not told whether the couple did too.)

One could repeat accounts of sightings until the brain goes numb. There is a weary sameness about them. At night or in broad daylight, the witnesses are certainly they were seeing cats. The size is generally compared to an Alsatian or doberman, or (say) 60 cm at the shoulder.

Where the colour was given, I counted 42 references to black animals and 24 to grey or brown ones. However, I suspect many people don't bother mentioning colour if it is nondescript, so the proportion of blacks to lights might be more equal.

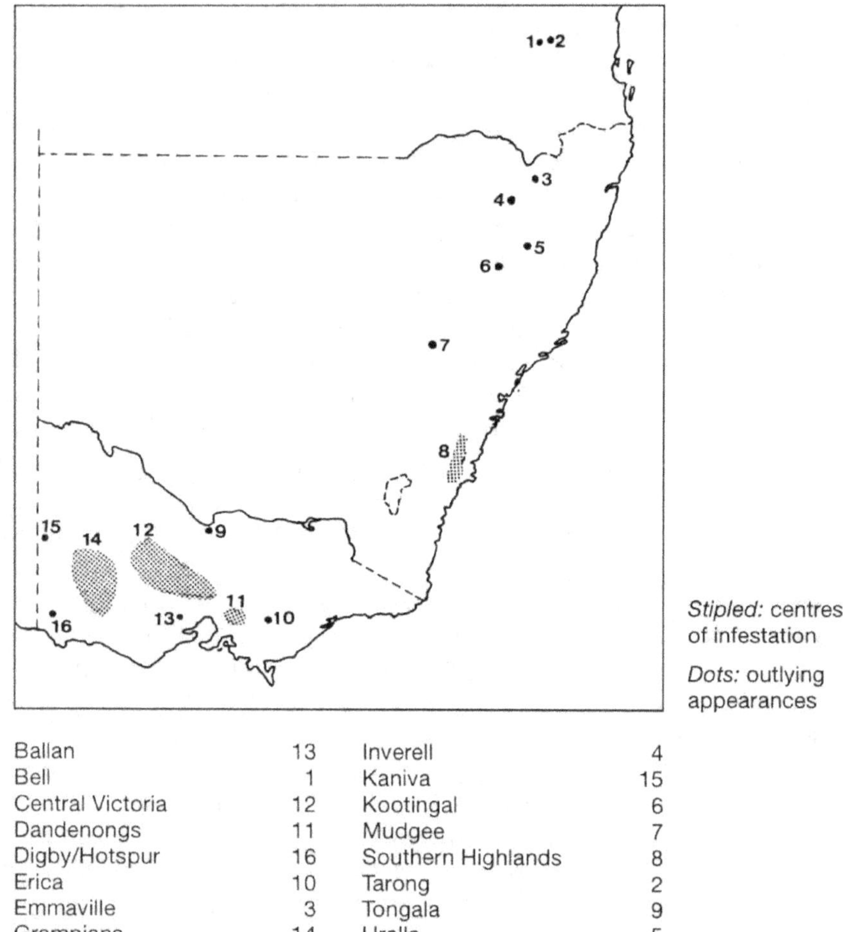

Ballan	13	Inverell	4
Bell	1	Kaniva	15
Central Victoria	12	Kootingal	6
Dandenongs	11	Mudgee	7
Digby/Hotspur	16	Southern Highlands	8
Erica	10	Tarong	2
Emmaville	3	Tongala	9
Grampians	14	Uralla	5

The Flinders and McIlwraith Ranges are outside the limits of the map.

Map 5B Big Cat reports from the Eastern States

It might be germane to ask where all these sightings are taking place? Southeast South Australia is geographically part of Victoria, and I have already mentioned the photo taken by a South Australian. This, you might recall, is thylacine country. I hope they leave each other alone. It would be a sad irony if the thylacine were to make a comeback on the mainland only to be wiped out by an introduced predator. It appears they are present even further west, in the Flinders Ranges. Wally Davies claims that the first sighting was at Parachilna in 1978, when a family was sleeping out on the veranda. A man awoke and thought he saw someone crawling on hands and knees among the sleepers. Then he saw the tail[45]. Wally himself saw the beast when he took some children to a gorge for a barbecue. The children went off down the creek to look for cougar tracks, and found them. Wally followed them to a rock formation, when out of the rocks came a roar like a speeding truck being thrown into low gear. After lunch they came back and saw a yellow cat about 50 yards away. He estimated its length as 6 or 7 feet [1.8 - 2.1 m]. He also made the point that cougars are not supposed to be able to roar. However, this appears to have been a call of aggression, rather than the deep roar given by lions and leopards as a territorial display.

The westernmost sighting I know of in Victoria was between Digby and Hotspur[46]. One hundred and fifty kilometres to the north, at Lemon Springs, south of Kaniva, on the edge of the Little Desert, Mrs Gwen Sambel heard the usual screeches, followed by throaty rumbles i.e. it was unlikely to be a barking owl. This is mostly low country. By and large, however, reports emanate from the forested highlands. The whole of the Grampians have produced innumerable reports, westward from a line from Natimuk, the Black Range, Glenisla, and Dunkfeld, and including the whole of the National Park (a frightening thought)[47]. From there the reports follow the highlands from the Pyrenees to Wedderburn, and east to Kyneton, Lancefield, Kilmore, Pyalong, Metcalfe, Redesdale, and everywhere in between. There is an isolated (?) sighting as far north as Tongala, near the Murray River[48], while further south a black beast "like a little Shetland pony" appeared on a farm 8km from Ballan, on the Western Highway[49].

It is sobering to think that one has a chance to see the mystery predator just a few hours' drive from the boundaries of Melbourne - in any direction. Rare Fauna Research did its early work to the east, in the Dandenongs, at such sites as Mt Evelyn, Montrose, Yarra Junction, Olinda and Emerald[50]. Indeed, one amusing story from the region of Emerald was told to me by the grandson of the witness. A quarter of a century ago, he was practising his hobby of painting when a black panther wandered out in front of him. With admirable aplomb, he calmly added the cat to the painting. I've been told it is still hanging in his widow's room in a southern nursing home. The easternmost record I have is Nick Costello's first encounter at Erica, already described. Since the centres of human settlement tend to thin out in these highlands, I suspect the scarcity of reports reflects a scarcity of witnesses rather than predators. Even so, it means an east-west range of 300 km - not bad for an animal that's not supposed to be there.

A major mystery of these alien cat outbreaks is that they are separated by such great distances. When I was still a student, in 1974, a zoology graduate told me of rumours of a cougar in the Kosciusko National Park, but I have heard nothing since. Other than that, the next closest centre is the Southern Highlands of New South Wales, from Mittagong south to Milton, and west to the Morton National Park. That's hundreds of kilometres from Victoria. Paul Cropper interviewed dozens of witnesses, most of whom had never spoken to the press, and some of whom requested anonymity[51]. Because his report was abbreviated, I was initially unimpressed. (After all, one likes more from a description than "cat like".) However, even in the unlikely event of farmers being unable to tell a cat from a dog, it is surely significant that the animals should be so big, and consistently black.

The earliest sighting appeared to have been in 1966, when Sam Knight saw in his paddock a huge black cat which put his two dogs to flight. That was in the early morning. The fat hit the fire in 1975 when retired naval officer, Raymond Noakes phoned the National Parks and Wildlife ranger. His 15 year old granddaughter had just seen a black panther, a metre high at the shoulder in broad daylight. Then his neighbour saw it. He had also glimpsed it a few months before. Altogether, ten people, including the ranger followed a trail of footprints for almost a mile [1.6 km]. A cement cast revealed them to be cat-like, four-toed, and 13 cm by 14 cm. Within the next few days 32 more people had reported sightings.

There is a distinct sameness about all the eyewitness reports. A sense of *déjà vu* settles in for anyone who has followed the Western Australian and Victorian scene. But I must mention the tale of Roman Sega. On 15 November 1977, he shot a black cat with a 60 cm tail in the Cambewarra Range, just north of Nowra. However, when Paul examined the skin, he felt it was nothing more than a large feral cat. Needless to say, there were many more footprints. One was "5 times the size of dingo prints", and Paul got a copy of a cast 4 inches by 5 [10 x 13 cm]. The sightings continued for years. It would be impossible to list all the reports. Sometimes the cats were jet black, sometimes fawny grey or brown. One witness saw a black one and a fawn one travelling together.

Mudgee became a new centre in 1992, when a woman saw a black panther cross the Ulan Road that January[52]. Then in March, Steve McLachlan of Green Gully was awakened by the barking of his dogs, and saw a large black animal on his property.

The Emmaville Panther became a local legend in the years 1958 to 1962, though I'm afraid I haven't sighted the original sources[53]. Haunting a stretch of New England 150 km long from Emmaville to Uralla, it was seen not only by locals, but passers through, such as Sydneysiders, Wallace Lewis (1959) and Mr E. Drewett (1962). In the period 1956-57, Clive Berry of Pretty Gully, near Uralla, lost 340 sheep. I shall spare you the familiar details of how they were killed. His neighbour, Mrs. S. Godley send a plaster cast of a footprint to Sir Edward Hallstrom, chairman of the Taronga Park Trust. The good knight at once offered £1000 reward for the maker, dead or alive, because the print did not resemble that of a dingo or dog. It matched that of the zoo's tiger.

The limited time span of the sightings would suggest transient individuals rather than a breeding population. Except - Paul Cropper knows of a second set of Emmaville sightings from 1969 to 1973. He also heard of a sighting at Watson's Creek about 1911. In 1989 or 1990 Wayne Spence saw what he thought was a black dog on the road near Tintinhull, also in the New England area. But when he got closer (it was dusk) he realised it was more like a panther. Next, a Tamworth man, Ron Campbell-Murdoch spoke up and told how he and his family saw something similar northwest of Inverell 15 years before - four times in fact[54]. Finally, Merv Thompson of Kootingal, wrote this letter to Paul:

> On the 28th July 1988, I was walking along the New England Highway. At 6.30 am in the morning, I noticed (the panther) walking in the paddock next to the road. It was about 50 mtrs away from me. I sneaked up behind a pine tree on the edge of the road to get a better look at it. The animal was walking very casually, then it kneeled down on all four paws. It was eating something. I watched it for about 2 minutes. It got up and started to walk towards the fence that was running up the hill to a corner post. It leapt on to the post and over the other side. The animal I saw that morning was too big to be a domestic cat. It was black all

You can't get it much plainer than that. The conclusion is obvious: New England is in the process of being colonised. Now it is Queensland's turn. On 15 February 1995 Robert Postlethwaite was driving between Bell and Kumbia, not far from Kingaroy, when he saw what he initially thought was a kangaroo with a black coat. Then it turned around, and he was looking at the face of a cat - a cat the size of a great dane, with a long tail and a glossy black coat. It was broad daylight - only 2 in the afternoon. The witness's uncle had also sighting something similar close to the nearby Tarong Power Station[55].

The other major sighting I know of from Queensland is a bit of a worry. It happened in the rainforest of the McIlwraith Range, nearly 1800 km to the north. In the early 1970s Dietrich and Patricia Stehle spent twelve months in Cape York making a documentary film, *A Vanishing Frontier* but - as usually happens - they did not have their camera set up when the following occurred:

In the face of all this evidence, can anybody seriously doubt that the southern states are in the grip of a mystery predator infestation? Even the doubters must surely concede that the high rates of stock loss make a thorough scientific study imperative.

What is it?

A marsupial? Hardly. The cat-like traits are too perfect. Admittedly, marsupials have exhibited remarkable convergent evolution with Northern Hemisphere mammals. There are marsupial mice which mimic shrews, a thylacine which looks like a wolf, and a Tasmanian devil which fills a similar niche to the hyaena. There was even a marsupial big cat, by the name of *Thylacoleo* (see Chapter 3). But in each case the similarity to the placental counterpart is only in overall structure. This animal is a cat in every detail.

A native Australian big cat? Even less likely. Australia is marsupial country. The only placental land mammals which arrived without the aid of man were bats, which flew here, and rodents. And the rodents themselves are descendants of only three invasions, by animals which are very small, and easily transported on floating vegetation. A big cat getting here is almost out of the question.

Both these hypotheses assume that the predator has been here all along. That would at least solve one perplexing problem: the vast distances between infestations. The animals, for example, would have crossed the Nullarbor in the days when the climate was more amenable. But it still leaves one big question unanswered: how come it was never noticed by the early settlers, despite its propensity for stock killing, and why did the Aborigines apparently know nothing about it?

No, it's got to be an introduced cat. And, by eliminating all those with manes, stripes and spots, we are left with two possibilities: the cougar and the black panther, of which the latter is simply a black variant of the leopard or jaguar. Now, it is unlikely that two big cats got in under the noses of the quarantine inspectors. Moreover, there is every indication that they are interbreeding, something which would never normally occur in the wild. In addition, the cougar is the one big cat which cannot roar, and with the exception of Wally Davies' account, I know no report of the cat roaring. The inevitable conclusion is that the black cats are in fact cougars. If so, a real biological novelty is developing because, as I mentioned earlier, the black morph of the cougar is so exceptionally rare in its homeland it is virtually non-existent.

How did it get here? There are two main legends. One that crops up on both sides of the continent is of a circus van which overturned, allowing a breeding pair of cougars to escape. O'Reilly[57] had heard that story, so he searched the newspaper files for the relevant years, and came up with an interesting discovery. There was no circus accident - at least not in Western Australia. Not only that, but every exotic animal entering and leaving the state must be registered, and all the cougars were accounted for. Considering the paranoia all state governments have about introduced animals, and the fact that circuses value their big cats highly, the circus escapee story must be written off as a myth.

The second rumour is of U.S. servicemen smuggling a cougar litter into the country as mascots, and then, when discovery could no longer be avoided, releasing them into the bush. This story is heard across the whole of the southern states. Researchers have met several people with personal memories of the incident, but their memories are so disparate there would have to have been several separate releases.

Unfortunately, these neat stories have a few inherent difficulties. In the first place, cougars are extremely reclusive animals, especially so since they are persecuted on their home ground. Even in the U.S. it would be difficult to get hold of a litter. Secondly, they would have to have been kept hidden in the close confines of the troop ship, because if the top brass knew about them, it is unlikely they would have conspired to deceive the Australian authorities. (Some versions of the story have the litter brought ashore by submariners who, of course, have plenty of space to store contraband cats.) Thirdly, the youngsters would have to learn to hunt without the assistance of a mother. I can't imagine they could have been released at under three months and have any chance of survival, and six months is far more reasonable. All the time they would be growing big and strong on milk and meat, neither of which was in oversupply during the war, even among the Yanks.

One other thing: the big cat stories don't all start with the Second World War. There are isolated reports throughout the country going back decades before. The value of these stories is problematical. Not all are as well documented as the modern ones, and in many cases they rely on memories which are half a century or so old. The most reasonable assumption would be that at least some of them were true, and that they represented the initial phase of the infestation which has now reached epidemic proportions.

Finally, in 1989, an old lady broke her silence[58]. Irene Addinsall, 78, told how she had worked in the Land Army in 1943 on her uncle's station south west of Hamilton, Victoria. Nearby was a U.S. mechanised unit, and one of the soldiers had a light coloured puma with four kittens, three light and one dark. As the kittens grew up the mother got savage, and so did the commanding officer. So one night, while he was away, they put the family in a truck and released them at a creek near Halls Gap. And so, with a mother to protect and feed them, they were able to survive and spread out over the land.

But think of what it means! On the voyage over they must have kept a fully grown catamount, with all the surliness of an expectant or nursing mother, below decks among the bunks and/or machinery, hungry for meat. And somehow they got her off the boat without anyone noticing. No, I'm afraid I don't think too highly of Miss Addinsall's story. To be fair, it should be recorded that two years before Miss Addinsall broke silence, Bernie Mace, of Rare Fauna Research, heard the exact same story from an elderly man who claimed to have taken part in the dumping, and even mentioned Miss Addinsall's name.

From Western Australia comes another story[59]. Brian Lambley heard from his father he had been on a US warship anchored off Albany in 1942. Other reports suggest it was the supply ship *Holland*, involved in servicing submarines[60]. Anyhow, it carried, not one, but two adult cougars, a brown female and a black male. (The latter must have been the rarest cat in North America.) When told to get rid of them, they pushed them overboard 3 km off Denmark, then watched through binoculars as they swam ashore. The rest is history.

Now we only need to discover is how they managed to cross the Nullarbor.

Looking at it all dispassionately, I have to admit that the idea of pumas roaming the Australian bush is impossible. Unfortunately, the facts are still there. And facts will not go away merely for want of an explanation. There are a darned sight too many impossible things happening in this world.

ADDENDUM

This is one area where the amount of additional information - sightings, photos, even official Government reports - has been overwhelming. You could fill a book with it. In fact, a book has been filled with it: *Australian Big Cats* by Michael Williams and Rebecca Lang[61]. Like this book, it is print on demand, and so permanently in print, so I would advise you to acquire it as the definitive work on the subject, leaving me to simply follow up some of the threads from the original chapter.

Shortly after the first edition came out, Nick Costello, of Australian Rare Fauna Research, sent me a draft of his proposed book, *Big Cats in the Back Paddock*. He later published it as a CD, covering a lot of the issues in the Victorian scene in particular.

One thing I found quite impressive was an initiative undertaken by Rare Fauna Research under the instigation of Peter Chapple. He reasoned that predators, like every other species, are creatures of habit, and therefore patrol their hunting grounds according to a timetable. By noting the date and time of sightings, the direction of travel of the animal, plus stock killings, and even the frenzied barking of dogs, it would be possible to establish its pattern of movements, and predict where it would turn up next. Thus, in 1986, they headed down one of the Dandenong country roads and - lo and behold! - a big cat crossed their path as predicted.

This was a genuine scientific investigation. If it had been undertaken, for example, in North America by qualified zoologists, the scientific community would have sung its praises. It is the sort of thing which should be written up in detail in a peer reviewed journal - say, the *Journal of Cryptozoology*.

The maps in this chapter were produced by my plotting all the sites I could find in the literature, but I have to admit that they were inadequate, Shortly after their publication, Peter Chapple told me that there would hardly be a town in Victoria which would not have had its sighting, and Williams and Lang's book also covered a lot more of New South Wales.

I myself live in Brisbane, and towards the end of the chapter I indicated that my home state was now in the process of being colonised. Unlike in the two southern states, big cats had received little publicity in Queensland (and that is still the case), so the witnesses were not interpreting their sightings according to social expectations. However, once the book was published, new information started coming in. In those days, once I had a lead, it was a simple matter of looking up the witness' name in the White Pages, but it might be more difficult these days, since many people no longer possess land lines, and mobile phone numbers are normally not listed, least of all with addresses.

In 1997 I was able to contact someone with unassailable credentials: a senior conservation officer with the Queensland Parks and Wildlife Service, called Bruce Thomson, who had collected, and in some cases, investigated, sightings on the Toowoomba Range, Haden, the Bunya Mountains, and south of Texas, which is on the New South Wales border.

One of the best encounters occurred near Miles in early 2000, possibly in February. Christine Stiller lives on a farm on the Darling Downs, but at the time was working in Miles, and she left work about half past five. The sighting would have occurred ten or fifteen minutes later, in broad daylight. Miles ends at a river. Six kilometres to the west, on the south side of the Warrego Highway, stands an historical site, a marker of pioneer graves. The sighting took place about 100 metres before that. The area is open woodland, and at the time the grass was green and lush. At this point the ground dips down about two or three feet from the edge of the bitumen producing, by design or default, a watercourse for the drainage of run-off. Christine referred to it as a "creek", but it would be better described as a depression running parallel to the road. She was driving along when she saw the animal feeding off a kill, possibly a kangaroo, in the depression, and immediately backed up for a closer view. The distance was no more than four metres at the very most. It raised its head, and she saw the blood on its muzzle. Although, when she later described it to her husband, he told her it was probably a pig dog, she was convinced it was a black panther. It was about the size of a pig dog ie it probably would have come up to her hip, but it was totally black, and sleek, whereas pig dogs are scruffy. There were no pointed ears, and the body and head were thick set. She later showed me a picture of a leopard, and said that the head was exactly the same, except black. Its tail was not dog-like.

I know Mrs Stiller well because, half a year later, I married her sister. I interviewed her in May 2001, and inspected the site two days after that, whereupon it became obvious that nobody could be mistaken at such a short distance in broad daylight.

Bit by bit, I started collecting reports from all over southeast Queensland, almost as far north as Bundaberg. However, as space is limited, I shall refer you to my blog, where the details are provided[62]. Apart from a couple of references by Williams and Lang, I have not found any evidence of big cats in the central coast area of Queensland (yet!), but there was a second cluster of sightings in the far north of the state. Several of them came from the Atherton Tableland, in the same general region as the alleged thylacine investigated by Dr. John Winter. I hope the new predator doesn't drive out the old! Both black and tawny cats were involved, and one report went back to 1974. I also interviewed witnesses from Cape York Peninsula, and the chief ranger of the Iron Range National Park shared with me the reports in his park's "sightings book".

The most remarkable witness I interviewed was Mrs Kerry Morgan, who lived on a property about 20 km from Cooktown. In 1998 she told me that, over the previous two years, her family had lost 50 to 55 goats. At one point she saw, in broad daylight, at a distance of about 150 metres, a big cat pick up a goat in its mouth and carry it away. Obviously, anything which could do this would have to be pretty big. Compared to the size of the goat, she felt it was as big as a lioness. Certainly, it was larger than a big, big dog. It was cinnamon in colour, and was smooth and silky, with an agile, catlike movement. The face was roundish and it had a fluffy tail. I asked some misleading questions about the tail, and got some misleading answers. She said it was bushier than a fox's. Later on she saw a second cat, which was sandy in colour.

Not only that, but reports have been coming in from Tasmania[63]. Back in 1989 three people saw what they thought was a black panther two metres long at Lake Gordon. Three "panthers" were seen walking together near Great Lake in 1980, and as far back as 1960 a farmer from Mt. Arthur near Launceston watched a two metre long black cat kill a calf and carry it away.

I tell you, there is a dangerous, intrusive predator threatening our wildlife and livestock all the way along the seaboard and a couple of hundred kilometres inland all the way from the far west to the far north. I hope the scientific fraternity and the state governments eventually get around to doing something about it.

In 1985 a lioness was found devouring a sheep in a roadside culvert near Broken Hill, and shot by a police detective. Where did it come from? Two decades after the event, folklorist David Waldron was able to track down three of the police involved in the incident, and interview one. It turns out it had escaped in transit from a Lion Safari Park based on Wingfield, S.A[64]. So escapees were not completely unknown! However, it is important to note that it requires a breeding pair to produce a colony.

Dr. Waldron reported this in *Snarls from the Tea-Tree*, which I referenced in the addendum to Chapter 3, in which he also detailed the wild and woolly days of the nineteenth century exotic animal trade, including (p 19) "an escaped tiger on Little Bourke Street in Melbourne pursued by members of the Chinese community to the merriment of European onlookers." One wonders about the merriment if it had been the tiger doing the pursuing.

But enough of the individual incidents; we should now turn to the issue of identification. Now it is certain that, both in Australia and overseas, photos of feral, or even domesticated cats (*Felis catus*) have been misinterpreted as black panthers, we should start there. According to Dr. E. Denny, who contributed the article on feral cats to the Third

Edition of the definitive handbook, *The Mammals of Australia*[65], the most common coat colour is striped tabby ie thin dark vertical stripes on a lighter background, but also orange, black, and occasion tortoiseshell can be found. The head-body length (HB) for adult males (the larger sex) is given as 448 - 740 mm [17.6 - 29.1 inches], while tail length ranges from 235 to 345 mm [9¼ - 13½ in]. That's quite a variation. To put this into perspective, the equivalent measurements for male foxes are HB: 610 - 740 mm, tail 360-450 mm[66]. Do you get that? There are feral cats in the bush which are as big as foxes!

Now compare it to the big cats in question[67,68]. Size is not the only determinant. Thus, a domestic/feral cat's ears are pointed, set high on the head, and relatively close together, while those of the puma, leopard (of which the black panther is a colour phase), and even the jaguar (which also has a black phase) are rounded, low on the head and wider apart. While a house cat's head is rather delicate in shape, the leopard's is solid and square jawed. As for the puma, its head is rather small compared to the leopard's, as per Fig. 5.1, with dark markings on its face.

A house cat has a relatively short tail: only 30 to 60 per cent of the head-body length (HB). With a panther the ratio is 60 to 100 per cent, and the tip often curls upward. A puma's tail is 50 to 70 per cent of its HB, and it is thicker or more fluffy, again as per Fig. 5.1, with a dark tip. On the other hand, the ratio of a jaguar's tail to HB is similar to that of a house cat's, but its tip also has a tendency to curl upwards.

As far as big cats go, the male tends to weigh an average of 40 or 50 per cent more than the female. I have always been intrigued by the way so many witnesses cite the total length of an animal. It is hard enough to estimate the height and body length, without adding on a flexible, moving tail. It is far better to try for the HB length, along with the proportions of tail and HB. With this in mind, a puma's HB ranges from 1.05 to 1.95 metres [3 ft 7 in to 6 ft 3in] and it stands an average of 67½ cm [27 in] at the shoulder.

The leopard is extremely variable in size, according to sex and race, with the jaguar is a similar range. The HB ranges from 1 to 1.9 metres [3ft 4 in to 6ft 3 in], with a shoulder height 45 to 80 cm [18 in to 2 ft 8 in]. However, although black panthers tend to come from Asia and such places as Ethiopia, the very biggest leopards hale from Sri Lanka. This is because that island has never possessed tigers or lions, so the leopards have evolved a larger size to hunt the prey which would have been the perquisite of these larger cats. It is an evolutionary process known as "niche expansion": something we will need to remember.

Believe it or not, but over the last quarter century a number of photos and video clips of our ABCs have appeared. When Dr. Darren Naish, a prominent British zoologist and science writer with a sympathetic interest in mystery animals, examined them, he noticed two things. Firstly, although it was difficult to estimate size, from the adjacent vegetation and other items, they appeared very big ie apparently exceeding a metre in total length. But the weird thing was that they didn't look like leopards or other cat species, but rather like "gigantic specimens of *F. catus*." He felt there was circumstantial evidence that feral cats in Australia had reached enormous sizes[69].

Finally, in October 2005 the Big Story broke, with photos of a huge black cat shot by 67-year-old Kurt Engel in June[70]. He was hunting deer in Gippsland at the time (the original story said "in rugged terrain near Sale", but later reports said Dargo, which is far more likely) when the monster charged out of the undergrowth. At the last moment it swerved towards the left, upon which he fired at close range, and a lucky shot entered its shoulder and smashed its head. Apparently, it didn't occur to him to call the press. Instead, seeing that the smashed head was no use as a trophy, he had some photographs taken with a disposable camera, then cut off, and skinned, the tail as a souvenir, after which he threw the carcass into a creek. He decided to go public only when a fellow hunter put Mr. Williams in contact with him.

At that point, the tail skin was sent to Dr. Hans Brunner, who has spent his entire career becoming Australia's leading hair expert, and he saw at once that it must have come from a domestic or feral cat.[71] Next, the tail went to Monash University, where a DNA test confirmed its owner's identity as a feral cat[72]. So now the truth was out: feral mega-cats really do exist, having evolved by niche expansion to take advantage of the larger prey available. But how big are they?

A British cat enthusiast claimed that giant cats were a myth, and that the genes for great size don't exist in cats. She also made the surprising statement regarding Engel's cat:

> The partially decomposed carcass was examined by a Rural Lands Protections Board vet, Dr Keith Hart, in 2006. The body was 34" (just under 3 ft) and the tail 14" (48" total length)[73].

I found that hard to believe because, firstly, I thought I would have heard about it myself, and because I knew Dr. Hart's jurisdiction was a long way from Gippsland, in the Sydney Basin and the adjoining Illawarra and Southern Highlands. Nevertheless, I wrote to him, and he replied that "It just goes to show you can't believe everything you read on the web." The only reason I mention this is that that specific piece of misinformation is still on the web.

So how big was Engel's cat? For this we have only two guides. The first is the skinned tail, with a reported length of 600 mm (?exactly). The second is the photographs[74]. Obtaining accurate proportions and dimensions from them is not easy, because of problems in perspective ie the cat was in the foreground, and the hunter in the rear. However, when Mr. Engel was interviewed by Williams and Lang, he showed them a photo of the cat hung from a beam of his cabin's verandah. Using this as a scale, they accepted his claimed measurement of 1850 mm [6 ft 1 in] from nose to tail[75], although later in their book (p 286) a figure of 170 - 176 cm was given.

This, of course, implies that the tail was half the HB length - which is about right for a feral cat, and consistent with the photographs, although it might have been a bit longer. As far as its length is concerned, two reservations have been expressed: (i) it is possible that the skin was deliberately or inadvertently stretched during tanning, and (ii) it would be possible for the length to be extended by including a strip of skin cut off from the back. Note that there are limits to which this chicanery can be performed. In any case, the second option can be ruled out. There exists a photo of Mr. Engel holding up the intact ie pre-skinned tail, and it is clear it had been cut off neatly at the base. Just the same, in comparison to his arm, my impression is that it was somewhat shorter - say 53 cm. However, I would not hold to this opinion.

Nevertheless, even if we reduce the overall length by ten per cent just to be on the safe side, it is obvious that this feline was far bigger than even the largest known feral cat, and within the lower size range for a leopard. Of course, there must be individuals of intermediate size linking the Gippsland cat with the known range of feral cat sizes. And, sure enough, on page 286 of their book, Williams and Lang introduce two specimens: shot by Larry Beppington in South Australia and "Alpine Man" in Victoria, whose total length were 117 cm and 123 cm respectively. Also, although it is difficult to estimate size at a distance, the most common comparison made by witnesses is that of a big dog such as a German shepherd. Moreover, I would like to take you back to page 192 of this book, which you probably passed over at first glance: how Paul Cropper examined the pelt of a cat shot by Roman Sega, and considered it was an overgrown feral cat. But the tail was 60 cm long, the same as for Kurt Engel's cat. And that was in 1977, in New South Wales.

So now the evidence is in. We know what the ABCs are. There are feral cats out there as big as foxes, as big as German shepherds, as big as small female leopards. Problem solved!

Or is it? There are still a few questions left unanswered.

1. With all the variety of coat colour in feral cats, the most common being striped tabby, why are these mega-cats all monochrome - in particular, black, fawn, or grey? I simply have no idea.

2. Are there, in fact, any mega-cats with more standard coat colours? Well, we might try the following article from Victoria in late 1955:

> A strange animal with a "blood-curdling yell," startled Fred Rollason, marine dealer, Inverloch Rd., Wonthaggi, and Mrs. Sturgess, at 7.30 a.m. Monday morning [28 Nov. 1955]. "And I hadn't been drinking," laughed Mrs. Sturgess, yesterday. "It was up a tree, big as a dog, large claws, large head, furry body, striped like a Zebra, and a long tail. When I heard the yell, I thought it was children looking for a lost calf. When it saw me it sprang 15-ft. to the ground and disappeared. I've seen goannas, wild cats and foxes, but was none of them." Asked if the animal resembled a tiger, Mrs. Sturgess said, "More like anything I can think of. I didn't get a long look at it." A circus passed through Wonthaggi last month, but did not report any missing animals. Mr. Crosbie Morrison said last night[76].

For the next eight months sporadic and confused reports came in concerning the "monster"[77]. To the extent that any resembled the original sighting, they were consistent with a very large feral tabby, but perhaps not in the mega-cat range. You can see why I said, in the addendum of Chapter 3, that I have reservations about modern reports of a marsupial tiger, at least outside of north Queensland. Nevertheless, reports of "tigers" are close to non-existent among ABCs, so one is forced to confess that striped tabbies, as well as tortoiseshells, hardly exist in the mega-cat range.

3. Is there any evidence of true big cats eg panthers or pumas, in addition to oversized feral domestic cats? Well, although size estimation at a distance may be unreliable, several close encounters are on file which imply much bigger animals. Remember Gerry Bowles near Bridgetown, WA, who had a big cat place its front paws on the top of his truck, its chest against the window. Admittedly, an Engel sized cat might have been able to do that in a pinch, but later he saw it at a distance of three metres - so close, in fact, that he was able to describe its features in enough detail to identify it as a puma. Then there was Peter Chapple's second encounter, of a cat which must have been a metre high and two metres long, because its body completely hid a certain log. Also, the ears of the first ABC he encountered were fluffy, like a koala's - which everyone knows are rounded, not pointed like a feral cat's. Remember, too, how Kerry Morgan watched a lioness-like animal carry off a goat in its mouth.

Goats, sheep, and wallabies are one thing, but what about larger prey? During 1982 and 1983, a series of stock killings occurred around Waterford, south of Brisbane, which the farmers attributed, rightly or wrongly to big cats. In December 1982 three sheep were found dead on one property. They had been herded into two separate dams and drowned, but their bodies were studded with puncture marks. More to the point, on the same night, on the neighbouring property of Gary and Shirley Russell, a horse had been attacked. The photo shows great horizontal slashes across it neck, left shoulder, and abdomen. No dog could have done that; I have to agree with its owners that a big cat must have jumped on its back[78]. And I doubt if even a mega-feral such Kurt Engel shot would have been big enough to tackle a horse.

In 2012 Drs. Menkhorst and Morison, of the Victorian Department of Sustainability and Environment, were tasked with producing an assessment of the presence of big cats in Victoria[79]. Their guarded conclusion was that: "The most parsimonious explanation for many of the reported sightings is that they involve feral individuals of the Domestic Cat *Felis catus*, such as the Kurt Engel specimen." Their guarded rejection of the existence of black panthers and pumas was based, in part, on the absence of specimens found on wildlife surveys, as well as their non-appearance in the hundreds of images taken by cameras triggered by heat and motion. (But then again, the feral mega-cats haven't been captured on camera either.) Nevertheless, they left the possibility open due to the reports of informed observers, and what they call the "Winchelsea faecal sample". And thereby hangs a tale[80].

It would be better to label it the "Wensleydale faecal sample", because it came from that locality some distance from Winchelsea, but adjacent to the Otway forests. In August 1991 a farmer reported unusual predation on calves and sheep to the Department of Conservation and Environment (DCE), as a result of which he was interviewed by a Land Protection Officer named David Cass. One thing led to another, and in November of that year Cass took possession of a dark, foul smelling turd which didn't appear to have passed through the bowels of either a dog, fox, or feral cat.

He promptly forwarded half the faecal sample to Dr. Barbara Triggs, the country's leading expert in mammal faeces. No doubt the average reader will consider this a rather bizarre speciality, but you can learn a lot from an animal's faeces about its food, parasites, and even distribution and population size, because it's a lot easier to locate faeces than the living animal. Thus, scatology, as it is known, is an important scientific discipline. It's a s****y job, but somebody's got to do it.

Once Dr. Triggs had received the sample, he also arranged for Dr. Helen McCracken, a vet at Melbourne Zoo to send her faeces from both a black leopard and a puma as a means of comparison. Cass also mailed the second half of the Wensleydale sample to Dr. Triggs.

Both the black leopard sample and the Wensleydale sample shared a strong, acrid stench quite different from any of the hundreds of dogs and fox scats she had dealt with previously. From the Wensleydale sample she managed to extract several black hairs which were presumed to have come from the animal's own fur, having been inadvertently ingesting during grooming. They turned out to be very, very similar to grooming hairs extracted from the known black leopard faeces. However, to be on the safe side, she forwarded the hairs to Dr. Brunner (remember him?) without providing any background information. He concluded that they were probably from a cat, *Felis catus*, but when told about the size and smell of the faeces, he replied that a panther could not be excluded.

And there the evidence initially rested. The hairs were sealed in a plastic bag, but in 1992 Cass turned them over to Dr. Stephen Frankenberg of La Trobe University. However, it was not until August 2000, when Frankenberg was in England, that he was able to analyse their mitochondrial DNA. It was almost identical to that of a leopard. He did not, however, publish it because of the very small possibility of contamination in Dr. Triggs' laboratory.

Nevertheless, from our point of view, on the balance of probabilities - indeed, on the basis of high probability - the hairs, and the huge, stinking faeces, came from a genuine black panther. And it is extremely unlikely that it was the only one in the area.

But let us leave that area for a while. There is another place which is not supposed to have any big cats - indeed, any feline natives at all - and that is the island of New Guinea. My wife, Esther grew up there. As she explained to me the day we met, she was born in New Guinea of missionary parents, and was carried home from hospital in a native string bag called a *bilum*. (She might also have added that she was protected from the monsoon by a cape of pandanus leaves, and was carried home over 30 miles of narrow, rugged jungle trails, and by horse and raft across flooded tropical rivers.[81]) Not long after we were married, a lady came to the front door collecting for charity. Noticing that she was carrying a bilum, Esther immediately said, "You come from New Guinea, don't you?" And that was how we discovered that another missionary offspring, also called Esther, was living just a few doors away.

Esther Ingram has also led an interesting life - not least of all being sent to Australia to start school at the age of five, and being totally unable to speak English, or anything except the local Papuan language. And one of her most remarkable experiences was the one she described to me on 4 October 2003, in the presence of her father, the Rev. Ronald Teale, also a witness.

The event took place in December 1999 or January 2000 ie nearly four years before the date of the interview, on one of their periodic returns to the Pitanka Mission Station in the Eastern Highlands province of PNG. On the night in question, they were returning from Goroka. Esther and her father were in the front seat of an old Landcruiser, being driven by Esther's native foster brother, Moses Teale. The sighting occurred about 11 or 12 miles from Kainantu, on the Kainantu-Okapa Road, about midnight (Esther checked her watch). Because of the roughness of the terrain, their speed was no more than what would have been expected in a built-up area at home. Their lights were full on. The road was a very rough bush track, 10 or 12 feet wide, the surrounding countryside dense jungle. On the right, the land descended to a very wooded gully with a stream at the bottom. On the left stood an almost perpendicular embankment 12 or 15 feet high.

Suddenly, about 20 yards in front of them, what looked like a huge cat came out of the jungle on the right, and "trotted" leisurely across the road. "What on earth is that?" cried Esther to her father. "Slow down, Moses, so we can see!" As they approached within about six feet of it, it sprang straight up the embankment and disappeared. The sighting must have lasted only a few seconds.

It was very solidly built, and the head-body length was about five feet [1½m]. Both Esther and her father were amazed at how huge it was. So, too, was I, when she stated that it was as high as the table around which we were gathered: about 2½ feet. Yes, Esther agreed, it was probably twice as long as high.

Esther, in particular, made an attempt to study as many details as possible. (Remember, it was *very* close.) The basic colour was white, with ginger "trimmings" on the tail and ears. Pale gingery, vertical stripes, not terribly well delineated, appeared on the sides, but they did not extend to the back, or dorsal surface, which was completely pale. She specifically noted that the forepaws were cat-like, rather than (say) hoofed like a goat's. She didn't get a glance at the rear paws. The tail was ginger and very long, hanging to the ground. I enquired about bushiness *etc*, to establish a comparison with a dog's. She said it was a bit coarser or fluffier than the body, but not much. On the body itself, the fur was smooth.

The head was broad, short, flattish, and definitely cat-like. It did not protrude like a dog's. The ears were ginger, mottled with white, and hung down. They were not as long as a spaniel's, but they were definitely long and rounded, and gave every indication of being naturally floppy. It was this feature which amazed both of them (and me as well, as it doesn't sound anything like a cat's). Esther also thought she saw whiskers.

At Esther's insistence, I wrote to Dr. Tim Flannery, who identified it as a tree kangaroo. In response, Esther said that this was impossible. Both she and her father were quite familiar with tree kangaroos. The animal was much larger than a metre - more like five feet, or a metre and a half. (Note that this did not refer to the total length, but merely the head-body length, which is always less than a metre in tree kangaroos.) The tail was quite unlike a tree kangaroo's, although it did reach the ground. It was thin like a cat's, with a bit of a tuft at the end. The hindquarters were not raised, as a tree kangaroo's would have been (because, although a tree kangaroo's hind legs are proportionally shorter than a regular kangaroo's, they are still longer than the fore legs). The forepaws resembled a cat's, not a tree kangaroo's.

So there you have it.

Then Esther recalled an event which took place at Pitanka a week or so before her sighting. The watchman told her he had approached the tea tree plantation when he heard dogs barking, and he saw a big white cat jump from one tree to another. Some of the people at the Pitanka school reported a white animal streaking into the bush. Some of the ex-pupils also spoke of black cats.

Back in Australia, still in 2000, Esther went to the airport to pick up a missionary's widow, Ruth B, who lived at Famu, just across the mountain from Pitanka. "You have white ones, and we have black ones," said Ruth. She had seen a photo of a black panther in a magazine, and claimed they existed at Famu.

So, what is going on? Do alien big cats now exist in Papua New Guinea, and if so, where do they come from? If not, what did Esther, her father, and her foster brother see? The watchman had no doubts about the identity of his white animal. It was a *masalai* (*muss*-a-lye): a hobgoblin or evil spirit.

I am not in a position to refute it.

REFERENCES

[1] Karl P.N. Shuker (1989) *Mystery Cats of the World. From blue tigers to Exmoor Beasts*. Robert Hale: London, updated and republished in 2020 as *Mystery Cats of the World Revisited: blue tigers, king cheetahs, black cougars, spotted lions, and more*. Anomalist Books.

[2] Anthony Bourke and John Rendall (1971) *A Lion Called Christian*, William Collins, expanded second edition 2009, Bantam Press

[3] David O'Reilly (1981) *Savage Shadow. The search for the Australian cougar*. Creative Research: Perth, and since republished, POD, by Strange Nation Publishing

[4] Eric R. Guiler (1985) *Thylacine : the tragedy of the Tasmanian tiger* Oxford University Press.

[5] Robert L. Downing and Virginia L. Fifield *Differences between tracks of dogs and cougars*. Pamphlet published by Worcester Science Center, Massachusetts Eastern Cougar Survey Team.

[6] Brian Pash *The Sunday Times* (Perth) 12 Nov. 1972, quoted in O'Reilly (ref. 3) pp 39-41

[7] Brian Pash *The Sunday Times* (Perth) 18 Nov. 1972, quoted in O'Reilly (ref. 3) pp 41-44

[8] Brian Pash *The Sunday Times* (Perth) 8 May 1975, quoted in O'Reilly (ref. 3) pp 44-45

[9] J. Richard Greenwell (1989) The eastern puma: evidence continues to build. *The ISC Newsletter* 8(3): 1-8

[10] Sharon West (1994) Mystery Animal Association of Western Australia, *Newsletter* no. 7, pp 5, 6, 9

[11] O'Reilly (ref. 3), p 216

[12] Pauline Staples (1991) 'New panther sighting.' publication thought to be the September 1991 edition of the *Albany Advertiser.*

[13] Rebecca Poultney, 'Sighting gives new life to mystery of southern panther.' *Albany Advertiser* 21 Jan. 1992

[14] Mike Edmondson, 'Beasts rip off lambs' heads.' *Australasian Post* 17 Nov. 1990, pp 3 - 5

[15] Shuker (ref. 1), plate 1, facing p 45

[16] Edmondson (ref. 14)

[17] Sharon West (1993) Mystery Animal Association of Western Australia. *Newsletter* No. 5.

[18] Sharon West (1993) Mystery Animal Association of Western Australia. *Newsletter* No. 1.

[19] West (1993), *Newsletter* No. 1, p 3

[20] West (1993), *Newsletter* No. 2, p 3

[21] West (1993), *Newsletter* No. 5, p 4

[22] West (1993), *Newsletter* No. 5, p 5

[23] West (1993), *Newsletter* No. 2, p 3

[24] West (1993), *Newsletter* No. 1, p 3

[25] West (1993), *Newsletter* No. 3, p 5

[26] 'A foundation to research our predator'. *Wedderburn Express* 10 May 1990. 'Sponsorship now sought.' *Maryborough Advertiser* (Victoria) 12 June 1990

[27] Graham Holdstock (1988) 'Night stalkers. The hunt is on for Victoria's killer pumas.' *People* 14 April 1988, pp 6 - 9

[28] letter to author from Peter J. Chapple, dated 18 Feb. 1987

[29] letter to author from Peter J. Chapple, dated 14 Oct. 1988

[30] Holdstock (ref. 27)

[31] letter to author from Peter J. Chapple, dated 14 Oct. 1988

[32] Denise Dalgliesh (1989) 'Pumas prowl our bush.' *Australasian Post* 20 May 1989, pp 4 - 6

[33] John Higgins (1987)   Unpublished memo dated 16 Sept 1987. (This, like most of the Victorian newspaper articles quoted in this chapter, was sent to be by Paul Cropper.)

[34] 'Puma mystery has thickened.' probably *The Age* (Melbourne) 27 June 1989

[35] Dr Colin Officer (1990) "Was 'scream' a barking owl?" letter to *The Kilmore Free Press* 1st Aug 1990

[36] John Higgins (ref. 33)

[37] For instance, 'A foundation to research our predator' *Wedderburn Express* 10 May 1990; 'Lambs start to go in numbers', *Maryborough Advertiser* 22 May 1990; 'Farmer's grizzly find' 19 May 1992, 'Farmer says stock killer is cat' 23 June 1992; 'Sheep death shock for farmers after puma attack' *Bendigo Advertiser* 5 May 90.

[38] letter to author from Paul Cropper dated 19 July 1990, plus articles in the *Maryborough Advertiser* 29 May 1990 and 1st June 1990

[39] 'Geoff's puma hunt hope', *Sun* (Melbourne) 15 June 1980, *The Weekly Times* 1st Aug. 1990, pp 5 - 6

[40] Mark Gardy 'Tracks give experts paws for thought.' *Melbourne Herald* 15 Sept 1989

[41] letter to author from Paul Cropper dated 10 Oct. 1989

[42] 'Big cat on outskirts of town.' *Midland Express* 15 March 1993. Don Gunn and Valerie Hornbuckle. 'Prints point to big black cat mystery?' *Kyneton Guardian* 18 March 1993

[43] West, *Newsletter* No. 7, pp 3 - 4

[44] Higgins (ref. 33)

[45] Wally Davies (1994) Mystery Animal Association of Western Australia. *Newsletter* No. 8, pp 4 - 6

[46] 'Puma sighting', *Hamilton Spectator*, 22 Nov. 1991

[47] 'Many see the Grampians puma.' *Horsham Mail Times* 28 Jan. 1987

[48] letter to author from Peter J. Chapple, dated 14 Oct. 1988 (ref. 29)

[49] 'It changes spots', *Sunday Press* 4 Sept. 1988

[50] letter to author from Peter J. Chapple, dated 14 Oct. 1988 (ref. 29)

[51] Paul Cropper (1980) 'The panthers of southern Australia'. *Fortean Times* 32: 18 -21 (Dr Karl Shuker alerted me to this article.)

[52] 'On the trail of the black panthers.' *Mudgee Guardian* 21 April 1992 (quotes earlier articles)

[53] B. L. Owens (1977) 'The strange saga of . . . The Emmaville Panther.' *Australian Outdoors and Fishing* April 1977, pp 17 - 19, 83. (The original sources were not mentioned. However, a detailed, fully referenced discussion can now be found on pp 70 -75 of *Snarls from the Tea-Tree* by David Waldron and Simon Townsend, 2012, Australian Scholarly Publishing)

[54] Peter Willcox (1990). 'Tintinhull - is it really a jungle out there?' *Northern Daily Leader* 10 Oct. 1990

[55] Warren Murray 'Bell-Kumbia panther sighting disturbs Kingaroy motorist.' *South Burnett Times* 17 Feb. 1995

[56] Owens (ref. 53)

57   O'Reilly (ref. 3) pp 73 - 5, 126 - 130

58   'Woman: I saw the Grampians pumas.' *The Mail-Times* (Horsham) 12 May 1989

59   West, *Newsletter*, No. 1, 1993, p. 6

60   West, *Newsletter*, No, 2, 1993, p. 5

61   Michael Williams and Rebecca Lang (2010), *Australian Big Cats, an unnatural history of panthers,* Strange Nation Publishing

62   https://malcolmscryptids.blogspot.com/search/label/ABC

63   Simon Bevilacqua, 'Ingrid lets cat out of the bag', *The Sunday Tasmanian*, 2 June 2002

64   David Waldron and Simon Townsend (2012) *Snarls from the Tea-tree. Big cat folklore*, Arcadia, Melbourne, pp 102 -4. (See ref. 36 of Chapter 3).

65   E. Denny (2008), 'Cat' pp 742 - 4 in *The Mammals of Australia*, Third Edition, Steven van Dyck and Ronald Strahan, eds., Reed New Holland

66   P. C. Catling and B. J. Coman (2008), 'Fox', pp 740 - 741 in van Dyck and Strahan (ref. 65)

67   Tom Brakefield (1993) *Big Cats. Kingdom of Might.* Voyageur Press

68   Menkhorst, Peter W. and Leigh Morison (2012), 'Assessment of evidence for the presence in Victoria of a wild population of 'big cats'. Arthur Rylah Institute, (PDF) Assessment of evidence for the presence of 'big cats' in Victoria. (researchgate.net) (assessed Dec. 2020)

Full address of link: https://www.researchgate.net/profile/Peter_Menkhorst/publication/28122 1781_Assessment_of_evidence_for_the_presence_of_'big_cats'_in_Vict oria/links/55dbe25208aec156b9aff6bc/Assessment-of-evidence-for-the-p resence-of-big-cats-in-Victoria.pdf

69   Darren Naish (2007) 'Australia's new feral mega-cats' https://scienceblogs.com/tetrapodzoology/2007/03/04/australias-new-fera l-mega-cats   (accessed Dec. 2020) Unfortunately, the original photos are

no longer on the site, but most can be found in Williams and Lang (ref. 61)

[70] Kevin Healey, 'Hunter's souvenir may solve bush riddle. I shot big cat.' *Sunday Herald Sun*, 9 Oct. 2005, p 3. More details are provided by Williams and Lang (ref. 61) pp 110 - 117

[71] Danny Butler, 'Big cat fight begins.' *Sun Herald,* Mon. 10 Oct 2005, p 9

[72] Tests reveal super-sized feral cat - ABC News Mon. 28 Nov 2005 (accessed Dec 2020)

[73] Sarah Hartwell (2012), 'The myth of giant feral cats' http://messybeast.com/giantferal.htm (last accessed Dec. 2020)

[74] Copyrighted, of course. But they were published by Williams and Lang (ref. 61), the newspapers (ref. 69 and 70, among others), and on the internet, which appears to ignore copyright.

[75] Williams and Lang (ref. 61) pp 110 - 117

[76] 'What was up that tree?' *Wonthaggi Express*, Thurs. 1st Dec. 1955.

[77] I published them on https://malcolmscryptids.blogspot.com/2014/10/the-wonthaggi-monster.html

[78] Frank Robson, 'Killer Cat', *People* 18 April 1983, pp 8 - 9

[79] Menkhorst and Morison (ref. 68)

[80] I have based the following discussion on Menkhorst and Morison (ref. 68), but more importantly, on the information provided to me personally by David Cass.

[81] Described graphically, along with a lot of other adventures, in my parents-in-law's memoires, *Savages and Saints, life and love on the New Guinea mission fields* by Leon and Theophila Philippi (2020)

CHAPTER 6

APES   DOWN   UNDER ?

At school you learned all about the major explorers, but most of the places on the map were discovered by ordinary people making short forays into the unknown. In July 1861 three men, Messrs Dempster, Clarkson and Harper decided to mount a private expedition into the hills and lake areas of south west Western Australia. On 19 July their diary recorded a second-hand account of three white men who had attempted the journey many years before with the help of a native guide called Boodgin. At a large salt water lake they turned back and "were either killed by the *jimbras*, or perished from want of water."

They heard the story again from the natives at Lake Grace. These men gave an account of the *jimbra*, or *jingra*, a strange animal, male and female, which they described as resembling a monkey, very fierce, which would attack men when it caught one singly. Thinking there might be a confusion of names, the explorers asked if the *jimbra*, or *jingra*, was the same as the *gingka* - the native name for devil. This, however, was not so, as the natives asserted that the devil, or *gingka*, was never seen, but that the *jimbra* was both seen and felt[1].

By now, you may have noticed that the chapters been moving gradually from the plausible to the improbable. But if there is one thing totally out of the question - one thing even more absurd than pumas and black panthers - it is the idea of a resident Australian ape. Yet people will keep seeing them. What the *jingras* were meant to be will probably never be known. The explorers had to use an interpreter who, as likely as not, spoke only pidgin English. It is unlikely that he used the word, "monkey" because he would never have seen one. This was an interpretation put on his description by the white men. And, as far as I know, the *jingras* have never been heard of since.

Strangely enough, however, a similar word, *Jingara*, is alleged to have been used on the other side of the continent, in the Cooma district, where it referred to a certain mountain haunted by a hairy man[2]. Which brings us to the next phase of our story: the apes may have kept clear of Western Australia, but they appear in more than a few tales from New South Wales in the second half of the last century. At that time, the word on the settlers' lips was *yahoo*, and there is a fascinating little story about its origin[3]. Apparently calcium was needed to make mortar, and an obvious source was the oyster middens at Port Hacking, just south of Botany Bay. A working party of convicts was sent to collect some, and two escaped, one tall and one short. The short one managed to grow a huge and luxurious beard, which would completely hide the other's face when he rode on his shoulders. Then, 2½ metres tall, four-armed and hairy, they would charge into the Aboriginal camps shouting, "Yarhoo!", and collect the food the terrified blacks had abandoned in their flight. I don't believe a word of it.

The name, of course, was adopted from the degraded human beings described in Swift's *Gulliver's Travels*. The same book lent the same word to a similar legend in the Bahamas[4]. Aborigines may learn to pronounce an "h" when conversing to white men, but the sound does not occur in their own languages.

As far as can be determined, the earliest reference to the legend is the 1835 *Travels* of J. Holman, who stated: "The natives are greatly terrified by the sight of a person in a mask calling him 'devil' or Yah-hoo, which signifies evil spirit."[5] But it was not till 1871 that any white man claimed to have seen one.

It is to Graham Joyner, a policy analyst from the A.C.T., that we owe the salvaging of many of these stories and legends. Anybody who has ever searched through old newspaper files knows how time consuming it can be. One can therefore only admire the remarkable job done by Mr. Joyner in culling the archives of many old and obscure local journals for references to hairy men. The result was a slim, privately published volume[6] which is a boon to both the folklorist and the cryptozoologist.

One thing he did establish was a tradition among the Aborigines of the southern coast areas of New South Wales, belonging to the Dharawal, Dyirringan, Dhurga and Ngarigo language groups. The word most frequently cited was *dhuligal*, in its various spellings, which tended to mean "wild blackfellow", or tribal renegade. In the two detailed legends where a *dhuligal* was described in detail, it appeared to correspond to the English ogre. Such monsters appear in the imagination of practically every race, and seldom have any basis in reality. Interestingly enough, the white men's accounts of yahoos came mostly from areas west of the dhuligal legends. Indeed, Joyner quotes a resident of Adaminaby who had questioned the Aborigines of the Murrumbidgee headwaters many times, and none of them had heard of a hairy man.

What about the stories told by whites? On this there has been not a little controversy. The prominent primatologist, Dr Colin Groves, believed they were just frontier myths, which faded when the first generation of settlers had passed. The eyewitness accounts he writes off as "a hotchpotch of shooters' campfire tales, unidentifiable apparitions seen at dusk, and various hairy horrids that frightened the horses and demoralized the dogs[7]." When challenged by Joyner, Groves performed an analysis of the reported sightings[8]. By a strange coincidence, I was independently working on the same project[9]. Both of us emphasized that the descriptions given did not produce a consistent pattern. Hair could be grey, white, dark, or tan, the body either slim or heavily built. Often details in individual accounts were so striking it was amazing no-one else reported them: a tan streak down the front of the body, arms reaching to the ankles, thighs much longer than the calf. I also made three other points:

- Most of the reports contained a remarkable lack of detail, even for features which should have been readily visible. Many were just a sentence or two. This suggests a lack of critical standards and a tendency to jump to conclusions.
- Two of the witnesses were children.
- Four of the accounts were second-hand, and many of the others were retold by a journalist without the witnesses' actual words being quoted. Often an indeterminate period had elapsed before the events were actually recorded.

From all the evidence I came to the conclusion that the *yahoo* or "hairy man" was just that: a hairy man. When we read the words, "covered with hair" we need not jump to the conclusion that it means "like an ape". It might mean, "like a hairy man". The Aborigines have just as much body hair as Caucasians, and some of the latter, one must admit, can be pretty striking. It is not uncommon to see on the beach men whose thick, curly hair extends from the chests down the abdomen and over the shoulders. Suppose an Aborigine like that was encountered in the forest. Suppose, too, he displayed no desire to interact with the white strangers. Those of south-east Australia tended to heavier built that the slim people of the north. Furthermore, all races possess "apelike" features which draw the attention of those who do not share them. With Aborigines, these include broad noses, heavy brow ridges, and forwardly protruding faces. Any exaggeration of such features would likely be called "apelike" by someone who had never seen an ape, or even a good photograph of one, but who was brought up on "ape man" legends. Such a person, while being in the outer limits of variability of the Aboriginal population, would not appear out of place in a native camp. Indeed, even alone in the bush, most white men would recognize him for what he was. Only those expecting to see a "yahoo" would make the mistake.

Impossible, you say. Nobody could mistake a man for an ape. Consider: in February 1987, police at Alice Springs received a call from Yambah Station, 50 km to the north, from a very frightened family. A man, a woman, and the woman's four grandchildren had gone rabbit shooting, and decided to have tea at a place called Top Bore. It was only 5 p.m., and still very bright. Just as they were busy passing around the food, a huge, apelike creature, two metres tall and covered with hair, leapt out of an empty tank and began walking towards them. As they turned and fled in their utility truck, it ran after them, grabbing hold of the truck before disappearing into the bush. The man, Frank Burns, believed it was a man. But the woman, Phyllis Kenny, who was too scared to leave the house for days, told the press she could tell the difference between a man and a beast, and this definitely fell into the second category. One grandson told how it ran like a gorilla, with its arms hanging down. Another described a apelike face, with big eyes, a large forehead, and a red colour all around the mouth[10]. The Central Australian desert is hardly the place you'd expect to find an ape. The following day the police searched the area and found a man, of unstated race, sitting by the road side quite naked. Although he stood 6 foot 8 inches [203 cm] in height and weighed an estimated 20 to 25 stone [127 - 159 kg], he came quietly, and was admitted to Alice Springs Hospital, presumably to the psychiatric ward.

Five months later police were called out to hunt the Woronara apeman, a 7 foot [213 cm] tall, hairy creature said to haunt the Heathcote National Park, south of Sydney, and which had even been sighted carrying a dead animal for food. However, locals quickly told them that the apeman had been coming into Heathcote Inn every pension day to pick up his liquor and vegetable supplies. It was, in fact, a Yugoslav migrant turned hermit, who had been living in the park as long as anyone could remember, and although not 7 feet tall, had "hair everywhere" and wore a bandana, jungle boots, stained jeans and a murky coloured shirt[11].

Of course, I suppose it is possible the small national park harbours both a human eccentric known to the locals and a subhuman primate unknown to science. But I prefer to think that both examples are indications that the age of credulity is not yet dead. I also pointed out[12] that every year during the hunting season North Americans are mistaken for deer - much to their disadvantage.

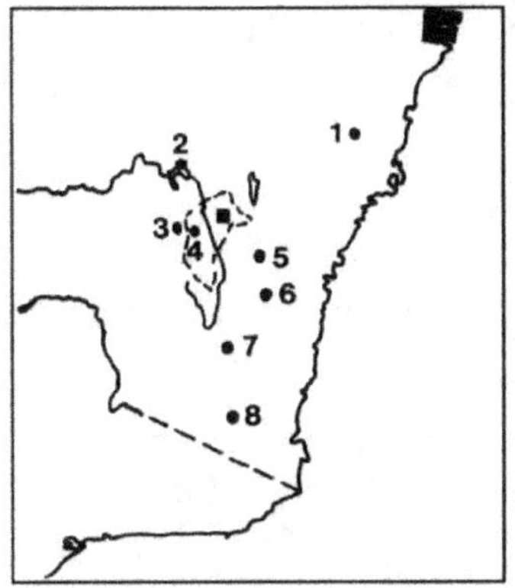

Sydney marked with a square in the north)

Avondale	1
Bombala	8
Brindabella Range	3
Captain's Flat	5
Jingeras	7
Snowball	6
Tidbinbilla Mt/Cotter R.	4
Yass/Murrumbidgee junction	2

The locality of the Currockbilly Range sighting was not precise enough for inclusion.

Map 6A   Approximate sites of early "yahoo" sightings

Let's have a look at the eyewitness accounts.

April 1871. Near Avondale, just after sunset, George Osborne saw an apelike figure climb out of a tree and head off on all fours. It was about 5 feet [150 cm] tall, with a human build, monkey features, and a coat of black hair over the whole of its body. It also had a tan-coloured streak from its neck to abdomen, and feet like an iguana's (goanna's) but 18 inches [46 cm] long. These two features have never been reported before or since, though they could hardly have been missed, and the feet must have made walking very awkward. For those reasons, I believe this was a hoax.

December 1871. In the Jingeras, near Cooma, a little girl met an old man with a bent back, hair all over his body, and enormously long nails.

May 1881. The Jingera hairy man was seen again, somewhat larger than a man, with the appearance of a monkey or baboon.

October 1893. Arthur Marrin actually killed a strange animal near Captain's Flat. The description was totally different from that of any other yahoo. Both Dr Groves and I agree that it was probably an oversized wombat, an opinion voiced by some of the witnesses to the carcass.

3 October 1894, near Snowball. A boy saw "a big man covered with long hair", run away from him.

1901. Brindabella Range. A Mr Cox was boiling his billy in the afternoon when he suddenly heard a loud cry, and out came "a huge animal in an erect posture tearing through the undergrowth."

1903 (reported). Also in the Brindabella Range. Joseph and William Webb were making camp for the night when out of the dense scrub came something the shape of a hirsute man with its head set deep on its shoulders, and bellowing gutturally. A slightly different version was told in 1927.

1903 (reported), between Tidbinbilla Mountain and Cotter River: "like a blackfellow with a blanket on him." (Perhaps that's what it was.)

1903 (reported), below the junction of the Yass and Murrumbidgee Rivers. A creature like a black man but covered with grey hair was killed by the blacks.

October 1912, near Bombala. A creature covered in grey hair was seen drinking on all fours in broad daylight. It stood up, picked up a stick, and walked away, revealing itself to be 7 feet [2.13 m] high, with the face of an ape or man, minus the forehead and chin, a broad trunk and arms nearly reaching its ankles.

1912. Currockbilly Range. My favourite: Charles Harper described an experience he had one night - it is not stated how long before - of something that came into the outer range of his camp fire light, not twenty yards away. The description of the monster, which stood "growling, grimacing, and thumping his breast" is vivid and detailed. It was as tall as a man, but of an enormous build, with long, black hair on its shoulders and back, and long brownish-red hair over the rest of its body. The head and face were very small, but very human, but with fangs protruding over its lower lip, and deep, piercing eyes (how could they tell at that distance?). There were two features which do not appear in any other account. The stomach hung like a sack halfway down its thigh. Perhaps it was wearing a sack-like loin cloth. Also, the thighs were much longer than the shins. As I pointed out, such an arrangement would be so inefficient, it is hard to believe any biped could be built that way[13].

For the full details, I shall refer you to Joyner's booklet, which also contains a wealth of information on popular beliefs not accessible elsewhere. Whether they can all be explained by hoaxes, and hirsute

Aborigines seen by uncritical settlers, I leave you to judge. Anyhow, that's my theory, and I'm sticking to it. Even if there is such a thing as a yahoo, the accounts are too unreliable to be used as evidence.

Some stories, of course, are so wild they have to be hoaxes. Take, for instance, the thing alleged to have been seen by a shepherd in the Pyramul district, near Mudgee, NSW in 1878. It was hairy, apparently bipedal, and four feet [1.2 m] high, but with a body as round as a horse, arms as thick as a man's thigh, and three claws on each foot. The head resembled a pig's, but turned upwards, and it threw the shepherd's dog (with its head or arms?) 60 yards each time the latter approached. The shepherd reported milk-white teeth under the monster's armpits[14].

In 1909, also in the Mudgee district, at a place called the Bar, people started hearing choking and screaming noises at night. Then, a bit after 5pm, several persons saw

> ...a peculiar animal, five feet [1.5 m] high, standing on his two legs, and at the same time brushing away with his claw-like hands the unkempt looking hair from his eyes. The animal is covered with long white hair and when seen was uttering the cries which had been disturbing the peace of the neighbourhood[15].

The police thought it was a prankster in a goat skin. If so, he was never found. But then again, the monster hasn't reappeared, either.

In all honesty, however, I cannot invoke such theories to explain the reports which have been coming in over the last two decades, under the title of *yowie*. This term was not attested in English before 1975, and its origin is obscure[16]. It might be a variant of *yuwi*, or "dream spirit", in the Yuawaalaraay language of the Walgett-Brewarrina district[17]. However, there is a Yowie Bay in Port Hacking, and it appears that *yowie* was a term used in the Blue Mountains and Bathurst districts for hairy giants. There also happens to be a village and a river called Yowrie. The comment by Kevin Gilbert is therefore relevant: "We had the legendary bunyip, the little people and the hairy youree - the huge shaggy man-like creature that the whites call 'yowie'"[18]. Gilbert belongs to the Wiradjuri, the largest tribal group in south-central New South Wales, and one of the Wiradjuri words for the little people (more about which later) is *yuurii* or "hairy"[19].

What relationship is there between the words, *yuurii, youree/yowrie* and *yowie*? The last has now entered the Aboriginal vocabulary with the same meaning as in English. Probably it was a mythological or folkloric term which has been misapplied, like calling a crocodile a dragon.

The responsibility for introducing the word into the Australian consciousness, and for the modern interest in the phenomenon, can be laid at the feet of one man: Rex Gilroy, the proprietor of a private museum in the Blue Mountains. As long ago as 1978 his Australian Yowie Research Centre was said to have files on 3,000 sightings[20]. Mr Gilroy must be regarded as one of Australia's true eccentrics, and he is certainly the most enthusiastic and relentless cryptozoologist in the country. He manages to turn up wherever mystery animals are reported, with the result that a great deal of useful information falls into his hands. At flushing out *yowie* stories he has no equal. Many of the tales I am about to relate were not collected by Mr Gilroy, but appeared in local papers after his visit to an area was reported, thus giving residents the courage to come forth.

Nevertheless, my impression has been that his enthusiasm overreaches his critical abilities. On occasions, when I've followed up his accounts, I've found them to be incorrect. When he has commented on classical sea serpent reports, for instance, the facts have been twisted to support pre-conceived theories. Furthermore, if we take him at his word, he has had some remarkable experiences. He claims to have seen a mainland thylacine, the Kangaroo Valley panther, and the Lake Taupo monster of New Zealand. Sometimes he will claim to have had only one yowie experience, at other times several - as well as having seen a yowie skeleton at a farm. In short, I am not prepared to accept any of Mr. Gilroy's stories unless they can be independently confirmed. But perhaps he will publish his findings in due course, and readers will be able to judge for themselves.

In fairness, it must be mentioned that he has a personal reason for his enthusiasm. It began on 7 August 1970, about half past three in the afternoon. He was busy eating pork and carrot sandwiches in a clearing near the Ruined Castle, a rock formation in the Blue Mountains between Mt. Sydney and Narrowneck.

> All was quiet, but I had a strange feeling that I was being watched. Then, almost immediately, this ape-like creature about as high as a small man broke from cover and ran across the open ground and disappeared into the bush on the far side[21].

He said it was about 18 metres away and 1.8 metres tall, and covered with orange coloured hair. It walked on two legs, and gave a scream[22].

Considering that the Blue Mountains have been the main gateway to the interior since 1813, it staggers the imagination to think that anything like this could have remained undetected there for so long. But apparently, tales of this nature have a long pedigree. Miss Lola Irish used to holiday in Katoomba as a child in the 1930s. One of the landladies was a bit of a tippler, but also a dedicated bushwalker, and her favourite story was of a giant hairy apeman which disappeared into the bush with the camp stores. That was at the Ruined Castle[23]. Judging from Gilroy's files, the Ruined Castle must be an interesting place[24]. In the same month as his own sighting, a group of hikers allegedly heard grunting near the base of the castle, and large, barely visible apelike footprints were found.

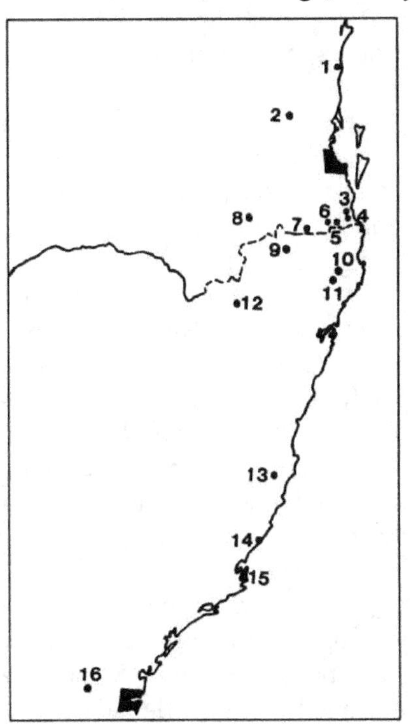

(Sydney and Brisbane marked with squares)

Blue Mountains	16
Dunoon	10
Kempsey	13
Kilcoy	2
Krambach	15
Lismore	11
Nerang	3
Oxley Island	14
Palen Creek	7
Springbrook	5
Tallebudgera Ck Rd	4
Tenterfield	12
Tewantin	1
Widgee Mountain	6
Woodenbong	9
Yangan	8

Emerald and L. Dulverton are beyond the limits of the map.

Map 6B Sites of modern "yowie" sightings

In July 1976 a Mr Jackson of Sydney had hiked to the Castle, turned a bend in the trail, and came face to face with a male *yowie* with almost humanlike features. On 13 April that year five bushwalkers - their names are given - reportedly encountered a female *yowie* in the Grose Valley, near Katoomba. It stood 2.4 metres [8 ft] tall, and was half that dimension across the shoulders, with pendulous breasts, an almost human face, dark brown hair several centimetres long all over its body, and a foul odour. On 18 September 1976, two boys camped at Mt. Solitary, south of the Ruined Castle, and saw "four hairy, manlike, apelike" beasts 1.5 metres high[25]. But as it was the middle of the night, could they be sure? The following month a rash of reports issued from around Kiandra, Tidbinbilla, Kosciusko and Cooma[26] - in fact, near the areas of the nineteenth century reports, except that the naked Aborigines were long since gone. The next year the Queanbeyan Council offered a $200,000 reward for a live *yowie*. It has yet to be paid.

But enough of this part of the woods. Let's travel further north, stopping at each district in turn to tell its stories.

Krambach, 70 km north of Port Stephens, NSW is a main-street-and-pub town where one would expect nothing ever happens. But in 1991 fourteen year old Julie Clark was riding on a nearby hillside where the horse reared up. Sitting on a road just three metres away was a grey something which immediately stood up and started towards her. Only by taking off at full gallop was she able to outrun it. According to Julie, "It was bigger than my horse (14 hands). It had humanlike skin but was covered in long, dark hair with patches of hair on the hands and most of its face was covered in hair"[27]. Julie, whose mother considers her practical and believable, later rode over to the same hillside with eleven year old Jodie Betts, and had the experience of the monster letting out a high-pitched scream, and disappearing before they could return with a camera. Other children told of having large stones thrown at them by the same creature. Paul Carney, 26 described a similar experience at the same site fourteen years before. An unnamed adult also told a reporter of seeing the monster disturb his cattle and dogs at night, but it took off before he could get a proper look.

No-one would suggest that Kempsey is sited in the midst of virgin wilderness. It is a thriving town surrounded by farms and rural residences, but also with narrow bands of forest, not necessarily interconnecting. Eleven kilometres south of the town, a narrow dirt road is flanked on one side by scattered properties, and on the other by steep, wooded gullies leading to the Ballengarra State Forest. It was about 5.30 pm, Sunday 22 January 1995. (Due to daylight savings, there would have been afternoon light.) Two boys, aged 10 and 11 - their parents request anonymity - were following the road when they heard a noise. By the roadside, just five to seven metres away, among the lantana and ferns, something huge was standing with its back towards them, hunched over. As it rose to its full height, moving its head from side to side, they watched in mute horror. Then they turned and walked away ... then they run.

When Paul Cropper interviewed them, separately, he found them sensible and uneffusive. Rather than indulge in flights of fancy, they resisted all attempts to make them provide more than the basic information. They had seen only its rear. They could remember no arms, legs or face. But it was 2.4 to 2.7 metres high, and massive, in shape intermediate between a man and a gorilla. Its dark brown hair was wild and scraggy, and several inches long.

Figure 6.1 Photograph of one of the Kempsey footprints. © *Paul Cropper*

But the amazing thing was this: although 13 days had passed before Paul arrived, a trail of 16 footprints was still obvious - each of them 30 cm long. The boys, being small themselves, and terrified, must have overestimated its height. Such prints indicate a height of only 2 metres. But they were not human. Although the individual toes did not stand out, the toe line did not curve back and outwards like your own; it formed a straight line in front. And the width was 18 cm: half as wide again as an equivalent human foot. A wildlife consultant who visited the site the following weekend could not believe that any living creature could have made them. They were 3 to 4 cm deep. Even by taking his entire weight on one heel, Paul could not achieve a depth of more than 2 cm. But then, I estimate the weight as three times his own: the weight of a fully grown male gorilla[28].

Paul later interviewed a man who had attended West Kempsey High School in the late 1940s and early 1950s. One day, after school, he rode his bicycle to a well-known lilly pilly tree in a small gully close to the present day site of the Kempsey airport. To his amazement, there stood a creature as big as a hefty man, but only 4 feet [1.2 m] high. He was only 6 to 8 metres away. He could see its flat face and snub nose, its droopy ears, yellow eyes, and yellow canines. Hair 3 inches [7½ cm] long covered its entire body, reducing to about an inch on its head. The animal appeared to have been feeding on the lilly pilly fruit; it had one hand - twice the size of a man's, with long claws - clutching a branch. The monster fled even before he did. In the same area he later found prints bearing four toes. His friends told him he had seen a bunyip.

In February 1977, at 11 o'clock in the morning, Mrs. Betty Gee looked out from her back door on Oxley Island, in the Manning River, NSW. Standing by the wharf 300 metres away was a yowie. Because of the lie of the land, it was visible only from the middle of the chest upwards, but when her 1.8 metre son stood on the same spot, not even his head could be seen. A week later, they came home to find their 1500 gallon [5677 litres] water tank overturned, and huge footprints everywhere[29].

From the above, it would appear that yowies know how to swim. But Oxley Island is at least a rural area. Nestled in the Macpherson Range, close to the Queensland border, Woodenbong is a town. It is also a town with a difference. The wildlife tends to wander into the streets at night. Wildlife that doesn't officially exist.

It was about 1 am, late November 1976. Unable to sleep, 48 year old Thel Crewe decided to go to the kitchen and read a book. However, the moonlight was so bright, instead of turning on the light, she just stood at the open window to admire the view. Just then, a yowie walked in from the vacant lot next door and stood in front of the window. Just three metres away, before her spellbound eyes, it stood looking her way for three or four minutes, flexing its arms alternately in front of its face. Then it moved three metres down the side of the house to the window of her bedroom. Much to her amazement, it was joined by a second creature, exactly the same, and together they stood by the window for a few seconds before crossing the yard and turning left down the street at the power pole. Only then did any fear set in, but when she woke her husband he told her to go to sleep. There were no footprints on the lawn the following morning. Mrs Crewe said there could be no possibility of error about what she saw. They were both about 5 feet [1.5 m] tall, and covered with a tan coloured hair, that on the arms being 6 inches [15 cm] longer than on the rest of the body. It gave her the impression of an Afghan hound, except that they were bigger and walked on two legs with a shuffling gait. Their heads were sunk low on their shoulders, and she could not make out any features[30].

Naturally, when she broke the story more than seven months later, she got a bit of kidding from the neighbours. But a man phoned her from Kyogle to tell about seeing the same sort of creature in a paddock more than thirty years before. A neighbour also told her of a nurse who saw a yowie in her headlights on the Woodenbong-Urbenville Road[31]. A day or two later a Ballina man phoned the local newspaper. No, he definitely did not want his name published, but back in 1935, when he was ten years old, he had been staying on his grandfather's farm in South Lismore. One moonlit winter's night, about 9 pm, he saw what looked like a man walking down from the hills. When the horses made a fuss, he called his grandfather. The old man immediately blew out the lamp, and grabbed a rifle. The family watched from the kitchen window as the "man" passed within 25 feet [7½ m]. It was thickset and hairy, with a hunched back and no neck. Walking bipedally, but dragging its feet, it hesitated near the sulky shed, and disappeared behind the dairy. His grandfather then told him how he had met it in a nearby gully four years before[32].

A bit of thought will convince you that if Mrs. Crewe had not been unable to sleep, none of this would ever have been recorded. I suppose the citizens of Woodenbong, like most people, are used to dogs barking at night for no obvious reason. No doubt if they did see a bipedal figure in the streets at night, they would assume it was a human being. One wonders how often these things had been wandering through the town without anyone noticing. Because, just seven weeks after Mrs Crewe told her story, it happened again - this time only a few hundred metres away, in Lindsay Street.

It was 2.30 am, 10 August 1977. A woman was lying in bed, not asleep, when suddenly she was startled by the yelping of her little terrier. Even more alarming, the yelping was mixed with an undoglike high-pitched screaming, as if a dog were killing her Siamese cat. Hurrying to the back door, she switched on the 200 watt outside light, and raced down the steps. There, only 6 feet [1.8 m] away, squatted an apelike creature, crushing the dog to its body with its folded arms. On seeing the mistress of the house, it dropped the dog, held up its arms, and backed off, not once taking its eyes off her. Once it got to a grape trellis, it stood for a few minutes, making deep, loud grunts before running off down the side of the house to the street, its arms hanging loose, not touching the ground. According to the woman, who requested anonymity, the intruder was 6 feet [183 cm] high, with a broad chest, narrower hips, and strong legs, and was covered all over with brownish hair. It had some features in common with Mrs Crewe's animal.

"The head was very small compared to the rest of its body, and the hair was close cropped and fell down over its forehead," she said. "The rest of the face didn't seem to have much hair over it. When the yowie held out its arms after dropping the dog I noticed that it had long gingery coloured hair hanging from the bottom of its arms. The hair seemed to be very well groomed, and flowing like a girl's would. The hair over all its body seemed to be pretty closely cropped except on the arms and over the shoulders. The shoulder hair was dark brown with a greyish tinge[33]."

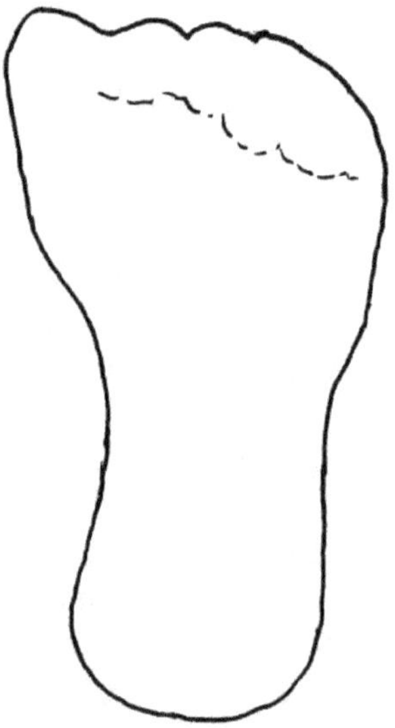

Figure 6.2 Outline of the Woodenbong footprint

Also, it had a vile odour, like a ferret's. She had to wash the dog with Dettol to remove it, as well as a greasiness left by its attacker.

A likely story! you say. But the woman contacted the press just three days later, and they were out the next morning, photographing everything in sight. Her husband supported her; he had heard the grunting. The next door neighbours had been awakened by the yelping, and heard the grunts. The dog still bore scratches and bruises from the encounter. And there was a footprint (Fig. 6.2). They had covered it with a bucket to protect it from the rain which had washed out two others. Its length of 22 cm was not exceptional. But the breadth of 11 cm was more than any human foot would make, especially since the greatest width was at the toes. There were five of them, fanning out almost in a semicircle, instead of sloping from largest to smallest as in humans.

Not only that, the reporter and photographer snooped around behind the shed where the yowie had passed, and found three strands of gingery brown hair, about 7 inches [18 cm] long caught on a splinter on an old post. However, nothing seems to have come of their plan to have them independently tested.

What's wrong with this story? Nothing, as far as I can see. It is the most convincing evidence I know for the existence of yowies. In criminal contexts, evidence like that has been known to send people to the gallows. How much more to we need to convict an unknown ape of the act of existing?

After that, things seem to have settled down at Woodenbong, but on 20 May 1981, two yowies made an appearance in front of three boys in the hills outside Dunoon[34]. The town is close to Lismore, in an area with a long history of white settlement. It took fourteen year old Craig Hatherell one and a half hours to lead his mother, teacher, fellow pupils, and a newspaper photographer to the site. The creatures passed between two trees and watched the boys for about 5 seconds. They stood 2½ metres tall, with long, brownish hair covering their apelike bodies, and rounded heads perched on top of neckless shoulders. They were not making it up. The eldest boy, the only one to actually make eye contact with the yowie, subsequently suffered from nightmares and inflamed eyes. According to his mother, human medicine was of no use. He was only cured when a clergyman laid hands on him.

The Queensland Gold Coast seems to have yowies periodically stepping out of the hinterland into the public view. Before 1975 the term didn't exist, so they called it a bunyip. (Refer back to Chapter 1). There was even the legend, familiar to folklorists throughout the world, that its feet pointed backwards. It was said to have been responsible for a set of footprints leading to (or from!) the edge of the Point Danger Cliff, but without any return set, or any body at the bottom[35].

Sixteen-year-old Alan Livingstone, of Melinda St, Southport had heard the stories. They came to mind when, over several weekends, he had seen glowing eyes when driving past a spot on the Tallebudgera

Creek Road. At that date this was just beyond the built up area. So, on Saturday 28 July 1973, he got together three friends, aged 15 to 19 - their names are on record - to investigate. They drove west of Fleay's Fauna Sanctuary, over a hill, and stopped at a wooden bridge at the bottom near a gateway. (So, hopefully, you'll be able to find the place yourself.) It was now 11 p.m. They left the lights on, and soon they saw the eyes. All but the youngest got out of the car. I shall let Alan explain what happened next.

> As soon as we got near it, the bunyip - or whatever it was came charging out of the trees towards us. It travelled at what seemed like a quick walk, moving its arms like a man. We could see the colour of its fur outlined in the light from the car headlights. But I couldn't see a nose or teeth or ears - only eyes. We could hear the pad of its feet, but there was no noise. No grunts or growls, no heavy breathing. My heart started to beat real fast as he came for us. We were all scared and took off like rabbits for the car[36].

They were no more than 15 to 20 feet [4½ - 6 m] away when the approach commenced. Its fur was reddish, and he estimated its height at 5 foot 8 inches [173 cm]. However, his courage was not completely exhausted. He came back the following Wednesday with four mates, three of whom had not been there and were sceptics. "Then they saw the eyes and the shape of a thing climbing a tree." The following Friday night dozens of people turned up with cameras, weapons and guns in a scene reminiscent of peasants in the old "Frankenstein" movies, but as far as I know, they came back empty handed[37]. One journalist did join the hunt, "fortified" beforehand, and saw it slinking between the trees. It began waving its hands like a traffic cop, but got away when they gave chase. However, his article was rather tongue in cheek[38].

The important thing to remember is that the *yowie* craze had not yet started, and up till then nobody, but nobody, had ever suggested there might be manlike monsters in the bush. It would not, however, be the last time they would be reported by youngsters, and not always at night.

In 1977 pupils of The Southport School claimed to have seen a yowie (it was no longer a bunyip) while on a camp at Springbrook. The 12-year-old editor of the school newspaper, himself a witness, decided to run the story, but headmaster Peter Rogers took him aside and told him it was out of the question. The young fellow was not going to stand for that. With an initiative that, in retrospect, can be seen as a portent of his future career, he went to the grown-ups' newspaper and told them:

<blockquote>

"About 20 of us saw it. It was about three metres tall, covered in hair, had a flat face and walked to one side in crab like style. It smashed small saplings and trees like matchsticks as it careered through the bush. We spotted it several times and once watched it through binoculars, so it definitely was there. We first saw the Yowie at 12.30 pm on October 22 and last saw it just before we returned back to Southport on the afternoon of October 23. It definitely was up there, but no-one will believe us. At one stage the Yowie came within 10 metres of our sleeping quarters, so we got a good look[39]."

</blockquote>

He said that the animal appeared to have no neck, and the footprint he measured was far too big for a human being's. Naturally, the press contacted the headmaster. All we wanted to do, he told them, was to prevent the younger students being scared by exaggerated stories. The staff had checked them out, and could find no evidence for or against the boys' tale.

"I bet he denies it," a friend said to me when I wrote to the chief witness 17 years later. In my heart I was sure he would. As an adult, he would find such a story embarrassing. Besides, it was one of those stories which ought to be true, but couldn't be. If it were, my whole outlook on Australian wildlife would be turned on its head. So, imagine my surprise when, one night two weeks later, the phone rang. It was the ex-schoolboy, very helpful and not a bit reticent. He confirmed everything in the original account and filled in additional details.

The site was Camp Bornhoffen, Springbrook, now known as Koonjewarre. It stands in a hollow, facing a hillside which, on the weekend in question, was covered with dry grass as tall as the boys' waists. Above it was the treeline of the national park. (By an amazing coincidence, he had only just met the man who lives on that hill. He had never seen anything, but had heard a lot of strange things.) All the boys were 12 years old, and supervised by a teacher. That afternoon the yowie suddenly appeared about three quarters the way up the hillside. They were able to watch it closely with both the naked eye and binoculars as it made its way through the grass and into the trees. His present day estimate of its height is 8 feet [2.4 m]. It was very tall, very broad and muscular, but with no visible neck. Except for its pale face, the whole of its body was covered with black hair. There was something non-human about its gait. Once it was gone, a large group of boys headed up the hill, and they found the impression in the thick grass where it had presumably been sleeping. Continuing to the top, they entered the forest, leaving three boys, including my informant, outside. Being seated looking down to the camp, they missed the spectacle. Those still in the camp watched the creature appear on the treeline a short distance behind them. That night, he saw a shape move past the dormitories, and assumed it was a teacher. There was a lot of noise, but he supposed it was the boys in another dormitory carrying on. Came the morning, and it was discovered that all the boys had attributed the noise to the others.

So, back up the hill they went. This time they found waist high shrubs torn out by the roots and tossed around. Even today, as a strong and fit athlete, he would not be able to uproot them. They also found a couple of footprints. Big ones. At this distance in time, he cannot be sure of the size, but thinks they would be much longer than 13 inches [33 cm], which would be consistent with a height of 2.2 metres. Furthermore, they were utterly non-human: almost trapezoidal in shape, narrow at the heel and very broad at the front - perhaps as much as 8 inches [20 cm]. (Compare the extreme width of the Woodenbong print.)

The monster made its appearance one last time before they broke camp that day.

What are the credentials of this witness man making this claim? His name is Bill O'Chee, and he is a prominent member of the Australian Senate. There is no question but that the event took place. Anybody who wishes to provide a mundane explanation is invited to try. "Nothing will ever convince me," the Senator said, "that what I saw wasn't a yowie." Even while we were talking he felt the hairs on his legs and arms stand on end.

Springbrook was also the site of the next occurrence, if we are to believe Howard Smith, of the Natureland Zoo at Kirra. He told how, on the evening of 28 January 1978, a man came to his zoo in a very distressed state and asked how to handle a yowie. The fellow, who refused to give his name, had been staying at a friend's home when a yowie wandered up to the front door and looked inside, grunting deeply. When the man threw a chair at it, it hopped or limped away.

> The man said the top of the Yowie's head was shaped like an egg, it was black in colour with deeply set eyes, a small screwed up nose and flat ears. It had a long round mouth and its cheek bones were high set. He said it was about two

metres tall and smelt like a badly kept public lavatory. "Its fingers were very long and held in a curled position and its eyes were very glazy, like porcelain," he said[40].

Although the man refused to give his name, he was able to show Mr. Smith a rather poor quality footprint, and his neighbour told how he (the informant) had broken into a cold sweat and refused to stay in the house by himself. Mr Smith offered a reward of $2 a kilo for the body of the yowie, which suggests that a publicity stunt should not be ruled out. The day after the story broke, a gorilla poked its head in the window of The Southport School library and grunted. It was suggested that an "old boy" had been playing a practical joke[41].

About 2.30 pm one Sunday in August 1978, 13 year old Shaun Cooper of Yarrayne Street, Nerang was riding his bicycle when he looked up the hill and saw it. Only 50 yards away stood a huge ape, 8 feet [2.4 m] high and covered with black hair, clawing at a tree with not too athletic movements. (The press were able to find the torn bark, but failed to mention the height.) He was not able to see its face. In fact, he waited only three or four seconds before fleeing for his life. His mother didn't feel inclined to search for the monster. No doubt she considered it a childish prank. Shaun realised he had to have proof. His home was on the edge of human settlement in the Gold Coast area. Gathering together three friends, aged 9 to 13 (their names are given), he set out to comb the countryside. And this is the point: after several weeks of searching, they found it: a series of huge tracks passing between the trees, up hill and down again, through a fence and down to a little waterfall. Not only that, the prints were still there when he contacted the press.

Now, I don't know much about the biology of yowies, but I used to be a 13 year old boy myself once. I know they if I tried to pull a stunt like that, I would not have been able to resist making a proper story out of it. I'd have provided a full, graphic description of the monster and its activities. I wouldn't have claimed to have hightailed it out after just three or four seconds. But I doubt if I would have been able to have faked a series of tracks well enough to fool any but the most amateurish reporter.

Be that as it may, the local newspaper took three photos of the tracks and published one[42]. It appears to measure 39 cm by 16 cm, which is consistent with the claimed height. But not only does it not belong to any known animal, it is hard to believe it could belong to anything. The heel is twisted very slightly to the side, though this might be an artefact of the way it adjusted to the slope. But what particularly bothers me is that the footprint - which is quite clear - displays only three thick toes. No monkey or ape has ever approached such a condition, and it is hard to believe one ever would. When walking upright one needs the stability of a full complement of toes.

Fig. 6.3. Sketch by Shaun Cooper

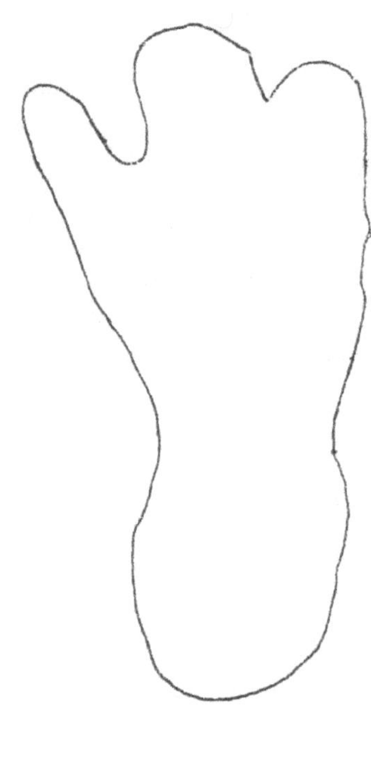

Fig. 6.4. Outline of footprint found by Shaun Cooper

A couple of years later a tour leader commented to me that a friend of his had toyed with the idea of dressing up as a yowie for publicity purposes but, he added, he probably changed his mind when the news broke of what happened up near Kilcoy. It was Friday 28 December, 1979. Two 16-year-old Brisbane boys, Warren Christensen and Tony Solano were out hunting pigs at Sandy Creek, 4 km from Kilcoy, near the headwaters of the Brisbane River. Just as they were having lunch, they heard the "thump, thump, thump" of heavy footsteps. Suddenly, there was a yowie, three metres high and covered with dirty chocolate coloured hair, and only 20 metres away. Warren grabbed his .22 rifle and fired from the hip. The monster took off. They heard the thumping sound as it circled round behind them, so they leapt into the creek bed to have a clear line of fire in case it attacked. But it never came back[43].

And that is all the description they gave: the height, the colour, and the fact that it left a faint sulphurous smell. But they did find large branches torn more than three metres up the trunks of trees, and tracks of what looked like two others. The upshot was that they brought their biology teacher, Jenny Bolman to the site, along with her husband, John, and the latter made a plaster cast of one of the tracks. The tracks and the cast were photographed by the press and a TV channel. The cast looked nothing like the five-toed Woodenbong prints and were even more improbable than the Nerang tracks. It too was twisted to the side, and appears to have only three lumpy toes. It is also elongated: 15 cm wide and 50 cm long.

Later that year a visit by Rex Gilroy inspired 76-year-old Redcliffe man, Bob Mitchell to contact the press. No, he didn't want his photo published, because people would say he was mad. But back in 1928 he was riding with two friends near Palen Creek when:

> "It was about 10 a.m. - the yowie was standing in a clearing not far from us and in that light there was no mistaking if for anything else," Mr Mitchell said. "It was about seven feet (2.1 m) tall, with a black human face and a gorilla-like body covered with thick brownish hair. It showed no aggression: it just looked at us for a moment, then turned and disappeared into the bush. It had really big feet and could move fast[44]."

This would have been only 25 km as the crow flies across the range from Woodenbong, the scene of such spectacular events half a century later. A few weeks later the same trio saw something similar while camping at Widgee Mountain about 32 km to the east. (Not to be confused with Widgee Mountain, near Gympie.)

His wife, Elsie then told how, in 1963, she had been in a car traversing an old bullock track 14 km south of Tenterfield, NSW. Three or four of the trees by the roadside had been cut off 1.8 metres or so from the ground. It was dusk, and she thought it was a peculiar way to lop trees. Then they moved, leaving behind a strong smell of rotting flesh and a low rumbling noise.

Apparently, Warwick had a bunyip early in the century (the mochel mochel, perhaps?), so that was what the press called the animal seen by a grain farmer outside the nearby town of Yangan on 24 October 1978.

> The farmer, who asked that his name be withheld, described the creature as being over 2.67 m (8ft.) tall, with what appeared to be hair covering its entire body. He made the sighting at dusk and across a paddock[45].

In that case, it is just possible it was a man. (Incidentally, the measurements are wrong; 8 feet equals 2.43 metres.)

One of the most recent sightings occurred on 12 October 1992. At about 2 am the police were called to Forest Drive, near the Golf Course at Tewantin, Queensland when a woman motorist reported a yowie 8 feet [2.4 m] tall[46]. There were alleged to have been similar sightings a few years back. How a large animal could remain unknown there is anyone's guess. This is the heart of the tourist strip, webbed by major highways, and next to a tiny state forest.

The most remote site on our survey is Emerald, central Queensland[47]. Mr Douglas Bombardieri of Mountford Rd, Kilsyth announced that he had made casts of two footprints found outside his front window. Measuring 21 cm by 16, they were markedly broader than any human foot, and about the same size as the Woodenbong print. More were discovered near the creek bed, 4 feet [1.2 m] apart. A friend of his, a plasterer called Vic, told him how he had been in the creek bed about four weeks before i.e. June 1979. All at once, he was being followed by noises "like an elephant running in galoshes." Running to his car, a Ford Fairlane, he tried to start it. It wouldn't move. He put in into third gear, but the beast was holding it back. Through the rear windscreen he could see a broad chest and two black arms. Finally, he reversed the car over it and made his escape. So, we must assume, did the creature, for there was no mention of a carcass. Mr Bombardieri appears to be genuine; he attempted to find a mundane explanation for the tracks. Perhaps, he suggested, they were made by conservationists to deter tree-fern thieves. Maybe. In that case, Vic must have seen a conservationist in a black jumper. If so, he should not be hard to find, for he is strong enough to hold back a Ford Fairlane.

That there are other sightings "out there" is quite certain. I know a gentleman who has a map of the Queensland Sunshine Coast hinterland marked with the yowie sightings he has investigated. He gets phone calls, often at night, from an acquaintance in the Blue Mountains, who believes he has a yowie living in the scrub behind his property. There are also reports of multiple witness sightings over many years in the Vulcan State Forest, near Oberon, NSW. I have not had time to follow up these leads, but I no longer simply scoff at them.

But the most southern sighting I know of was at Lake Dulverton, near Oatlands, Tasmania.[48] If yowies live there, they must have arrived during the ice age, when Bass Strait was dry land. And when I say "at" Lake Dulverton, I really mean "in". When campers, Stella Donahue and Bill Johnstone woke up, they saw the 2½ metre ape standing waist deep in the water just 20 yards away. As the great brute waded ashore, the moonlight silver on its streaming body, they fled for their lives. That was 2 am. 2 January, 1987.

With that, you should have some idea of what a yowie might be. Let's have a look at what we've got. Some of the accounts are hoaxes, needless to say. I shall let you take your pick. But, for the sake of argument, let's assume that all the witnesses are telling the truth as they see it. It should be noted that some of the features of last century's reports, such as long nails and arms reaching the ankles, are missing. It is equally obvious that the descriptions are meagre, and leave much to be desired. The face is seldom described in any detail, the limbs hardly ever. But what we have makes it clear that the animal is not a marsupial, however problematical. It can only be a primate - an ape - and a close relative of man. Man is the only known primate to habitually walked erect. (I said "known", for there are plenty of reports from America and Central Asia of unknown bipeds.) On the other hand, it cannot be too close to the human line, because of its social life. Only very rarely are more than one seen together. Like all the mystery apes from the Caucasus to California, the yowie is basically solitary.

One gains the impression that they are normally heavily built, have little in the way of a neck, and often emit a foul odour (the last trait being shared with the North American bigfoot.) However, only two features are regularly described: hair colour and height. Unfortunately, they are inconsistent. Hair colour varies from reddish to ginger to dark brown and black. To be fair, this is well within the range of normal species variation, especially since many of the observations were made at night. But height is a different matter. A species should not have half its members as tall as a medium sized man, and the others towering giants. Yet the fact is that there are excellent accounts of animals a metre and a half tall, and others 2½ metres - or more. If the former are youngsters, one would expect to see them in the company of their mothers. The few black ones were reported from the north. Also, the paler ones were all man-sized, though the reverse was not the same. Apart from that, there does not appear to be any correlation between colour, size, geography, or whether the witnesses were adults or teenagers.

To put it all in perspective, it should be added that a similar situation exists in the former Soviet Union. A Russian biologist, Valentin Sapunov, has analysed 200 reports of "snowmen", as they are called in Russia. He found that they come in four colour phases, but in different proportions to those of yowies. They also readily formed two height groups, one averaging 156 cm, the other 204 cm. The educational levels of the witnesses made no difference[49].

If such things exist in Australia, how have they managed to official detection up to now? I would tentatively attribute it to three characteristics which are not shared by the other higher primates, but which they appear to hold in common with all the other mystery apes of the world. Firstly, they are, at least in part, nocturnal. Secondly, they are solitary. A troop of gorillas would never be able to avoid notice by human beings, but what about a single gorilla, especially a shy one? And this brings us to their third saving feature: despite their size and strength, they are inoffensive, and shy of human beings almost to the point of phobia. In nearly all cases, they have moved off at the first sign of man.

Australia's native forests have been fragmented to an alarming extent by human settlement. This self-evident fact causes us to overlook an equally obvious fact: that the forests which are left are often very dense and inaccessible. Indeed, it is their very inaccessibility which has prevented settlement. We also tend to forget how we use these tracts of bush. In national parks we simply follow the beaten tracts. In state forests, if they are being used commercially, we use access roads and make a lot of noise. The patch of scrub behind the farm is probably not visited at all or, if it is, it is because we have chosen a few favourite picnic spots or meditation points, connected with unofficial trails. In other words, we tend to treat the bush like a terrestrial sea: moving over a few, well-used, traffic lanes and leaving the rest to its animal inhabitants. If one of those inhabitants wanted to avoid us, it would be largely successful. A big inhabitant would want to go roaming sometime, and the deep woods tend to be connected by belts of trees along the sides of rivers and roads, and patches of open scrub left for grazing livestock. These can easily be negotiated at night and, indeed, it is at night that most of the sightings close to human habitation have occurred. Yowies probably eat a fibrous diet, and their excrement would be more likely to be mistaken for that of horses than of human beings. Unlike gorillas and chimpanzees, they probably do not build nests, but curl up to sleep in dense, inaccessible hollows, which they also choose for their long, final sleep. Besides, how many kangaroo skeletons have you seen in the bush?

There is, however, a more serious problem. In North America the tracks of Bigfoot are seen far more often than the live animal, which is what would be expected. The reverse is true in Australia. True, the Australian soil is more likely to be hard and dry, but one would still expect more than do occur. When prints are found, they are tend to be unlike anything any plausible animal could be expected to make, and certainly unlike one another. Feet are a pretty fundamental part of a species' adaptation to its ecological niche. A species may have four different hair colours, but it simply cannot have several different types of feet. On the other hand, there are four prints - those of Woodenbong, Kempsey, Springbrook and Emerald - which do agree in general proportions, and are far too wide to be human.

Furthermore, a major problem is presented by the distribution of sightings. It is hard to believe, or example, that there is a breeding colony of black yowies at Emerald, nearly 550 km from the closest other colony and 300 km from the coast. Indeed, the sites of yowie reports have only two things in common: they are widely separated from one another, and are in areas where white settlement has been heaviest and most persistent, leaving little scope for a large, unknown animal to pass undetected.

Finally, there is the sheer improbability of an ape resident in Australia. As explained in the last chapter, this is marsupial country. No non-marsupial bigger than a rat has ever got across without human assistance. In other words, the whole thing is preposterous. The trouble is, I still can't find a way to debunk the second Woodenbong sighting. Nor can I imagine why a Senator would go out on a limb with a similar story if it was not true. And if those two are genuine . . .?

So much for the yahoos and the yowies. To my knowledge, they did not figure highly in Aboriginal lore. What they do have are tales of hairy dwarfs about a metre high[50], which fill the niche occupied by elves and goblins in the land of our forefathers. In Carnarvon Gorge, Queensland, they are apparently known as Junjuddis, for the most recent report is of a former National Parks and Wildlife Officer, Grahame Walsh out looking for them[51]. He has heard bushmen talk of seeing them around their camps at night. He himself found some footprints near the headwaters of the Maranoa the size of a five year old child's. It's amazing what you can see in the Australian bush. Which brings us to the next two stories.

The first was told by Kempsey resident, George Gray[52]. It had happened in 1968, when he was aged 57, and asleep in a bush hut near the village of Kookaburra. It was only eight years later, when he heard of Rex Gilroy's quest that he broke his silence. It was a moonlit night, when suddenly he was awakened by a hairy mannikin trying to drag him to the door. It was 4 feet [122 cm] high, web-toed, and covered with dirty grey hair, bristly like a pig's. They wrestled on the floor for many minutes. The animal did not appear angry, it made no sound, and hardly seemed to breathe. Its skin was loose; his fingers sunk in. It was like trying to hold something slippery. He could feel its fleshless bones, but the dwarf was nevertheless very strong. Its shoulders and chest were deep, and it shook him like a dog before eventually deciding to let go and shuffle out the door. The moon must have been very bright that night, and Mr Gray unusually observant. Despite the darkness, and the parlous state he was in, he was able to note the deep creases under the thing's humanlike eyes, the copper colour of its hairless face, and its large, flat nose.

The second incident was almost as dramatic, and took place more than 1300 km to the north. It became public in February 1979 when 19 year old apprentice baker, Michael Mangan rushed into the Charters Towers police station "ashen-faced and visibly upset."

One night six months before, he and his girlfriend had been parked on Towers Hill, a 100 metre high prominence just outside of town. Looking across to the passenger side, he saw, to his horror, a black, hairy face, small and drawn back like an ape's. They both screamed. The thing was about a metre tall, covered with black hair, and looked "half-man, half-ape". As he strove to get the car moving, the ape man raised its hand and smashed the passenger side window. Neither of them said anything to anyone else at the time, for obvious reasons, nor did they have any intention of going back. But when a friend told him about a similar sighting, he decided to gather a group together to search the hill.

Which is where the police came in. One of the group got separated from the others in the dark, and when they heard his screams, they went for help. The police found him 3 km from the town centre, running down the road leading to the hill. He told them he had just fought off a hairy monster with stones, and according to Sergeant Gill Engler, he had blood on his leg which was not his own. Towers Hill is not uninhabited. It is pitted with old mining shafts, and several hermits live in the ruins and the caves. However, a thorough police search revealed nothing[53].

Michael Mangan was subjected to a great deal of ridicule immediately afterwards but, according to his mother[54], he maintained the truth of the story up to the date of his death a few years ago. The police are inclined to believe he was the victim of a practical joke by his friends. If so, they would have to have played it on two separate occasions.

There are so many sightings of little people all over the world, one wonders if there is not something in them. One of these days I would like to write an article on the subject. It would start with the little hairy men of Africa, which are more plausible. After all, our short hairy ancestors lived on that continent not so long ago. It would continue with the eight hairy figures, only 60 cm high, which appeared near a school in Fiji, and go on to modern sightings of English fairies, some of which were quite minute. Then I would mention the 50 green froglike men who appeared one night in France, the little man "not much bigger than a Coke bottle" which turned up in North Carolina, the tiny man picked up in a rain-swept gutter in Ohio, and the four beings, just 20 cm high, under a bridge in Colombia. It would finish with the tale of the Peruvian who was saved from drowning in a swamp by four 3-fingered entities less than a metre high and covered with green scales[55].

I have never known what to make of such tales. Neither fact nor folklore, they exist in a special limbo of stories too wild to be accepted and too interesting to be let go. So, unless one of Mr Mangan's friends comes forth with more information, the Charters Towers mannikins will have to join them. They will not lack company.

I should add that the South Island of New Zealand also had its hairy man, though nothing seems to have been head of him since 1844, when the following was penned:

> Behind Totuki, he [i.e. the settler] may explore the mountain dreaded by the natives, on account of its being the favourite residence of the *mairoero*. This is a wild man of the woods, strong, cunning, and mischievous, and addicted to running

off with young people and damsels. His body is covered with coarse and long hair, which also flows down from the back of his head nearly to his heels. To compensate for this excessive quantity behind, his forehead is said to be bald. He was vividly described to us by a Maori who had seen one long ago, when he was a little boy, and was of opinion that "there is not a more fearful wild-fowl than your *mairoero* living."[56]

This chapter would not be complete without a reference to "the headless blackfellow". Apparently he lived in the Northern Rivers District of New South Wales in the second half of last century. So strange was his deformity that by the 1920s it had reached mythical proportions. An old Lismore resident draw a sketch of a man with abnormally large eyes set in his chest, two holes for nostrils, and a mouth, incapable of closure, set in his stomach and armed with tusks instead of teeth[57]. He was said to have been held in great fear by the Aborigines, and his burial place was kept secret. In point of fact, the Richmond River Historical Society has a tape of an interview with nonagenarian, Frank McQuilty made in 1954. He gave the name of the headless blackfellow as Nindiann or Nindjiann, and told how he used to hide his deformity under an old, tattered blanket. He was intelligent and athletic, and well protected by his brothers, Jerry and Tarah. His tribesmen steadfastly refused to betray the site of his grave, despite offers of rewards up to £15, which would have amounted to several weeks' pay even for a white man[58].

Of such things are legends made. Needless to say - and despite the rantings of second rate science fiction writers - it is quite impossible for a man's face to form part of his chest. The human body cannot be put together that way. Obviously, the unfortunate Nindjiann suffered from some spectacular deformity which he was highly successful in concealing. What it was we shall never know, but in its way, it is even more intriguing than any number of yahoos or yowies. May he rest in peace.

ADDENDUM

What is the most fantastic: a ghost, a flying saucer, or a yowie? Obviously the last! After all, we know little about the intermediate state of the soul, we know even less about life in outer space, but we *know* that having a great, hairy ape tramping around Australia - and undetected by science, to boot - is *impossible*. Australia is marsupial country. A thing like that could only arrive with human help. And apart from the sheer improbability of such an event, where would it come from? The yowie can be shown to be more or less the same as the North American bigfoot, or sasquatch, and while there are rumours of unknown bipedal apes in the parts of Asia nearest to us, they are allegedly not the same sort of ape.

So you should not be surprised that I began this chapter as an unbeliever, and half way through became a believer. I can pinpoint the month when my mind changed, and the two reports which changed it were the second Woodenbong encounter, and the testimony of the Senator. Apart from that, there was the simple accumulation of evidence. As I stated in another book: how often do people have to report something fantastic before we accept that something fantastic is going on? We might even consider a more mundane example. It might be perfectly reasonable to reject an allegation that your husband or wife is unfaithful, or your son in involved in criminal activity, but as more and more evidence keeps coming in, at some point you will have to accept the unpleasant truth.

With that in mind, I have to revise my assessment of the nineteenth century reports, as discussed in the first part of the chapter. The criticisms I made are still valid: that they lack detail, that some are second-hand, and some witnesses were children. Nevertheless, if the twentieth century reports are reliable - and they appear to be - then we must accept the earlier ones as well. Likewise, I must reconsider my scepticism of the Woronara apeman. It appears there really was a yowie in the national park, as well as a human hermit.

One correction I really do need to make concerns the 1979 incident at Emerald. As a Queenslander, I leapt to the conclusion that the town in central Queensland was involved. I hadn't realised there was one of a similar name in Victoria, where the event took place.

I also have some reservations about my suggestion that their excrement would be fibrous, and possibly mistaken for that of a horse. I was thinking of gorillas, but a yowie's faeces may be somewhat closer to a human's. Nevertheless, I stick to my comment: how many kangaroo skeletons have you seen in the bush? They may be rare, but you do find them occasionally, for two reasons. The first is they are very numerous. The second is that they don't choose their place to die ie they are killed and eaten, and their bones left where they died. But a big, rare animal at the top of the food chain chooses its own place to die; it curls up in some deep, hidden spot. Prof. Grover Krantz made this point concerning the

North American situation: judging from sightings and footprints, there must be a hundred bears for every sasquatch (bigfoot), but one practically never finds the remains of dead bears.[59]

But enough of corrections and reservations! Since the first edition of this book, a comprehensive work on all aspects of the phenomenon had been published - print-on-demand, like this book, which means it is constantly in print. This is *The Yowie* by Tony Healy and Paul Cropper[60].

They were, for example, able to find a reference to the term at least a dozen years before being popularised by Rex Gilroy, and confirmed that it was a genuine Aboriginal word from the Blue Mountains. As well as discussing all aspects of the phenomenon, they produced a catalogue of 282 cases, and personally interviewed 120 eyewitnesses. Where did they come from? Apart from a couple of dubious cases from Western Australia, reports ranged from southeast South Australia, all the way through the eastern states, to far north Queensland, the "top end" of the Northern Territory, and even the desert area near Alice Springs! And, of course, Tasmania. Not bad for a species which is not supposed to exist!

In the face of so much material, there is not much for me to do but to tie up a few loose ends. Take, for instance, George Gray's fight with a little yowie which attacked him at night. At the time I thought it strange that, despite the parlous state he was in, he was able to remember such fine detail of his assailant. As it turns out, his description was perfectly accurate; it was just not what he thought. It took Ed Skoda, a yowie sceptic, to finally establish that Gray was the victim of a practical joke[61]. A workmate, Ray Lawrence, who was "a bit of a lout" pounced on him that night dressed in a woman's fur coat, gloves, and flippers. That explains some of the odd features of the "yowie", features not present in any other encounter: the webbed feet, and the loose skin, with hardly any flesh on its bones.

With respect to the Kempsey footprints, I suggested the maker would have been 2 metres high and as heavy as a male gorilla. Dr. John Napier, who was then one of the foremost experts in the world on moneys and apes, once wrote a book entitled, *Bigfoot,* in the fifth chapter of which he calculated heights by multiplying the length of the print by 6.6.[62] Yes, we know that people of the same stature can have different shoe sizes, but he was able to show that, for human beings, it was an accurate estimate of height to within a few inches, which is all that matters. I had therefore been using that figure. However, what works for a human being may not be applicable to a very heavy animal with a broad, flat foot and a different stride. Since then, a scientist called Wolf Fahrenbach has used mass of scientific data to provide tables which are more plausible[63].

Using his calculations, the Kempsey footprint would have been made by a yowie 7 feet [2.1 m] high, and weighing 222 kg, which is in fact the weight of a big male gorilla. The prints found by young Shaun Cooper would equate to a height of 7 ft 9 in, or 2.3 metres, while the 33 cm [13 in] cast shown in Fig. 6.5 would imply the maker stood about 7 ft 3 in, or 2.2 metres, high. I photographed it at the Homestead Restaurant in Springbrook in 2002. It was cast by the manager, Andre Clayden and his friend, Gary Maguire from a set of nine they found in the mud.[64]

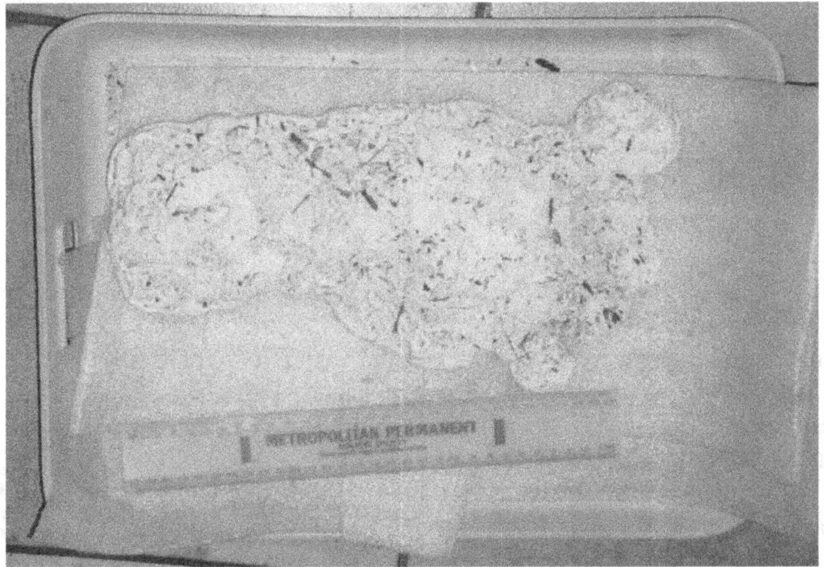

Fig. 6.5. *Cast of footprint held in the Homestead Restaurant, Springbrook* (© Malcolm Smith)

In the immediate aftermath the publication of the first edition, further reports from southeast Queensland drifted into my files. Compared to Healy and Cropper's catalogue, they are hardly worthy of filling up space here, so I shall just skip through the highlights and refer you to my blog[65].

In 1998 I was called to interview a father and adult son in the small town of Gatton. They were fearful, completely ignorant about yowies, and insisted on complete confidentiality, because their position in the community would leave them extremely vulnerable to ridicule. Close to midnight, a couple of weeks beforehand, they had been driving along the road separating the suburbs from farmland. They were only a couple of hundred metres from home when the creature climbed over the wire fence of a farm, ran across the road, and into a front yard. Specific landmarks permitted a precise identification of the site. The animal was humanoid in shape, covered in hair, and judging from height of objects nearby, it would have been 2.4 metres [8 feet] high. Surprisingly, they claimed it was as slim as I was, whereas yowies are normally described as heavily built. It was clear that it lived in the state forest a couple of miles away, had crossed the open fields, and ventured into the yards of the suburbanites. I wonder what they would have thought if they knew that![66]

There was also the experiences of a family who lived on a farm near Stanthorpe, and who desired confidentiality. Various strange happenings suggested to them that they were being checked out by an inoffensive yowie. Then one night the youngest child, a girl of 12, was going to the toilet and when she walked past the sun room with its big glass windows looking out into the patio area with three big stone arches, she saw a tall hairy creature sheltering from the drizzle under the middle arch. Its head and shoulders were wet with rain, and it was standing quite erect and looking into the room. The family and their neighbour, who provided the information to me, measured the height she felt it reached against the arch, and it came to 7ft 6in [2.3 metres]. It had no neck, long black and dark brown hair with dreadlocks coming down to its shoulders, with much shorter hair on its chest, and beautiful tan coloured hair on its legs, a little puffy at the knees and long hair down over its feet like the feathers of a draft horse. It was a bit fluffy in the groin area. It had a flat nose with two round nostrils meeting in the middle like a gorilla's nose. From where she stood, through the glass to where it stood, will have been approximately 5½ to 6 metres.

The oldest child, a boy of 15, scoffed at his sisters' stories, until one day he was taking a short cut through the bush to catch the school bus, and almost ran into a hairy man. It was only 15 metres away, and again, of an estimated height of 7ft 6in. Another time, had brought an armful of firewood into the house and had returned for the next load when he was terrified at seeing the hairy man bending over the wood pile no more than two metres from the door.

Mrs Roma Ravn belonged to a group called Omega International Research, investigating anomalies in their home districts, and in 1997 she was kind enough to send me some of their reports - with the names removed, of course. The most remarkable took place near Kandanga, which is not far from Gympie. The witness had been working at Kandanga Forestry on and off for 20 years from the late '50s into the early '70s. His job was collecting seed and nuts directly off the trees. One morning, very early because of the promised heat to come, he had set out carrying a longish pole type affair with runnels down each side of it, rather like a fishing rod, and fine twine threaded through them, in order to manipulate the clutch type affair at the collected end. The sun had not yet penetrated the forest, so he was working in semi-dark, and looking up he noted a series of strange lights fairly high above the forest. These lights were not moving, quite stationary, and he rested this pole against the tree while he moved backwards to try for a clearer view of this *thing*. It was large - about 150 feet [46 metres] across, with a row of white lights around the edge - and it seemed to him about every fourth light there was another red, smaller one directly above it. In other words, he had a close encounter with a flying saucer, although he did not report it as such. The red lights were flashing, and he simply stood and stared for several minutes. Then, when this thing was not going to move, he stepped forward once again to the tree that he was working on. He moved slightly around the tree, and once again looked up, and froze. He was attempting to look through the heavily laden branches, which radiated out at roughly nine feet [2¾ m] above the ground, and he found himself staring into a pair of eyes. He shook his head, rubbed his free hand over his eyes, and looked up again, and he could then make out the head shape, which he stated was as big as a bucket, eyes very large and very round with no whites, just brown or black, and the rest of facial features were also in shadow against the lighter sky. He actually decided he was seeing things, when he jagged the pole, which startled the animal, and it took off into the forest, breaking branches and making a lot of noise as it went. He estimates it to have been 10 feet [3 metres] high, and probably 20 odd stone [280 lb/127 kg] in weight. He could not say whether it was hairy, naked, etc. On his return to camp he told other men about the experience, and four of them stated he had seen a yowie. They had seen them many times, but as they always ran away at great speed, they *knew* them to be harmless. However, they also agreed that they often saw strange lights in the sky before or during their yowie sightings.

Personally, I don't think the yowie had any connection with the UFO except being in the same place and time. However, his experience, and that of his friends, confirms what I said before: that these unknown apes are shy of man, and generally inoffensive. But not always.

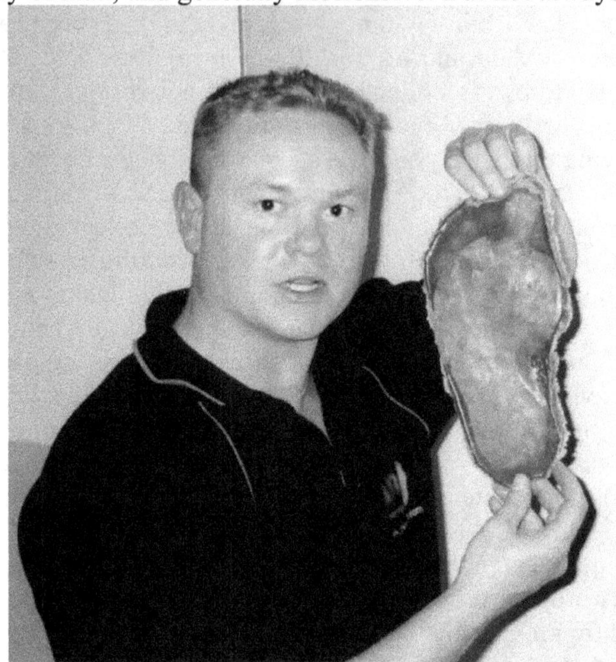

Fig. 6.6 Dean Harrison with cast of a yowie footprint.
© Malcolm Smith

In July 1997, 27-year-old Dean Harrison was in a field near Ormeau on the Queensland Gold Coast at 11 o'clock at night talking on his phone when he heard what appeared to be three people crashing through the bush behind him. Then came the sounds of something carefully stalking him. He waited. Then, as the thing reached the tree line about 25 metres away, a chill passed through him from head to toe. He turned, and saw a huge, shadowy figure squat behind a bush. It would have been about 7 feet [2.13 m] tall. (It was interesting that, although brought up and raised under metrication, he nevertheless thought in imperial measures.) Dean counted to three, then made a mad dash for the road, with the monster in fast pursuit, roaring and screaming, attempting to cut him off from the road. Following the tree line, it had twice the distance as him to cover, but it made no difference. However, just as he reached the street light, it stopped, and retreated into the bush. Its power and aggression was horrific, and he knew it could easily have killed him if it had wanted to.[67]

You might think this would put anyone off yowies, but for Dean it was the start of a fascination. One thing led to another, and in 1999 he created Australian Hominid Research, the name later changed to Australian Yowie Research (A.Y.R.), with a website where witnesses can tell their stories. I have included it among the Useful Links in Appendix 2.

Fig. 6.6 shows Dean holding the cast of a yowie footprint at the 2001 "Myths and Monsters" conference in Sydney in 2001. Some unusual ideas came out of that conference. For example, I can't imagine that any mammal, even a beaver, would have teeth and jaws strong enough to bite a piece out of a hunk of wood. Nevertheless, I was shown the branch of a tree with a section removed which, for the life of me, really did look like it had been bitten off with an ape-sized pair of jaws. The belief was also expressed that yowies dig out beetle larvae ("witchetty grubs") from timber with their fangs, just like cockatoos do, and that they also dig out the grubs with twigs. When I asked about this, I was told that the twigs have been found on the ground under such openings in the bark, along with wood dust from the opening.

My scientific background cries out: Whoa! These are wholly unsystematic observations. We require a lot more before we accept any of this. Nevertheless, if any professional zoologist out there wishes to investigate, there are people in the A.Y.R. who would be prepared to lead him to the appropriate sites. If he does, however, I can make two predictions:

1. If he discovers nothing out of the ordinary, it won't be considered worthy of publication.

2. On the other hand, if he considers there is something in the theory, then he had better direct his story to the *Journal of Cryptozoology* because, if he happens to mention "yowie" or "ape" in the paper, no formal zoological paper will accept it.

REFERENCES

[1] Ernest Favenc (1888) *The History of Australian Exploration from 1788 to 1888*. Sydney: Turner & Henderson, facsimile edition, Golden Press 1983, pp 188, 202.

[2] Aboriginal dialects: Cooma sub-district, *Science of Man* , vol.7 (7):

p104, 23 Aug. 1904, quoted by Graham C. Joyner (1977) *The hairy man of south eastern Australia*, 27 pages, privately printed. Joyner points out that there was no indication given as to how the word was collected.

[3] Mr F. Cridland *Story of Port Hacking, Cronulla and Sutherland Shire*, quoted by Fred Reilly in a letter to the editor of the *Sydney Morning Herald*, 9 Sept. 1978.

[4] Michel Raynal (1985) Yahoos in the Bahamas. *Cryptozoology* 4 p106

[5] Colin P. Groves (1986) The yahoo, the yowie, and reports of Australian hairy bipeds. *Cryptozoology* 5 pp 47 - 54

[6] Graham C. Joyner (1977) *The hairy man of south eastern Australia*, 27 pages, privately printed.

[7] Colin P. Groves (ref. 5)

[8] Colin P. Groves (1988) On type I and type II errors in cryptozoology; or, Was Proteus a yahoo? *Cryptozoology* 7: pp 123 -128

[9] Malcolm Smith (1989) Analysis of the Australian "hairy man" (yahoo) data. *Cryptozoology* 8: 27 - 36   For the controversy these two articles produced, see Joyner: *ibid.* 8: 136 - 139 and 9: 116 - 117, Smith: *ibid.* 9: 117 - 119.

[10] 'Desert family sticks to "monster" claim'. *Sunday Mail* (Brisbane) 22 Feb. 1987

[11] "Apeman" turns out to be "Rambo" the hermit. *Telegraph* (Brisbane) 28 July 1987

[12] Smith (ref. 9) p 31

[13] Smith (ref. 9), pp 34- 35

[14] *Freeman's Journal* (Sydney) 13 April 1878, quoted by Paul Cropper in 'On the trail of the black panthers'. *Mudgee Guardian* 21 April 1992

[15] *Mudgee Guardian*, June 1909, quoted by Paul Cropper in 'On the trail of the black panthers'. *Mudgee Guardian* 21 April 1992.

[16] Ron Shaw 'Why can't they leave monsters alone?' *The Bulletin* 17 May 1975   (This is the first use of the term according the Australian

National Dictionary, but it appears to have been used by Gilroy slightly earlier.)

[17] C. William (1980) *Grammar of Yuawaalaraay*   p 156, quoted by Groves (ref. 5).

[18]   Kevin Gilbert (1977) *Living Black*, p 241, cited by the *Australian National Dictionary*

[19] Frank Povah (1990) *You Kids Count Your Shadows, Hairymen and other Aboriginal folklore in New South Wales*, p 4. published by the author.

[20] Don Boyd 'Zowie! where's the YOWIE?' *Australian Outdoors and Fishing* June 1978, pp 82 - 83

[21] James Cunningham, 'On the trail of the abominable yowie.' *Sydney Morning Herald* 2 Sept. 1978

[22] Shaw (ref. 16)

[23] letter to the editor, *Sydney Morning Herald* 9 Sept. 1978

[24] Don Boyd 'Zowie! where's the YOWIE?' *Australian Outdoors and Fishing* June 1978, pp 82 - 83

[25] Boyd (ref 24)

[26] Boyd (ref, 24)

[27] 'Rock-tossing 'monster' terrifies bush kids.' *Australasian Post* 29 Feb. 1992

[28] Letter to author from Paul Cropper dated 13 Feb. 1995

[29] *Northern Star* (Lismore) 2 July 1977

[30] Gary Buchanan, 'Close-up sighting of yowies made by Woodenbong woman.' *The Northern Star* (Lismore) 4 July 1977

[31] Gary Buchanan, 'Report of Woodenbong yowies brings mixed public reaction.' *The Northern Star* (Lismore) 5 July 1977

[32] Gary Buchanan, 'Yowie report: Lismore 1935' *The Northern Star* (Lismore) 7 July 1977

[33] Gary Buchanan, 'Clear sighting of yowie at Woodenbong.' *The Northern Star* (Lismore) 15 Aug. 1977

[34] Gary Buchanan, "Return visit to 'yowie country'" *The Northern Star* (Lismore) 3 June 1981

[35] 'Ban on bunyip!' *Gold Coast Bulletin* 14 May 1965

[36] 'The bunyip hunt is on again.' *Gold Coast Bulletin* 3 Aug. 1973

[37] 'Burleigh bunyip on the run again.' *The Sunday Mail* (Brisbane) 5 Aug. 1973

[38] Des Haughton, 'Bunyip hunters are 'none the wiser" *Gold Coast Bulletin* 7 Aug. 1973

[39] 'Yowie sighting was kept secret'. *Gold Coast Bulletin* 17 Nov. 1977

[40] 'Yowie is sighted again at Springbrook.' *Gold Coast Bulletin* 2 Feb. 1978

[41] "'Gorilla' scare for boys in school library." *Gold Coast Bulletin* 3 Feb. 1978

[42] Des Houghton, 'Terror-stricken boy tells of strange encounter with the 'Yowie' kind.' *Gold Coast Bulletin* 25 Aug. 1978

[43] Andrew McKenzie, 'Campers see 'yowie' in Brisbane Valley.' *Courier-Mail* (Brisbane) 4 Jan. 1980

[44] 'Hunt plan protest 'Save the Yowie' plea.' *Sunday Mail* (Brisbane) 9 Nov. 1980

[45] 'Bunyip alive and well.' Clipping of unidentified Brisbane newspaper of 25 Oct. 1978, provided by Peter Hansen of *The Sunday Mail*.

[46] 'Woman reports Yowie sighting at Tewantin'. *Noosa News* 13 Oct. 1992

[47] Paul Robinson and Peter Roberts, 'A mountains monster runs loose.' *The Age* (Melbourne) 9 July 1979

[48] *Melbourne Herald,* 6 Jan. 1987, quoted by Tony Healy and Paul Cropper: *Out of the Shadows, mystery animals of Australia*, Pan McMillan

[49] Valentin B. Sapunov (1988) A mathematical analysis of "snowman" (wildman) eyewitness reports. *Cryptozoology* 7 : 61 - 65

[50] Povah (ref. 19), pp 4 - 8

[51] 'In search of a hairy quarry.' *Courier-Mail* (Brisbane) 29 Jan. 1994

[52] "Desperate fight with 'ape man'" *Sun-Herald* (Sydney) 12 Sept. 1976

[53] 'A 'Littlefoot' for Charters?'   *The Sunday Mail* (Brisbane) 11 March 1979

[54] From information supplied to the author from Joy Zeller, 1st July 1992

[55] For those who are interested the references are:

Africa - *On the Track of Unknown Animals* and *Les bêtes humaines de l'Afrique* by B. Heuvelmans.
Fiji - *Fiji Times* 19 July 1975
England - *The Fairies in Tradition and Folklore* by K.M. Briggs, and *Fortean Times* 71 p39 (1993)
France - *Flying Saucer Review* (FSR) 22(6) p 21 (1976)
North Carolina - *Pursuit* 10(2) p 50 (1976)
Ohio - *FSR* 26(6) p32 (1981)
Colombia - *FSR* 21(5) p31 (1975)
Peru - *FSR* 23(5) p iii (1977)   (Despite the title of the journal, none of these entities were seen in conjunction with a flying saucer.)
I myself have discussed many of these cases, and more, on my blog: https://malcolmsanomalies.blogspot.com/search/label/fairies
There will also be a long section on them in my up-coming book, *Apparitions*.

[56] D. Monro, *Nelson Examiner* 20 July1844, reprinted in Appendix C of *Contributions to the Early History of New Zealand*, by T.M. Hocken (1898) pp 262 - 3. ("Wild-fowl" means "wildlife", for the Maoris had no experience with land mammals.)

[57] 'Freak of early days.' clipping from *The Northern Star* (Lismore) of the 1920s, quoted by the same newspaper on 6 June 1981

[58] 'Historical society records tally with article on 'freak man'.' *The Northern Star* (Lismore) 13 June 1981

[59] Grover S. Krantz (1999) *Bigfoot Sasquatch Evidence*, 2nd edition, Hancock House, p 250

[60] Tony Healy and Paul Cropper (2006) *The Yowie, in search of Australia's bigfoot*, published by Strange Nation in Australia, and Anomalist Books in the U.S. and U.K.

[61] Ed Skoda, 'The unmasking of George Gray's yowie'
http://home.yowieocalypse.com/George_Gray_Yowie/ (accessed 2020)

[62] John Napier (1972), *Bigfoot*, E. P. Dutton and Co.

[63] Wolf H. Fahrenbach (1998) Sasquatch: size, scaling, and statistics. *Cryptozoology* 13: 47 -75

[64] Healy and Cropper (ref. 60), pp 74 - 75

[65] https://malcolmscryptids.blogspot.com/search/label/yowie

[66]
https://malcolmscryptids.blogspot.com/2019/11/the-gatton-yowie-1998.html
This is also case #226 in Healy and Cropper (ref. 60), p 281. The sketch was actually made by the son, not the father.

[67] https://www.yowiehunters.com.au/queensland/1317-ormeau-qld-1997

(In the original, 1999 website, Dean gave his name, but not the name of the locality.)

CHAPTER 7

A NEW ZEALAND MYSTERY

Yes, I know this is supposed to be about Australia's unknown animals. Yes, I am sure that New Zealand has its own quota of mystery animals I know nothing about. But I am equally mindful of Emerson's adage that a foolish consistency is the hobgoblin of a small mind. I also know that this is a story too good to let pass, and you will probably never hear it if you don't read it here. So, here goes.

New Zealand is a land mass, or rather two, which has been separated from the rest of the world since the days of the dinosaurs. It might even have kept a few dinosaurs if it had stayed in the tropics during its wanderings. It even has a relic of those days: the tuatara, which looks like a lizard, but is really the sole survivor of a group whose other members preceded the dinosaurs to extinction.

So isolated has it been, that since that time nothing has settled there which could neither swim nor fly. It is a land of birds which have become flightless, and the only native land animals are two species of bat. But ever since last century there have been rumours of a third. Earlier than that, in fact: when Captain Cook stayed in Dusky Sound in May 1773. Several of the crew claimed to have seen an animal the size of a cat, with short legs, a mousey colour, and a bushy tail. One even likened it to a jackal[1]. It is possible, of course, that it might have been a Maori dog.

The next reference was in 1844 when an expedition heard of animals frequenting the lakes at the source of the Molyneux (now the Clutha) River. From a description given by "one very intelligent native" of their swimming, diving, and building houses on the bank, they felt sure they were beavers[2]. One expedition member firmly located the beaver lodges on the east side of Lake Wanaka[3]. Four years later, the "beaver" received a name. In a letter to his father, Walter Mantell referred to information he had obtained in 1838:

About ten miles [16 km] inland of Arowenua Bush [i.e. Arowhenua Bush, near Temuka] there is a lake where an indigenous terrestrial quadruped, called Kāurehe, is said to exist; another reported habitat of this animal is inland two days' journey from Te Taumutu[4].

Maopo, the headman of Te Taumutu, at the southern end of Lake Ellesmere, told him that the animal laid eggs as large as a duck's, and added:

> 'Our forefathers used to catch them, and keep them as pets: when they broke loose, as they frequently did, they would return to the place they had been taken from. They still exist a day and a half's journey inland. We are afraid of them. There are two kinds, - one living on the land; the other is amphibious.'

From Tarawhata, a descendent of the Ngatimamoe tribe, he received a more detailed account:

> He informed me that the length of the animal is about two feet [60 cm] from the point of the nose to the root of the tail; the fur grisly [sic] brown - thick short legs - bushy tail - head between that of a dog and a cat - lives in holes - the food of the land kind is lizards, of the amphibious kind fish - does not lay eggs.

To Mantell's questions, Tarawhata denied that it had any pouch. Mantell offered a reward for a specimen, but had no luck. It has been suggested that the reference to egg-laying was a confusion with the tuatara. The animal, after all, was rare, and the locals need not have been completely *au fait* on its biology[5]. In a briefer, earlier account, the term *kaureke* had been used, and the animal said to be "covered with coarse gristly hair". This may be very significant.

Four years after Mantell, i.e. in 1848, the animal received another name. The Rev. Mr. Richard Taylor recorded *waitoreke* in a little Maori dictionary as "otter (uncertain, perhaps seal)", and this term seems to have gained prominence over *kaureke*, despite the letter's priority.

Later, Taylor himself interviewed two witnesses. A man named Seymour claimed to have seen the animal several times near Dusky Sound, and referred to it as a muskrat because of its strong smell. Its tail he likened to a ripe *pirori*, a fruit with a flattish shape like a beaver's tail. (This suggests he was being honest, and not just answering leading questions about beavers.) A Maori, Tamihana te Rauparaha, confirmed the shape of the tail, and nominated a size twice that of a European rat. A whaler/sealer called Tom Crib, familiar with Dusky Sound for 25 years, told Taylor he had never seen the animal, but had found little streams dammed up, with houses like beehives on either side, with entrances above and below the dam. You might note that this is the same area as the sightings by Cook's crew. However, these dams and houses, like those of Lake Wanaka, pose a problem. They do not appear in later accounts. It has been suggested that the floating nests of the great crested grebe may have been attributed to the little known aquatic animal. However, a bird would not dam a stream. Furthermore, the houses are not constructed like a true beaver's lodge.

The next report comes from a letter dated 6 June 1861 to Prof. Ferdinand von Hochstetter from Sir Julius von Haast, a very prominent biologist, and founder of the Philosophical Institute.

> At a height of 3500 feet [1067 m] above the level of the sea I frequently saw its tracks on the upper Ashburton River (Prov. Canterbury, South Island), in a region never before trodden by man. They resemble the tracks of our European otter, - only a little smaller. The animal itself, however, was likewise seen by two gentlemen, who has a sheep-station at Lake Heron not far from the Ashburton, 2100 feet [640 m] high. They describe the animal as dark-brown, of the size of a stout cony [rabbit]. On being struck with the whip, it uttered a shrill, yelping sound, and quickly disappeared in the water amid the sea-grass[6].

Sir Julius made further observations:

> Traces of a quadruped of smaller size, of nocturnal habits, and the stride of which was between seven and eight inches [18 - 20 cm], and indicates that its mode of progress was by jumps or springs, was discovered by me in the riverbed of the Hopkins, the stream which forms Lake Ohau, and as there is every reason to believe that this animals still exists in great numbers, hundreds of tracks having been found in one night in the fresh-falled snow, we may hope that some specimens of this entirely unknown quadruped will soon be obtained[7].

His hopes were to be unfounded. However, as Pollock[8] pointed out, an expert of Haast's experience would be familiar with the five-toed spoor of an otter, and could distinguish them from those of the four-toed wild dog. Otter tracks can also be confused with those of the introduced Australian brushtailed possum, but it would have been impossible for it to have spread to that area in Haast's time[9].

Haast apparently got hold of a *kaurehe* skin in 1868. Bailed up by dogs in a flax bush near the banks of the Selwyn, it had been knocked on the head, skinned, and the body and skull thrown to the pigs. (Readers should understand that the skull is the most diagnostic feature of an animal, and should never be discarded.) Even the skin had been torn by the dogs after being hung on the killer's wall, till only the head, parts of the back and one foreleg remained. The scientist found it to be light brown and covered with white spots. The foot was not webbed. He sent to it to Dr. Krefft in Sydney for identification, and nothing more was recorded of it. Presumably Krefft recognized for for the common Australian marsupial cat, *Dasyurus* sp., for two had been liberated in New Zealand by the Canterbury Acclimatization Society the same year.

And that is just about all the information available on the mystery animal from last century. The names themselves have been the subject of much debate. Recently, however, a New Zealand anthropologist called John Colarusso appears to have solved the problem, and his conclusions are startling. Taking all the variant spellings, and juggling all the possible components from the Maori language, he found that the only ones which make sense involve the root, *reke*, meaning "bone pin", "knob", "quill", or "spur". It implies an important feature of the anatomy not previously commented on. The names, he discovered, were known to only a few persons in restricted areas, fitting an animal equally rare and elusive. *Kau-reke* would mean "many spurs/quills" e.g. "very spiny". The variant, *kaurehe* actually means "monster" or, sometimes, "tuatara", and had apparently been substituted for the original because the informants found it a more familiar term. The other name, *wai-tō-reke* (with a long *o*) means "water diver (with the) spur(s)", and follows an old pattern of word formation. A less likely interpretation would be "the one with the spur(s)/quill(s)".[10]

Since Haast's time the *waitoreke/kaureke* has been largely ignored by science, though it had been the subject of intermittent correspondence in the *Southland Times* in the early part of this century. Recently, however, G. A. Pollock has come forth and collated the available data. Much of it emanated from what he calls the Henderson papers, a file of clippings and correspondence in the possession of L. E. Henderson (in 1970), after passing through two other hands. In addition, he had himself accumulated an number of accounts from more recent years. Pollock's articles are so detailed, they really should be quoted in their entirety. Although they themselves merely recorded the most striking reports, only a summary can be provided here. The evidence, in short, has been very much attenuated, and will therefore lose much of its compelling force[11].

A. E. Trapper, of Clifton Station, Lower Waiai, and later Grassmere, near Invercargill, liked to go fishing in lonely sites. That was how he managed to see the animal six times between 1890 and 1921. An animal a "dark mousey" colour, nearly as large as a half-grown rabbit was seen on the bed of a creek, searching under stones for food. One day, near dusk, a biggish animal with a small, round head like a seal's swam against the current to within two yards of him. Another time, he saw an animal the size of a brushtailed possum in a broadleaf tree on a bank, but when he approached, it dived into the stream and disappeared. In 1912 he and a friend watched two animals playing or fishing 100 yards away for 15 minutes. Something with a small, round head was also seen swimming in a swamp on the Waikiwi River, near Invercargill.

The 1921 sighting, from an old bridge over the Waikiwi, Pollock found particularly significant. Although Trapper claimed no knowledge of otters, the "dark shadowy form 18 in. or two feet [45 - 60 cm] deep" he witnessed left a trail of bubbles typical of otters. Some months later he found a hole in the bank the size of a rabbit's burrow at the site when it had vanished. Pollock was even able to find the old bridge in 1968, but by then the river was horribly polluted. One more rare animal had decamped unrecognized.

Many other observations could be cited. Dr. J. Garfield Crawford was fishing the Dunsdale Stream in 1936 when a small animal darted between his friend's legs and immediately submerged. It was furry, "mousey" in colour, and 7 to 8 inches [18 - 20 cm] long and 2 inches [5 cm] broad, with feet 1½ to 2 inches [4 - 5 cm] long, a rounded head and flattish tail. Mrs. O. Linscott, of Thronbury, watched an animal swim across a lagoon draining the Aparima River in 1957. It had a dark, "browny-purple" face, with small pop eyes and flat, rounded ears. She could see only the head and forequarters. No neck was visible, but the head appeared small, the fur cat-like, but with longer guard hairs, and short, stout whiskers on the head. Previously, her father-in-law had watched two animals playing in the same lagoon.

Bob Thompson originally lived beside the River Yare in Norfolk, where otters abound. But in December 1968 he was in a holiday hut near the Whakaea River, close to Waikaia. At daybreak, awakened by possums on the roof, he looked outside and saw an otter emerge from the creek, look cautiously around, and then signal to three three-quarters grown young, which followed her up the bank and behind the shrubbery. P. J. A. Bradley was familiar with New Zealand wildlife. In 1971 he was hunting deer on the Hollyford River. For a quarter of an hour he watched an animal climb the bank and slide down - four or five times in all - as only an otter will do. His description: smooth, short, dark brown fur, small head, no noticeable neck or ears, tail thick, short and tapering, overall length 36 to 42 inches [91 - 107 cm].

For the period 1968 to 1971 Pollock cited three observations in the province of Canterbury, by two men each with experience with otters in Britain. One came so close to an animal eating a fish on the banks of the Opihi River that he was even able to see the webbing on its forefeet. Horace Sinclair owns much of a swamp on the Taieri Plain. On 26 April 1971 he listened to a radio announcer reading a description of otter tracks from an article previously written by Pollock. That very day he and a friend were inspecting a drain on his property when they found identical footprints in the mud. They were the size of a matchbox, and even the webbing was clearly marked. The year before he had fired at an animal he at first thought was a rat, but even as he was squeezing the trigger he realised his mistake. Not so much as a drop of blood was found. Except at close range, an otter's hide is highly resistant to shotgun pellets.

In April 1973 Pollock himself visited the area. In a swamp where no terrestrial animal would go, he found a system of tunnels through the reeds, some enlarged by excavation, a nest chamber, and an emergency tunnel leading vertically to the top of the bank: all characteristic of an otter's holt, and nothing else.

It is hard to read Pollock's article without agreeing that the *waitoreke* is, in fact, an otter. He even feels he can identify the subspecies: *Lutra lutra barang*, the *simung* of Indonesia, Thailand and Vietnam, frequently domesticated in those countries and trained to catch fish. There is evidence that Indonesians visited New Zealand centuries before the Europeans, albeit probably not intentionally. They were more likely to be storm-tossed castaways. One of those boats may have carried a pair of simungs. He even suggests a possible date: some time before the arrival of the Ngatimamoe tribe in the 16th century, because they knew the animal, but had no knowledge of its origins.

Nevertheless, I can see problems. Whether the Indonesians arrived deliberately or accidentally, they would have been aboard an ocean-going vessel. Why would they be carrying a fresh-water animal like an otter? And why both a male and a female? Just the same, it is more plausible than the theories propounded to account for the Australian cougars. The areas involved are Southland and western Otago north into the Canterbury Plains to at least the Ashburton River. Otters are shy, elusive and secretive, easily missed by those not actually looking for them. It would not be difficult for them to remain unnoticed for so long. The lack of spraints (faeces deposited as territorial marks) can be explained by their low population densities, making territorial defence less necessary.

All the same, Pollock did note some ecological problems. Its present distribution would suggest that it had managed to cross extremely high mountain passes, in a most un-otterlike fashion. Tarawhata, you will remember, claimed there was a land variety of kaureke which fed on lizards, and this would virtually be a requirement in their travels away from water. But such a habit has never been recorded of otters. Cook's men almost certainly saw native dogs. But even with this exclusion, you will note that certain features of Maori tradition are absent from modern descriptions. What about the flat, beaver-like tail? An otter's tail is really nothing like a beaver's but it is is flattish, and if a Maori said "flat", a European would think beaver rather than otter. However, a European witness, Seymour, did emphasize the beaver similarity. And what about the conspicuous nests? What about the characteristics implicit in the derivation of the names?

The *waitoreke* has go to be found. Naturalists should make every effort to check streams for indications of its presence whenever they are in the relevant areas. Anyone who sees the animal or its signs should be prepared to report them to the scientific authorities. The latter should take them seriously. If the *waitoreke* is an otter, it has become an established member of the fauna. Any damage it may have produced in the environment is now over and done with, but it is itself threatened by the havoc wreaked by man and his domesticated animals - just as it is in Europe.

But there is an even more compelling reason for finding it. There is still a slim chance that it is actually an indigenous mammal. If so, it is even more threatened for having evolved in a land without native land predators. Terrible things have happened to New Zealand's lizards and flightless birds for that very reason. Many have already gone down the memory hole of extinction. An indigenous New Zealand mammal would be the zoological discovery of the century. It would not be your common, or garden variety of mammal, but a leftover from the days when mammals were scurrying under the feet of the giant reptiles. It might well be a monotreme, a distant relative of the platypus and the echidna. Chief Maopo may have been right when he said it laid eggs.

Better still, it might be a representative of those small groups of primitive mammals, experiments in the evolution of mammals, which are known only from incomplete fossils, most of which were extinct before the great explosion of mammal evolution began. Indeed, Colarusso has suggested that the "reke", or spines, spurs, quills etc., which form the basis of the Maori names, could logically refer to the coarse body covering which would have preceded the evolution of hair in the most primitive of mammals[12].

Isn't this going beyond the evidence, you might ask: a romantic dream of the perennial optimist? Very likely. But consider. When the vocabulary of Maori natural history was being collected, there were found three reptile names which did not match up with any specific reptile. These were *ngārara, kumi* and *kawekaweau*. The first appears to be a generic term for reptiles. The second was a fabulous (?) reptile 5 feet [1½ m] long, with six legs. But the *kawekaweau* is a different matter. It has just been found.

It was not, I hasten to add, in New Zealand, but in the Natural History Museum of Marseille, France: an unlabelled specimen of the world's largest gecko. At 370 mm from snout to vent, and 622 mm including the tail, it was 54% longer than the previous record holder, and almost three times the length of 97% of the world's geckos. Newly christened *Hoplodactylus delcourti*, and bearing no label, it is believed to have been collected sometime between 1833 and 1869, a period for which the museum's records have been lost. While the exact site in also unrecorded, the obvious assumption is the North Island of New Zealand, because it fits the traditional description of the kawekaweau exactly[13]. Think of it: the world's largest gecko, extinct before the world knew anything about it! Or is it? The hunt is now on, and several witnesses of unusually large lizards in the forests of the North Island have come forth[14].

The lesson is obvious: if the *kawekaweau* proved to be more than a legend, why not the *waitoreke*? And what on earth was, or is, the *kumi*?

REFERENCES

[1] J.S. Watson (1960) The New Zealand 'otter' *Rec. Cant. Mus.* 7 : 175 - 183 (Many of the early documents are not easily accessible in this country. They can be assumed to have been quoted from this summary unless specifically stated otherwise.)

[2] D. Monro, *Nelson Examiner* 20 July 1844, reprinted in Appendix C of *Contributions to the Early History of New Zealand*, by T.M. Hocken (1898) pp 262 - 3.

[3] Watson (ref. 1), p 176

[4] Gideon Algernon Mantell (1851) *Petrifactions and their Teachings; or a Handbook to the Gallery of Organic Remains of the British Museum London*, pp 105 - 106 (spine-title: *Mantell's Fossils of the British Museum*)

[5] G. A. Pollock (1970) The South Island otter - a reassessment. *Proc. N. Z. Ecol. Soc.* 17: 129 - 135 **and** (1974) The South Island otter - an addendum. *ibid.* 21: 57 - 61

[6] Ferdinand von Hochstetter (1867) *New Zealand, its physical geography, geology and natural history with special reference to the results of the Government Expeditions in the provinces of Auckland and Nelson.* Stuttgart, p161

[7] H. F. von Haast (1948) *The Life and Times of Sir Julius von Haast.* Wellington, p 225

[8] Pollock (ref. 5) p 129

[9] Pollock (ref. 5) p 129

[10] John Colarusso (1988) Waitoreke, the New Zealand "otter": a linguistic solution to a cryptozoological problem. *Cryptozoology* 7: 46 - 60

[11] Pollock (ref. 5), pp 130 - 2

[12] Colarusso (ref. 10)

[13] Aaron M. Bauer and Anthony P. Russell (1986) *Hoplodactylus delcourti* n. sp. (Reptilia: Gekkonidae), the largest known gecko. *N. Z. J. Zool.* 13: 141 - 148

[14] Aaron M. Bauer and Anthony P. Russell (1990) Recent advances in the search for the living giant gecko of New Zealand. *Cryptozoology* 9: 66 - 73

CHAPTER 8

ODDS AND ENDS (MOSTLY ODDS)

What an amazing country Australia is! Not only are our known animals unlike anything in the rest of the world, so are our mystery animals. We have thylacines on the mainland which don't really look like thylacines. Our big cats look just like pumas and black panthers, but they cannot be either, because they hunt together and interbreed. And they definitely could not have got here. We have apes unknown to science which quite literally could not have got here in a million years. Even the sea serpents visiting our shores are stranger than those of more mundane nations. And sometimes, just sometimes, we take it for granted.

Many of those who saw the North Queensland tiger (chapter 3) assumed at the time that it was a normal part of the fauna, not worthy of reporting to science. The same can happen with far better known species. My own brother once came upon a wombat while motoring in the Gympie/Nambour area of Queensland. He didn't think it strange, because no-one had told him that wombats are not supposed to exist much north of the New South Wales border. Of course, he is not a zoologist, but how many degrees do you need to recognize a wombat?

For that matter, it is not certain that Ian Offer, the owner of the Wellesley Road Wildlife Park, north of Bunbury, knew that wombats do not exist in Western Australia. So when foresters told him of one sighted close to his sanctuary in 1972, he naively set a cage trap for it. And just as naively caught it. There has been some suggestions that it had been introduced from the east by persons unknown. He believed it was a new subspecies. The jury is still out[1].

Ignorance can also produce the reverse effect: an animal which completely mystifies its discoverer can turn out to be quite commonplace. On 2nd March 1871 some men caught a small creature at Corio Bay, near Geelong, Victoria. It had been in the water making for the beach when some boys pointed it out, and heading for a nest in the cliff when they finally caught it. Neither they nor the press could work out what it might be. It was reportedly a foot and a quarter [38 cm] long, with a tail as thick as one's second finger. Its fur was glossy, like a beaver's, its head somewhat flattened, its feet webbed, its nose like a ferret's or rat's, with front teeth which overlapped like a rabbit's[2]. Weird, wasn't it? But the identity is perfectly clear: it was the common water rat, *Hydromys chrysogaster*. The only thing unusual was its presence in salt water.

The moral of the story is: if ever you come across an unusual specimen, whether bird, beast, fish or insect - and it's dead - don't hesitate to take it to your local museum. If it is a common animal they can identify it right away. If it isn't, they'll want to know about it.

Then, of course, there are the wild cards, like *Ompax spatuloides*[3,4]. In 1879, a museum director in search of lungfish, stayed at Gayndah station on the Burnett River. When a fish was served for breakfast, he was so amazed, that he had it drawn by a passing road-inspector before consuming it (see Figure 8.1). The details were then dispatched to the French Consul, Count F. de Castelnau, who gave it its official name. The first was taken from the Eleusinian Mysteries of ancient Greece. For the second he followed the frowned-upon practice of combining Greek and Latin to refer to its spatula-shaped head, for the fish was 18 inches [45cm] long, of a dirty mahogany colour, with ganoid scales, a fringe-like tail, and a spatulate bill. The story remained a standard joke in the Burnett district for half a century, until an old timer spilled the beans. Apparently *Ompax* had been constructed by local stockmen from the head of a platypus, the body of a mullet, and the tail of an eel or lungfish. As my old university text book pointed out[5], the universal desire to make a fool out of an expert has introduced more such hoaxes into the zoological literature than is normally realised. No doubt a few have crept into this book as well.

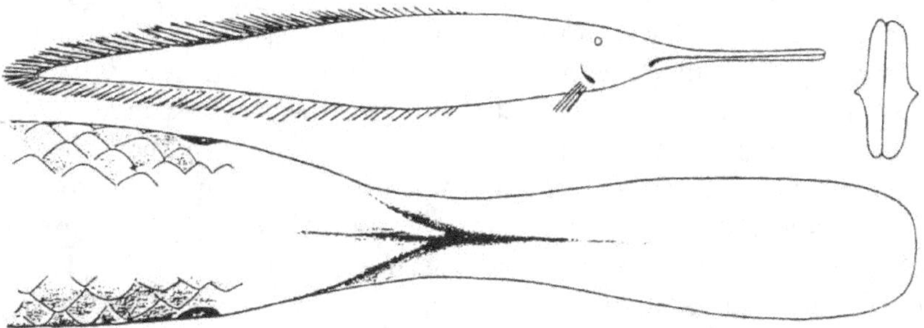

Figure 8.1 Ompax spatuloides

With all this in mind, let us now examine a few stories which do not warrant chapters of their own. You have all heard of the abominable snowman, but what about the Spinifex Man? His tracks were found by Peter Muir, a government "dogger" near Laverton, W.A., about 250 km E.N.E. of Kalgoorlie in 1970. In 30 years in the desert he had never seen anything like them: prints 15 inches [38 cm] long, consisting of just two toes. Almost at once it was pointed out[6] that only one animal fits the bill: the ostrich. No, that's not as ridiculous as it sounds. There had been unsuccessful attempts at ostrich farming in South Australia in earlier decades, and some might have been set free. There is a lot of desert between there and Laverton, but ostriches are desert birds, and capable of wide wandering. Witnesses would be few and far between in the desert. Also, any ostrich seen at a distance would be mistaken for an emu which, incidentally, has three toes. Since ostrich farming is making a comeback, desert travellers should keep their eyes peeled.

Diprotodonts. Imagine a wombat the size of an ox and you have some idea of what a diprotodont looked like, although diprotodonts were not really closely related to wombats. The last ones were still around for the coming of the first Aborigines, who probably hastened their extinction. (The idea that primitive man lived "in harmony with nature" is a romantic myth.) The discovery of their huge bones last century produced instant speculation that some might survive in the still unexplored interior. Ludwig Leichhardt was said to be looking for such evidence on his ill-fated expedition to the north.

The only evidence I know of is a comment by Dr Heuvelmans[7] that prospectors' tales of rabbits 10 feet [3 m] long had reached the ears of "the great Australian naturalist", Ambrose Pratt. I would hardly have graced Pratt with that title. I came across his best known work, *The Call of the Koala* when I was myself studying koalas, and it was enough to destroy any naturalist's credibility. It received terrible reviews when it first came out, and I have to concur with the other koala specialists that it was a load of unmitigated rubbish. A letter from Heuvelmans informed me he had obtained the information from the American cryptozoologist, Dr Ivan Sanderson, presumably in the 1940s or '50s. That is not much to go on. As far as I am aware, there is no evidence of any diprotodont surviving to modern times. Which is a pity.

Giant goannas. The extinct goanna, *Megalania prisca* was probably the largest land predator in the world in its time. At 6 metres in length, only the very biggest crocodiles could now compare to it. Today's biggest lizard the Komodo dragon, is only half as long. Nobody can imagine how overpowering the sight of such a monster would be without personal experience. The Queensland Museum has a *Megalania* exhibit which is so realistic that they were forced to erect a warning sign. Apparently, it was scaring the daylights out of small children. Furthermore, no such a monster could go undetected for long. Far from skulking in the undergrowth like a yowie or a marsupial tiger, it would need to bask in the sun in good reptilian fashion.

So how do you feel about goannas half as long again in areas where white settlement has been longest and most intense? In 1979 Rex Gilroy published an article on these giants[8]. He had collected reports of sightings - close up and under excellent viewing conditions by reliable people - from the Watagan Mountains near Cessnock, N.S.W., the Blue Mountains, the district of Capertee, west of Sydney, down to the Victorian border, up to the Lamington National Park in southern Queensland, and even - though he gave no details - to the rainforests of north Queensland and Papua New Guinea. One was even seen crossing a bush road near Beenleigh, south of Brisbane.

The area of Loadstone, 7 miles [11 km] south of the Queensland border, seems to have been a hive of activity. Stan Lomond often had to put down cattle whose legs had been bitten off by the monsters. In 1955 loggers had moved into the cedar grove on the Lomond property, and quickly became acquainted with the goannas. One man had two fingers bitten off. Indeed, the loggers would only work in the early morning and late afternoon to avoid the brutes. All this appears to have gone unrecorded by the press. Immediately I read the article I wrote to Mr. Lomond's widow, and received the following response:

> The whole article is just a lot of garbage. There is only one line of truth in it, & that is, that Loadstone is about 7 miles from the Queensland border. We have no cedar trees, no scrub, & certainly no giant lizards. We would like to know where Mr Gilroy got his "facts" from.

As I said before, I've never been impressed by Rex Gilroy's pronouncements.

Crocodiles. Now, there's a subject we can all feel at home with. They're related to alligators, and most of us have heard the tale of the sewer alligators. According to this widespread urban myth, baby alligators brought as pets to New York or Washington, or maybe both, end up biting the fingers that feed them, and are then angrily flushed down the toilet. However, they manage to survive the journey to the sewers, where they grow to immense size by feeding on sewer rats and the occasional unwary sewer worker. They even made a film about it. Somewhat better documented is the case of the Over-Norton crocodiles. Apparently, young crocodiles were reported on four separate occasions near this village over a period of decades in the 1800s. One wonders how they got there. Over-Norton is in Oxfordshire, England[9].

Be that as it may, the estuarine crocodile of our far north is capable of remarkable journeys. It does not actually live in the sea, but if one is swept away from shore or for some reason loses its bearings, it may survive to turn up a long, long way from home. The Cocos-Keeling Islands, the New Hebrides, and Fiji are all well over 1000 km from any crocodile habitat, but all have recorded strays[10].

But these islands are all in the tropics, of course, and a long way from the Logan River, south of Brisbane. So when locals started seeing "alligators" in that river in the early 1900s, it occasioned not a little scoffing. When a swimmer was dragged down, spectators claimed an alligator had taken him. In early 1905 a resident not only claimed to have seen one, but to have shot at it. Then, several months later, on 22 June 1905, a Mr. A. G. Hinds happened to see a crocodile floating dead under a willow tree near the old Logan Village ferry. With the help of his brother and another man, he dragged it to shore, where it was photographed and found to measure 12 foot 7 inches [3.8 m] in length. It had apparently been shot a few days before by persons unknown[11].

You may remember from chapter 1 how Carl Lentz had claimed, in 1965, that the Burleigh "bunyip" was a crocodile. He then narrated his adventures in 1934[12]. It was the year of the big dry. He had been ridiculed for reporting strange noises in a river in the Gold Coast hinterland. Nevertheless, his friend, Bob Veivers had lost nine cows. One of Lentz's own cows died in the creek. Three days later the whole carcass was gone except for a strip of hide. Something very strong must have dragged it out of the hole.

Three days later one of his cows was bellowing "something awful", but he found nothing. However, that afternoon eight of his cows were missing at the muster. One was found in the creek, its belly ripped open and its unborn calf gone. The next morning the carcass was gone. When a noise was heard, halfway between a bark and a roar, his neighbour, Barlow Duncan said it was a bunyip.

That August he went stalking along the creek and - lo and behold! - there was a crocodile whose left hind foot was as big as a dinner plate. Unfortunately, he was not able to get into a suitable position to shoot it.

Another time, he shot at a crocodile which he found caught by an uprooted tree in a narrow channel. No doubt he missed, for the reptile make a terrific commotion, snapped off a branch, and got free. As the hunter went to shoot, it scrambled over a rock barrier and was gone. Whether it deserted the Gold Coast completely, I cannot say. Mr Lentz did, however, claim that it once took 17 cows plus a heifer in a single month. That, however, is beyond belief. Crocodiles are cold blooded, and need to eat only a fraction of the food their hot blooded colleagues require. The eat a full meal only 50 times a year, and consume no more than the average cormorant[13]. The cattle presumably went missing for far less sinister reasons. Just the same, he also claimed to have searched for bunyips in the Merrimac Swamp in 1887. Two of them could be heard calling at the same time, half a mile [0.8 km] apart. That does sound like a pair of crocodiles.

Unobtrusive Angourie Beach, just south of Yamba in the Northern Rivers District of New South Wales, became the centre of a short-lived crocodile hunt at the end of 1939. A small railway line ran there, and the driver, Max Rutledge, was surprised to discover that a "log" next to where the train had stopped was, in fact, a 15 foot [4½ m] crocodile. Both croc and train took off in different directions[14]. Soon it became apparent that on two earlier occasions local residents had seen something strange at night, but hadn't mentioned it[15]. This is typical where mystery animals are concerned. Furthermore, a recent ex-resident, Captain Fraser, told how he had often been kept awake at night by a booming noise from the swamp. (Remember the Burleigh bunyip in Chapter 1?) Now the search parties were out in force, combing a patch of swamp said to measure only four square miles [10½ sq.km.]. They managed to kill numerous snakes, plus a 5 foot [1½ m] goanna, and obtain a plaster cast of a footprint. A zoologist at the Australian Museum, J.R. Kinghorn compared the cast to a reproduction of a crocodile in the museum[16]. It appeared to be the left hand paw of a crocodile about 12 feet [3.66 m] long. But the crocodile itself managed to disappear without trace.

That, of course, was before the great crocodile shoot-out had virtually emptied north Queensland of the animals. But as late as 1980, stories were circulating of crocodiles sighted on the Gold Coast, and even in Brisbane itself[17]. An amateur fisherman, for example, saw a small crocodile slip into the water when he was fishing at the mouth of the Pine River and Hayes Islet. This is the stretch of water separating Brisbane from Redcliffe. It is also very close to my house, so I was not a little taken aback by such a report. It was confirmed by a boat hire proprietor, John Zamper, who had a tenant tell him he saw one in the mangroves at the same place. Jeanette Covacevich, the Queensland Museum herpetologist, had irrigation and water supply workers tell her they had seen a crocodile a metre and a half in length in Currumbin Creek, on the Gold Coast about 1978. She had also heard of a crocodile found crossing a road in the Brisbane suburb of Fairfield in 1970. Keeping young crocs was banned in 1974, and some pet owners no doubt liberated some into the wild. That was the reason Bob Irwin, the owner of the Queensland Reptile and Fauna Park, gave for the presence of crocodiles which he believed definitely existed on the Gold Coast.

Who knows what people can see and mistake for crocodiles? Goannas perhaps - or real crocodiles, either released pets or strays from the far north. I am not prepared to rule out the last possibility. But it would appear certain that no individuals have set up permanent homes south of the Tropic of Capricorn.

At any rate, no one can deny that crocodiles are gradually making a comeback. Newswatchers of 29 August 1989 may remember seeing a three metre long female being caught in the heart of Rockhampton right in front of the Channel 2 cameras. So when half a dozen reports of another three metre croc in the Noosa River were made in 1993, the coastguard at least took them seriously. Of course, it did not escape their notice that the first sighting occurred on April Fools' Day[18],[19]. The latest I have heard is of an ex-policeman residing at Banksia Beach, on the Sunshine Coast, who was walking his dog what he thought was a 1.5 metre log in his path turned out to be a crocodile. It appears three other locals have seen one too[20].

The Barcoo alligator was said to have been 4 or 5 metres long and was "armour-plated and knobbled, and bellowed like a bull"[21]. In other words, it was just like a normal crocodile, only a long way from home. However, I have not been able to sight the original report, and know nothing more, not even the date. Windorah, for those who don't know it, is a west Queensland town about 800 km from the nearest coast, but adjacent to Cooper Creek, also known as the Barcoo. It was there, in mid-January, 1992 that some tourists found a dead crocodile in an illegal fishing net[22]. At 1.85 metres, it was fully grown, perhaps 15 or 20 years old, for this was the non-maneating, freshwater species. A zoologist speculated that it had been kept illegally in a dam which overflowed, or that it came down from the Longreach district on a flood. How it got over the mountains was not speculated.

The above sightings are at least plausible, but there is one report which really puzzles me. It is dated 1867.

CROCODILES IN GIPPSLAND

Not long ago the *Gipps Land Times* startled its local readers by publishing a statement to the effect that some of the Gipps Land rivers were infested by a species of crocodile or alligator. A correspondent at the Crooked River supplies our contemporary with some corroborative facts:

Several times, he writes, I have read a description of a reptile styled the fresh water crocodile, in the columns of your paper. I am in a position to give a truthful account of this strange beast, which you are at liberty to publish. Last Wednesday morning, while walking along the Wongungarra River, about two miles an three-quarters [4½ km] below Winchester township, being out on a fishing excursion, I noticed unusual and new tracks, looking like the marks by the feet of an enormous eagle, in the sand by the river side. While examining these curious tracks, I was suddenly alarmed by a rushing sound through a bed of reeds in front, and a reptile (which, no doubt, must be the often spoken of fresh water crocodile) rushed out and, looking at me fixedly for a few moments, with jaws opened to a frightful extent, and uttering sounds like a plaintive bellow of a calf, plunged into the river. Although much startles, as you may suppose, I am perfectly sure as to the identity of the reptile, as I had ample time to observe his proportions. I am positive he measured close on twelve feet [3.6m] from the snout to the tip of his tail. His colour was that of a dark brown on the back, and greenish under the belly. On the back, from the neck down, he had horny fins in the shape of the teeth of a cross-cut saw, and presented altogether a most repulsive and formidable appearance . . .[23]

The correspondent suggested that it could have inspired the bunyip legend. What he didn't know was that, if his estimate of the size of anywhere near accurate, this couldn't have been a harmless freshwater crocodile. It would have been a saltwater croc - a potential maneater. And this was in Victoria!

And now for my favourites, the *pièces de résistance*, the *crème de la crème*. The first comes from David Heppell, a mollusc specialist from the Royal Museum of Scotland, who had the task of sorting out the museum's mermaid collection. Don't laugh. One of the peculiar customs of the nineteenth century was the forging of grotescue mermaids out of fish tails and similar material, for sale to mariners. He was also involved in collating accounts of mermaid sightings, of which there are more than you might expect. Anyhow, I was able to help him with a photograph of a very unusual mermaid specimen[24], and he came back with the following story.

The witness was Shane, aged 26, a body builder and security guard and, according to his mother, a very down to earth person who would not say anything that was not true. The family lived in Melbourne, but in 1989 they bought some land at Bundaberg, Queensland, and went up for a holiday. One afternoon, after fishing off the beach, the parents went home to prepare dinner, but Shane decided to stay longer. When he finally returned, he was bubbling over with the following tale. As his mother described it:

> After about one or two hours Shane thought it was getting late, just on twilight, and he had better go home. He packed up his line, *etc.*, and, when he stood up to go, this beautiful being was walking at the edge of the surf. He was about 6ft [183 cm] high - green scales, instead of skin, and webbing (like ducks') on hands and feet. A fin reached from his wrist to the waistline. Also, a fin from the centre of the forehead reached down the back. He seemed to speak telepathically, saying 'We are watching you - do not be afraid'. He lifted his hands above his head and crossed his hands as he seemed to speak. As Shane moved closer he moved back slowly, then stopped. Then Shane stayed in the one position. When Shane made no movement he just stood there. Shane thinks it was about a quarter of an hour or 20 minutes he was there. Then he put his arms by his side, and dived into the sea, and swam just the same as the dolphin swims. Shane ran closer to watch him swim. He was about 25 to 30 yards away from Shane at that time.

And that is why it is important never to throw out any information, no matter how ridiculous it sounds. Immediately I read that story, I knew I'd read something similar from the other side of the Pacific. Actress Shelley Winters had been at a party at Malibu Beach, California in World

War II when she saw what she first thought was a frogman emerge from the sea. Instead, it was a red, humanoid creature, which gave her a thrill by wrapping its webbed hands around her. Shelley told that story on American TV in 1991[25]. Whether Shane or his mother ever heard it, I don't know. But why would a film star make up such a wild story?

Something even stranger appeared beside the Wakehurst Parkway beside the Narrabeen Lakes. In other words, it was in the northern suburbs of Sydney, and even in 1968 that was not virgin wilderness. Yet at 1.15 p.m. on 3rd April that year, Mrs Mabel Walsh was driving down the parkway with her nephew, John when they saw the creature standing with its feet in shallow water.

> It was a bit over 4 feet [122 cm] tall, with dark grey, tough leathery skin, like an elephant's. It had small front legs and walked on its hind legs which were thick and round like an elephant's.
>
> It ambled out of the lake and ran into the scrub. It had a strange shuffling walk, but was quite fast. It shocked me. It was a peculiar looking thing. I've never seen anything like it. We saw it for only a few seconds.
>
> I stopped the car, but had to wait for traffic to pass before I could back up. But the thing had gone. We were in a hurry. We wanted to have a swim. Then I had to get John to the airport and go home for tea before going to gemology classes I didn't have time to call anyone and check on it.
>
> I didn't notice a tail or ears, but it had small eyes and smaller front legs or arms. Its head reminded me of an ant-eater's. Its trunk was rigid, squared off at the end and stuck down and out at an angle[26].

Perhaps it was not a coincidence that UFOs turned up in the Sydney sky a fortnight later[27]. And perhaps, too, the Narrabeen critter was a relative of the one observed by two fishermen in a boat three years later by the light of a kerosene lamp. It was also grey, with a trunk like an elephant's, and was walking on its back legs on the water[28].

Do I believe such stories? I heard it once said that if you keep your mind sufficiently open, people will dump a lot of rubbish into it. My motto is to believe nothing that has not been corroborated, but to file everything, no matter how bizarre. Every now and then I look over my files. And sometimes a wry grin creeps over my face. I imagine drawing an appropriate cartoon. The captain of a flying saucer is reprimanding one of his crew. "You idiot!" he shouts. "Don't you know to keep the mascot on a leash when you take it for a walk?"[29]

ADDENDUM

The is not much to add to this chapter. In 1995 Rex Gilroy's book, *Mysterious Australia* came out[30]. At no time did either he or his publisher consider that documentation, or even an index, might be appropriate, and locating his alleged witnesses was next to impossible. In it, he introduces even more fanciful accounts: of a monster in an outback Queensland lake never more than two metres deep, of a (relatively) small sauropod dinosaur in a swamp near Singleton, New South Wales, and of a monstrous tyrannosaur-like flesh-eating dinosaur in Arnhem Land. Compared to these, the chapter on giant lizards sounds almost pedestrian. Mostly they were only in the 30 foot [9 metre] range (still half as long again as *Megalania*), but one allegedly seen ripping up a cow in the Cessnock district of New South Wales was 45 feet long, and stood 9 feet [2.7 m] high on all fours.

Where he gets these stories is a total mystery to me. I can only agree with my friend, Paul Cropper who commented to me that, in the many decades he had been researching mystery animals, he had never heard such a story, he had never met any other researcher who had heard them, and, in fact, he had never ever come across a bad hoax concerning giant lizards. They appear to be something only Rex Gilroy hears about.

Crocodiles are another matter. One historical record I missed occurred in 1938 on Queensland's Gold Coast. At the end of June, a sanitary inspector named Charles Finamor "encountered a crocodile 10 feet [3 m] lying in the long grass close to the rubbish tip at the depot, at the northern end of the Merrimac swamp". Following the crocodile into the undergrowth, Mr. Finamor discovered the bones of a cow scattered all over the place. He decided to carry a spear whenever he was working in the area.[31]

The Director of the Queensland Museum said it was an escapee from captivity, but that can hardly be the case with modern sightings. It is clear that stray crocs have ended up a long way south of their breeding grounds, which is supposed to end at Boyne River, near Gladstone. In 1995, for example, retired police officer, Bill Amps was walking his dog near the Pumicestone Passage, which separates Bribie Island from the mainland, when a crocodile lunged out of the water and attempted to take

274

his dog. A group of teenagers tried to drive it away by throwing rocks at it.[32]

However, I didn't realise how many reports come from the 21st century alone until I looked back on my files.

2001: On 11 November 2008, after a flurry of reports from the Fraser Coast, I telephoned Mr. Ken Raddunz, the owner of Hervey Bay Fishing Charters. He told me that, about 7 years before, in the early morning, he had come across a crocodile about 6 feet [1.8 m] long in the back waters of the Mary River, perhaps 10 km from the sea. He was only 30 or 40 metres away.

2003: A 60 cm crocodile, probably two years old, was caught in Centenary Lake, in the middle of Caboolture. It was suggested it had been dumped.[33]

2006: Another 60 cm saltwater crocodile had apparently been living for several months in a natural spring at Dee Why, in the northern suburbs of Sydney, before it was captured by Craig Adams of the Australian Reptile Park. How did it get there? It would not have been expected to survive the winter[34].

2008: Sightings on what is called the "Fraser Coast" of Queensland were plentiful this year[35]. A Victorian man took photographs in the sand at Hervey Bay of footprints consistent with a crocodile 4.8 metres long. Seven weeks before, there had been a sighting of a 2.5 metre croc at Baffle Creek, 150 km to the northwest. A fisherman, Stan Pappin, who lived at Maaroom Creek just south of Maryborough, claimed to have seen three crocodiles in the creek. And they weren't babies either; he estimated the smallest at 12 feet [3.6 m], and the largest 16 feet [4.9 m]. Others were reported from the western side of Fraser Island.

2009: In February, a 1.6 metre crocodile was sighted near Middle Road, Logan City (south of Brisbane), captured, and taken to the Fleay Reserve. Being well fed, it was assumed to have been an illegal pet.[36] That was in February. In April, Michelle Palmer saw a crocodile *on her lawn* near Kin Kin, before it went into the nearby creek. Authorities declared that this was the fifth sighting in the general area in the previous few months.[37]

2010: That year something big appeared at Nudgee Beach, near the mouth of the Schulz Canal, on the northern suburbs of Brisbane. First, on 16 or 17 September, a fisherman called Tim Barr saw a 3 metre crocodile a short distance away. He called another fisherman, and the both witnessed it rise again, turn left, and head up Jackson Creek.[38] A couple of weeks later, a man kayaking at Nudgee Beach happened to video it. Although it was not possible to identify the subject, it was moving around, and it was not easy to see what else it could be but a crocodile.[39] Finally, Belinda Biebrick and her father saw it when fishing where the mouth of the Schulz Canal met Nudgee Beach. It came up vertically out of the water just 15 metres away, exposing its whole head and eyes to their view.[40]

2013. In November, a 3 metre crocodile was captured in the Mary River.[41] A freshwater crocodile also appeared in a waterhole near Birdsville, in the far west, well beyond the river systems of the Great Dividing Range[42].

2014. On 28 February a witness phoned radio station 4BC to report that he had seen a crocodile emerge from Bulimba Creek in Brisbane's southside.[43]

2015. It was back to the Mary River this time. A night camera had been set up to photograph nesting turtles at Tiaro, and recorded a crocodile as well.[44]

2017. In February a Mr. Tristan Van Rye was driving past the Mount Crosby Weir on the Brisbane River when he happened to see something which made him stop and get out. It appeared to be a 2 metre crocodile.[45] Finally, at the very end of the year a one metre long freshwater crocodile was found in Melbourne, of all places.[46]

All of this indicates that fairly large juvenile crocodiles, perhaps pushed out by their bigger conspecifics, have a tendency to move southwards, often several hundred kilometres, from their natural breeding range, while the very small ones may, perhaps, be the subject of illegal human activity.

REFERENCES

[1] David O'Reilly (1981) *Savage Shadow. The search for the Australian cougar.* Creative Research: Perth p48 (since republished, POD, by Strange Nation Publishing)

[2] 'A strange animal.' *Sydney Morning Herald* 14 March 1871 (Paul Cropper alerted me to this.)

[3] Gilbert Whitley (1940) Mystery animals of Australia. *Aust. Mus. Mag.* 7 : 132 - 9 (1 March 1940)

[4] T.J. Parker and W.A. Haswell (1967) *A Text-book of Zoology* (7th edition) vol. 2, p 364

[5] Parker and Haswell (ref. 4) *ibid.*

[6] 'The abominable spinifex man' *Pursuit* 4(1) pp 9 -10 (January 1971), quoting an unidentified press clipping. (*Pursuit* was the journal of the Society for the Investigation of the Unexplained.)

[7] Bernard Heuvelmans (1958) *On the Track of Unknown Animals* Rupert Hart-Davis, p 206

[8] Rex Gilroy 'Our fantastic lizards' *Australasian Post* 20 Dec . 1979

[9] Charles Fort (1931) *Lo!*, chapter 7

[10] C. A. W. Guggisberg (1972) *Crocodiles. Their natural history, folklore and conservation.* Wren, Victoria, p 40

[11] Ken Blanch 'Man-eaters on our doorstep' *The Sunday Mail* (Brisbane), 2 Jan1994, quoting *The Queenslander* of 22 & 24 June 1905.

[12]'Pioneer claims that "bunyips are crocs"'. *Gold Coast Bulletin* 12 May 1965

[13] Guggisberg (ref. 10) pp 95 - 96

[14] 'Crocodile near train line'. *Sydney Morning Herald* 30 Nov. 1939

[15] 'More crocodile reports.' *Sydney Morning Herald* 5 Dec. 1939

[16] 'Crocodile theory supported.' *Sydney Morning Herald* 9 Dec. 1939

[17] *Australasian Post* 11 Dec. 1980

[18] Channel 7 News (Brisbane) 3 April 1993

[19] 'Croc Poser', *Sunday Mail* (Brisbane) 4 April 1993

[20] Toni McRae, 'Beast of Buderim', *Sunday Mail* (Brisbane) 18June 1995

[21] Pam Shilton (1980) 'Mythical monsters of Australia.'   Unidentified Brisbane newspaper of 27 April 1980, clipping provided by Peter Hansen of *The Sunday Mail.*

[22]   Brian Williams, 'Windorah nets a new attraction.' *Courier-Mail* (Brisbane) 23 Jan 1993

[23]   'Crocodiles in Gippsland', *Sydney Morning Herald*, 25 March 1867

[24]   If you're interested, it was published in the *Truth* (Brisbane) 9 Oct 1960. I was able to borrow the original from the present owner and deduce that it was taken in England some time after 1874.

[25]   'Fishy lover for Shelley' *Sunday Mail* (Brisbane) 2 June 1991

[26]   *Sun* (Sydney) 5 April 1968, quoted by Bill Chalker and Keith Basterfield (1976) *An Australian Catalogue of Close Encounter Type Three Reports,* published by UFO Research Inc., S.A.

[27]   Chalker and Basterfield (ref. 26)

[28]   *Sunday Mirror* (Sydney) 25 April 1971, quoted by Chalker and Basterfield (ref. 26)

[29]   Many a true word has been spoken in jest. I told that joke to a friend after reading about the "mothman": an armless, headless humanoid creature with eyes in its shoulders, and wings, which plagued West Virginia in 1966 (John Keel: *The Mothman Prophesies*). Imagine my surprise to discover that a similar monster appeared in the vicinity of a UFO in Kent, UK in 1963 (*Flying Saucer Review* March/April 1964). In 1976 a strange animal was seen coming out of a landed UFO in Wales, but one of the crew shooed it back inside (*ibid.* May/June 1979).

[30]   Rex Gilroy (1995) *Mysterious Australia*, Nexus Publishing

[31]   'Bunyip-crocodile found at Merrimac swamp', *Courier-Mail* (Brisbane) Tues. 5 July 1938, p 3

[32]   Richard Gwynn-Seary (1996), 'A croc in my passage' *Fortean Times* 85: 26-27 (Feb/March 1996). (The author lived on Bribie Island and interviewed the witness.)

[33]   Channel 10 and Channel 7 news, 6 Nov 2003. Also:
Glenis Green, 'I'm just teasing, my teeth don't hurt' *Courier-Mail* (Brisbane) 7 Nov 2003

[34]   'Sydney saved from 60cm croc', *Courier-Mail* (Brisbane) Fri. 24 Feb. 2006

[35] 'Crocs reported moving southwards' *The Australian*,10 Oct. 2008
Loretta Bryce, 'No shock if croc made its mark', *Fraser Coast Chronicle,* Mon. 13 Oct. 2008
Glenis Green, 'Warning signs are 'no croc'', *Courier-Mail* (Brisbane), Sat. 27-28 Dec. 2008, p 1

[36] Channel 10 News, Fri. 20 Feb, 2009.
'Pioneering crocodile gets way too close for comfort' *Courier-Mail* (Brisbane) Sat 21-22 Feb, 2009, p 3

[37] Channel 10 News, Thurs. 16 April 2009

[38] Channel 10 News, 5pm Fri 17 Sept 2010.
'Brisbane on croc alert', *Sunday Mail* (Brisbane), 19 Sept. 2010, p 11

[39] Sky TV News, Sun. 3 Oct 2010.
Anthony Templeton, 'Channel Nine footage raises questions about crocodile in waters around Brisbane Airport', *Courier-Mail* (Brisbane), 10 Oct. 2010.

[40] 'Croc sighted on northside', *Sunday Mail*, 24 Oct. 2010, p 38

[41] Channel 10 News, Thurs. 7 Nov. 2013

[42] Channel 10 News, Tues. 13 Aug. 2013

[43] 'Is it a croc or a crock?' *Sunday Mail* (Brisbane) 2 March 2014

[44] Kathleen Donaghey, 'Red alert on killer from the depths. Monsters on march', *Courier-Mail* (Brisbane) Wed. 29 July 2015, p 12

[45] 'Brisbane River croc tale holds water', *Courier-Mail* (Brisbane) Fri. 3 February 2017

[46] Channel 10 News, 26 Dec. 2017

CHAPTER 9

SO, WHERE DO WE GO FROM HERE?

Now our expedition is over. We have blazed a trail through a jungle of folklore, fantasy and fact, often in danger of losing our way, and have encountered the most amazing wildlife. What, you may ask, do I think of it all? That is the wrong question. The real issue is: what do you think of it all? I have given you the data. You now know as much as I do. It is a fallacy that the researcher is an expert compared to the reader. Any scientist worth his salt presents his data in such a thorough and objective manner that any arguments against his conclusions can be based on his own evidence.

Just the same, I know a lot of readers will still place special value on the researcher's final opinion, and will want to hear it. To this, I can only say that I am a sceptic. This is not synonymous with "unbeliever" or "debunker". The Greek word, *skeptomai* means "I consider". A sceptic is one who is not prepared to accept popular beliefs, whether they be venerable traditions, the latest trendy craze, or established scientific dogma. He thinks about, and submits them all to critical, open minded examination. In the field of anomalous data, whether it be bunyips, ghosts, or flying saucers, one may be a sceptical believer or a sceptical unbeliever, but a sceptic no matter what.

For myself, I am a sceptical believer in sea serpents and alien big cats, a very puzzled sceptic with regard to yowies and mainland thylacines, and a sceptical unbeliever about some of the lesser reported animals. I do not believe that the final word has been said about any of the topics of this book. I have changed my mind on some of them before today, and am quite prepared to change it again if need be. Of course, to be a good sceptic, one has to conquer certain psychological traits. There are some people - and I confess to being one - who are romantics at heart. It satisfies something deep inside to think that out there, on the borders of our secure, well-planned, geometrically ordered existence, there lurks a world of mystery and wonder, which fires the imagination - the Goblin Universe, as the late Prof. Napier once called it. Others, on the other hand, suffer from exactly the opposite mental block. They like the world to be secure, well-planned, and geometrically ordered. The Goblin Universe is an affront to them. It cannot be true. It must be fought - preferably with logic, but at the last resort, by simply turning one's back on it.

Now, much as we might feel a warm inner glow by belonging to one or other of these camps, it must be admitted that both are irrational. So when a refugee from the Goblin Universe arrives on our shores, instead of embracing him like a long lost brother, or driving him out like an alien invader, let us ask what a good sceptic should do. Suppose you happened to see something really extraordinary - say a mermaid combing her hair on the beach. Whom would you tell? Your next door neighbour? The fellows at the pub? The local newspaper? Not if you knew the term, "laughing stock"! The odds are you would keep it to yourself. And so would the next person to see one. And the next. The information would never accumulate. For all we know, there might be mermaids preening themselves all the way down the coast, but nobody is ever game to say so.

Now you see why I announced in the introduction that I am unwilling to reject a story just because it is fantastic. Put it in your file. If there is no substance to it, it will eventually die of loneliness. If there is, then bit by bit its fellows will drift in to lend support. But, you will counter, we are not dealing with anything as unmistakable as a mermaid. We are dealing with shadows in the night, shapes in the undergrowth, blurred footprints, things which might be something and could be anything. Not only that, but the witnesses are self-selected. Those who cannot tell chalk from cheese are the first to come forward.

True. The solution is to cull the reports. Select only those made by apparently good witnesses under conditions conductive to good observation. Take, for example, Geoff Woess, who claims to have seen a black panther walk out in front of his car (chapter 5). If that is not what he saw, then either he his hoaxing, hallucinating, or mistaken in his observations. Since Mr Woess owns a private zoo with big cats, the third possibility is not likely. On his honesty or his sanity, I am in no position to comment. But I dare say if he reported anything as mundane as a bank robbery, the police and jury would take his evidence very seriously. The law assumes that most people are reasonably reliable - at least as far as the big picture goes. Remember that when you hear it said that all this evidence is "anecdotal". Anecdotal evidence puts people in gaol.

But I still hear a voice of protest. Every lawyer will tell you that even apparently faultless witnesses can turn out to be unreliable. Of course. In practice we tend to balance the weight of the testimony against the likelihood of the allegation. Let us assume there is one chance in ten that the testimony of a witness, not known to be a liar or a lunatic, is incorrect. I think this is erring on the side of scepticism. The world would be a very frightening place, and the legal system would jam up, if more than 10 percent of the population could not be trusted. However, the probability that there really are big cats loose in Australia is very low - say one in a million. That's less than one in ten, so on the balance of probabilities we will have to reject Mr Woess's testimony. But what about Rob Wallis, a former zoo keeper who claims to have seen the Grampians pumas three times? Is he a liar or a lunatic as well? The chances of both of them being wrong are 10 percent of 10 percent, or one in 100. The existence of feral big cats still stands at one in a million. What about the local councillor who saw a big cat climb through the trees to escape him? The odds are now one in a thousand. It only needs three more good witnesses and we are down to the one in a million mark. After that, the bets are on the big cats[ii].

Do you get the drift? Maybe some of you have a lower opinion than mine about the reliability of witnesses. But it makes no difference what figures you use. No matter how unlikely an unknown animal might be, a point will be reached where it becomes even more unlikely that all the witnesses are wrong.

So what should we do about these reports? The first thing I ask is that the scientific fraternity take them seriously. To use one example: the alleged pumas of southern Australia. The undeniable fact is that a lot of stock are being lost, and it is costing the farmers a lot of money. If they are not being killed by big cats, then it is by something else mistaken for big cats. And they must be stopped. We owe it to the farmers to investigate them. If an astute mammalogist or vet arrives at the scene soon after a kill, he should be able to tell whether it was made by a dog or a cat. Whichever it is, he should be able to study their ecology and recommend a method of fighting them. Not only that, there is always the possibility that out there is a rare and truly unknown species, which is

---

[ii] When I originally wrote this, I assumed that most people understood this basic principle of probability, but I turned out to be mistaken. I don't know how to make it clearer. The chance of two things happening is the multiple of their probabilities. Thus, if there is one chance in 2 of a coin turning up heads on the first throw, the chance of getting three heads in a row is one in 2 x 2 x 2 = 1 in 8. Thus, if the chances of a witness being completely unreliable is one in 10, the chances of three being unreliable is one in 10 x 10 x 10 = 1 in 1,000. The chances of six being unreliable is 1 in a million.

going extinct while we are ignoring its existence. Remember the giant gecko of New Zealand.

How often have we often heard it said: "There have been no confirmed sightings of ..." whatever? Rarely is it stipulated what would count as confirmation. In most cases, I doubt if the speaker has even addressed the question. Whether it is a dead specimen you want, or a photo, or a good cast of a footprint, one thing is certain: you are more likely to obtain it if you go out looking for it. Zoologists attached to museums or to the national parks or primary industry administrations are often the recipients of reports and queries from the public. Several times in this book scientists have been quoted as keeping files of anomalous reports. I would like to encourage them to share them with the rest of us. Even if one man's file is insufficient to make a case, when linked to a second's it could be significant.

I should also add that the International Society of Cryptozoology is planning a conference in Australia in the next couple of years. You are all invited.

The second thing I want is to encourage witnesses to come forth. However, at this point I have to add a word of caution. Remember what I said in chapter 4: when strange animal fever strikes, the population's critical faculties collapse. The last thing I want is to inspire my readers to go off half-cocked. We all know what happens when you go off half cocked. You shoot yourself in the foot. So, if you happen to see something peculiar, *think*! Could it have a mundane explanation? If, after your second thought, you are still convinced it cannot be explained, write down what you saw at once. If you haven't any notebook, jot down the cardinal points on a newspaper, paper towel, or whatever, until you have time to produce a full account. If you are utterly out of writing material, at least rehearse the whole event in you mind until you have time to write it. In your account, be specific. Don't say "it looked like a cat". What made it look like a cat? Its face? Its shape? Its movements? At the same time, don't be too definite. If you are uncertain about a particular feature, say so. If you are in a group, do not discuss it among yourselves until you have put it on paper. If you do, you may well influence one another, and your testimony will lose its value.

Where it is possible to photograph the tracks, include in the photo something of known size. Try to get both close ups of the best prints, and photos of two or more prints together. If you have no camera, try sketching them.

If you clip a story from a newspaper, it is important to record the name of the paper and the place of publication, because many newspapers have similar names. The date should also be recorded, as should the day of the week. This last is important because the sighting will often be said to have occurred (say) last Friday, and not everybody has a ready reckoner to determine what date that was.

At present there are a lot of enthusiastic amateurs performing investigations in the field. So my third plea is for them to adopt systematic scientific methods. We live in the age of computers and data bases. In any collection of information, there is always a certain amount of "noise" among the "signal". However, if we go about it correctly, it should be possible to find the underlying consistencies. From that, one can determine whether any set of sightings refer to a known or an unknown species. More than that, it will be possible to discover useful patterns, and gain clues to the species' identity and ecology.

To give one example, it would be useful to know whether the black and grey types of "puma", and the alleged thylacines are observed in the same areas, whether one type is more likely to be seen at night, the seasons of the years in which most sightings occur, any possible connection between the sightings, the killings, and the nocturnal screams, and so on. When I mentioned this to one investigator, she replied that it had simply never occurred to her. When interviewing witnesses, let them tell their story, then ask for further information. Stress the importance of providing full details, but also to state when they are not sure. Do not offer any suggested explanations until the interview is over. Do not ask any leading questions. (Ask misleading questions if you wish.) Ask them to draw a picture if possible, regardless of their artistic skill. When you have completed your check sheet of information, it is permissible to show pictures of animals you suspect might have been responsible. If there are multiple witnesses to the same event, make sure that they are interviewed separately, and request that they not discuss the matter with one another until it is over. A variation of this technique can be used to produce a questionnaire if the interview has to be performed by correspondence.

Frequently, when reading newspaper accounts, I have been pained to note how much useful information has been left out, either for lack of space, or due to lack of skill on the part of the journalist. There are certain data which should be obtained if a report is to be of maximum value.

1.   The date of the interview. It might be years before it is published; so you ought to have some record of the time elapsed between sighting and recording.
2.   The names and addresses of the witnesses.
3.   The status of the witnesses: sex, age, occupation, any special qualifications in observation or identification. In other words, why should we believe them?
4.   The date and time of the sighting. It is often difficult to tell from newspaper reports even whether it was day or night.
5.   Weather and lighting conditions. Readers of the paper the next day will know whether 6 pm was just after sunset of just before. The researcher in another state a couple of years later will not.
6.   How long the observation lasted.
7.   The maximum and minimum distances between animal and observer. Did the latter have any objective method of estimation?
8.   The terrain. Even if the sighting was on a road, was the surrounding country farmland, open scrub rainforest, or what?
9.   The size of the animal, both height and length, with and without the tail. Again, was there any way to estimate it objectively?
10.   Colour - on both upper and lower parts of body.
11. Any distinguishing marks, such as stripes, spots or blotches. Be specific. A thylacine's stripes are quite different from a tiger's, and different still from the fortuitous stripes of feral cats and dogs.
12.   The shape of the head, particularly whether the muzzle was long or short, pointed or truncated, or whether any marks could be seen on the face.
13.   The size and shape of the ears.
14.   The shape of the hindquarters.
15.   The shape, length and carriage of the tail.
16.   The behaviour of the animal.
17.   Names and addresses of anyone else who may have had a similar experience.
18.   Anything else the observer might think relevant.

When marine animals are involved, certain other data are also important.
19.   The condition of the sea. Again, be specific. A landlubber doesn't know what a "low swell" might be.

20.   Whether the skin appeared furred, smooth, or scaly. Information like this is essential in determining to which group of animals the creature belongs.
21.   The shape of the head, with the presence and position of visible eyes, ears, breathing tubes etc.
22.   The length, thickness and shape of the neck. Was it clearly demarcated from the body and/or the head? Was there any mane?
23.   The presence or absence of any humps, their relative size and spacing, and whether they appeared to be integral to the body shape, or merely an artefact of the body's undulations.
24.   Any fins or paddles, and their positions. Do not infer their existence if they are covered by water.
25.   Shape of the tail, if visible. Again, do not infer its existence because of the wake. A seal would merely have a pair of flippers attached to its rear.
26.   Method of propulsion: paddling, sculling, or undulating. (As a general rule, mammals undulate vertically, other life forms horizontally.)
27.   Method of surfacing and submerging. (Most animals will dive, but certain types of sea serpent simply sink like a stone.)

Then there are the yowies. It becomes rather tedious reading reports which list only the height, colour, and the fact that it looked like an ape. So if they really exist, and if you have the freakishly good luck to see one, remember: you will probably never be so lucky again, and you have only a very short time before it gets away. (All the evidence suggests that it will run away from you.) Stop shivering, stand still, and give it a very thorough once-over. As well as the obvious features listed above, take note of the following:
28.   The proportions of the body. Are its arms and legs longer or shorter in relation to its trunk than a human being's? Is it slim or heavily built? Does it have a protruding belly?
29.   The facial features. What shape is the face? Is the nose flat, long, broad, or pug-like? Do the brows project? Are the lips full like a man's, or thin like an ape's? Is the chin prominent or recessed? What about the ears?
30.   The pattern of hair. Are there any parts where the hair is longer than others? Is there any hair on the face? Is there a beard? Is the chest bare or hairy? Details like this are clues to its relationship to ourselves.
31.   Presence and size of genitals and/or female breasts.
32.   Shape of the hand.

33.   How many toes does it have?

34.   Does the footprint differ in any way from ours?

If you have the presence of mind to record all that, you will be rewarded with a memory that will stick in your mind forever. You will also deserve a medal. More to the point, if you are interviewing someone, at least ask those questions. They might end up remembering more than they originally volunteered.

The next step is for the information to be gathered together. At the end of this book I have listed a number of contacts who are happy to act as collection agencies for reports. In the southern states mystery predators are the major, but not sole concern, and there are many active investigators in the field.

For my own part, I am particularly interested in events in Queensland and northern Australia, and in anything that will help solve the mystery of the Queensland tiger, the yowie, and the sea serpent. If any readers can shed any light on any of the events mentioned in this book - for, example, if they are unnamed witnesses to an event - I would be delighted to hear from them.

I am also concerned about documentation. If you check the bibliographies of chapters 1 and 2 in particular, you will note that many of the stories are quoted from secondary sources. Some of the sea serpent incidents are known only by name. The early history of the bunyip is very poorly documented. Somewhere, in the archives of minor regional newspapers, and even more obscure journals, the original stories lie buried. If any of you can lay hands on them, please, please let me know.

(On the other hand, you may have a query, or merely wish to say how much you liked the book - or how much you hated it! If so, and you want a reply, please remember that an author's royalties do not amount to much. A stamped reply envelope would therefore be appreciated.)

Finally, there is the issue of publication. At intervals throughout this book there has been mention of individuals who have undertaken local investigations. Probably because the animals in question have not come to light, the information gathered has never been published. Those files will do any good sitting in your closet. I have therefore included the address of the International Society of Cryptozoology. The editor, I know for a fact, is only too eager for papers or progress reports from anyone who can submit them in a format worthy of a scientific publication. If you think you can, don't hesitate to write to him. If you are not sure of your abilities, talk to someone with scientific training. Besides, the

Society's journal makes fascinating reading in its own right.

One last word of caution. If you ever go to the gem fields, you will hear stories along the following lines. A man stakes a claim, brings in earth moving equipment, spends a small fortune hollowing out the land, and eventually gives up in disgust. Along comes some simple prospector, takes over the claim, digs a metre further on, and strikes a bonanza. Moral of the story: if the treasure doesn't have your name on it, there is no way you will get it.

The same thing applies to cryptozoology. In Tasmania numerous official and amateur expeditions have set out on the quest for the Tasmanian tiger. Invariably they have come away empty handed, while the beast in question has strolled out in front of some unsuspecting hiker a few kilometres away. Hunting unknown animals can be as addictive as prospecting, or searching for sunken treasure, or gambling. There is always the feeling that if you look just that little harder, if you follow just one more lead, you may strike lucky. Already there are people in the field who are devoting all the time they can spare to the quest, plus time they cannot spare, even at the risk of marriage and career. I want to remind you that it isn't worth all that. The goal is excellent. It is worth the try. Success will not come without hard work. But it will also not come without the one thing no-one can rely on: luck. If there are species out there which have remained undiscovered, it is for a very good reason: they are rare, and extremely elusive. They will not give up their secrets readily.

Appendix 1

Help Wanted

As explained in the last chapter, if you think you have seen an unknown animal, I would like to hear about it. The list of contacts provided in the first edition is no longer valid. However, I run a cryptozoological blog at https://malcolmscryptids.blogspot.com/. At the top you can click on the button marked, "How to report a sighting". Alternatively, you can go straight to the page: https://malcolmscryptids.blogspot.com/p/how-to-report-sighting.html. This will lead you to my e-mail address.

Even if you wish to send a written report, or photographs, by snail mail, it would be appreciated if you would use the e-mail initially. Please let me know if you do not wish your name to be published.

If you are interested in the *Journal of Cryptozoology*, the issues can be ordered through Amazon.

Appendix 2

Useful Websites

Malcolm's Musings: Cryptozoology. I operate a number of blogs, most of which are prefixed with the words, "Malcolm's Musings", and so can be easily located with any search engine. My cryptozoology blog is: https://malcolmscryptids.blogspot.com.

Here are a number of other websites relevant to Australian mystery animals.

Centre for Fortean Zoology (Australia). A blog on Australian cryptids, plus a lot of links. http://www.cfzaustralia.com/

Gary Opit's Cryptozoological Australia. Gary Opit is a professional zoologist who is even more eccentric than me! His website covers the full range of Australian mystery animals - not to mention extraterrestrials! http://garyopit.com/

Myths and Monsters 2001 Conference. This can be downloaded in PDF form (along with other reports) from http://www.strangeark.com/cryptozoology-resources. (Note: my own contribution involves a huge fish and a manta ray. I now realise that there was nothing unusual about the manta, and have resiled from that part of the paper.)

Strange Nation. A website run by Michael Williams and Rebecca Lang, it contains a number of interesting items on mystery animals. http://www.strangenation.com.au/

Bunyip and Inland Seal Archive. Peter Ravenscroft digs into the newspaper archives at http://pandora.nla.gov.au/pan/97461/20100202-1526/www.pool.org.au/text/peter_ravenscroft/the_bunyip_and_inland_seal_archive_of_australia.html. It is taken to the 20th century at https://webarchive.nla.gov.au/awa/20100203215518/http://pandora.nla.gov.au/pan/97461/20100202-1526/www.pool.org.au/text/peter_ravenscroft/seals_observed_inland.html

Thylacine Research Unit. https://www.thylacineresearchunit.org/

Australian Big Cats. Several reports. http://www.australianbigcats.com/

Australian Rare Fauna Research Association. https://www.arfra.org/

Tasmanian Devils on the Mainland. http://mainlanddevils.com.au

Big Cats Victoria by Simon Townsend and John Turner.
http://www.bigcatsvic.com.au/

Where Light Meets Dark. Looks at marsupial carnivores, especially on the mainland. www.wherelightmeetsdark.com.au

The Fox in Tasmania. This is as much a cryptozoological issue as the thylacine. http://www.tasmanianfox.com/Tasmanian_Fox/HOME.html

The Fortean, run by Paul Cropper, with the occasional post by Tony Healy. It covers mostly yowies and poltergeists. https://thefortean.com/

Australian Yowie Research, run by Dean Harrison.
https://www.yowiehunters.com.au/

Australian Yowie Project. Photos and artefacts which you may or may not find convincing. http://theaustralianapeproject.blogspot.com/

Yowieocalypse. Edgar Skoda does his best to debunk the yowie, and thereby provides a useful foil to some of the other websites.
 http://home.yowieocalypse.com/

For your interest, I have bequeathed my own documents to the University of Queensland, the Queensland Museum Library, and the State Library of Queensland, in that order, depending on who will take them.

Other Books by the Author

The following books are all in print, and available from Amazon.

The Stranger from the Stars. A science fiction novel about a group of hikers who rescue an injured alien from a crashed flying saucer. Having followed the UFO scene for more than 50 years, I have ensured that the story is "realistic", in that all the phenomena described have been reported many times in the literature.

Savages and Saints. This is the story of my parents-in-law, Leon and Theophila Philippi: a farm boy from Nebraska, and a pastor's daughter from the Eyre Peninsula of South Australia, who were thrown together under unusual circumstances, married after a whirlwind courtship, and set out for New Guinea as missionaries. The sort of experiences they went through are beyond the imagination of the present generation.

The Truth About Bunyips. Every Australian has heard about bunyips, but no-one knows what they are supposed to look like. Based on a huge number of recently digitalised old documents and newspapers, this short book should be the definitive work on the subject.

Australian Sea Serpents. Sea serpents really exist, and have been visiting Australian shores for a long time. I have now trawled through dozens to digitalised newspapers to produce what I expect will also become the definitive work on the subject. More than half of the case histories are new - that is to say, they have never been published in book form by other researchers.

Forgotten Sea Serpents. This is an adjunct to the above: a large collection of reports of sea serpents outside of Australia which have, apparently, been missed by other researchers. The book should be welcomed by cryptozoologists looking to complete their documentation on the subject.

Forgotten Bigfoots Around the World. Here I provide translations of articles and reports in little known foreign language journals about mystery apes on five continents.

Trials of a Tourist. I've been an international tourist for most of my adult life, visiting remote places even millionaires haven't seen. So now I have written a humorous account of the quirky things I have experienced, as well as the "plot against tourists", by which the world conspires to make travelling as inconvenient as possible.

Apparitions: tulpas, ghosts, fairies, and even stranger things. This is not an ordinary book on ghosts, but coves a whole range of paranormal apparitions: tulpas and other creations of the mind, ghosts, fairies, and things which are more bizarre - but all fully documented.

Paranormal Planet. A companion book to the above, documenting effective sorcery, ESP, spontaneous human combustion, alien abductions, demon possession, miracles, and many other even stranger things.

A Zoologist Looks at Science Fiction. H. G. Wells said that the essence of science fiction was the suspension of disbelief. As a zoologist, I have a bit more difficulty than most. In this short book I examine the mistakes made by science fiction writers in their creations of monsters and aliens, not to mention robots.

The Gospels: Harmonized and Annotated (two volumes): Here I present the four gospels together in chronological order, with parallel texts side by side, and with a discussion of the situation in first century Israel in which they were embedded.

The Repat Racket. An insider's report on Veterans' Affairs. Originally published in 2010, and now republished, it reveals the way in which good intentions for compensating ex-servicemen resulted in a grotesque legal system open to enormous abuses.